OECD Tax Policy Studies

Housing Taxation in OECD Countries

No. 29

OECD
BETTER POLICIES FOR BETTER LIVES

Please cite this publication as:
OECD (2022), *Housing Taxation in OECD Countries*, OECD Tax Policy Studies, No. 29, OECD Publishing, Paris, https://doi.org/10.1787/03dfe007-en.

ISBN 978-92-64-45792-8 (print)
ISBN 978-92-64-86268-5 (pdf)
ISBN 978-92-64-78625-7 (HTML)
ISBN 978-92-64-76292-3 (epub)

OECD Tax Policy Studies
ISSN 1990-0546 (print)
ISSN 1990-0538 (online)

Photo credits: Cover © selensergen/Thinkstock.

Corrigenda to publications may be found on line at: www.oecd.org/about/publishing/corrigenda.htm.

Foreword

Housing taxes are of growing importance given the pressure on governments to raise revenues, improve the functioning of housing markets, and combat inequality. As they emerge from the COVID-19 pandemic, many countries are looking to restore public finances by raising tax revenues while supporting the economic recovery. Many governments are also under increasing pressure to address rising inequality and declining housing affordability, which is more acutely affecting low-income and young households. In addition, in the context of growing international mobility of both capital and people, governments may aim to raise more revenues from less mobile tax bases, in particular real estate. This increased attention on housing taxes reinforces the need to design them effectively and fairly.

This report provides a comparative assessment of housing tax policies across OECD countries. It covers all taxes levied on the acquisition, ownership and disposal of housing assets. The report shows that while housing taxes play an important role in OECD countries, there is significant scope to enhance their efficiency, equity and revenue potential, and the report identifies a number of reform options to improve their design.

The report builds on previous OECD work on the taxation of housing. In particular, an OECD Taxation Working Paper on "Measuring the Effective Taxation of Housing" was released in January 2022. The report is also part of a wider work stream on personal capital taxation, which includes the recent publication of reports on Inheritance Taxation in OECD Countries (2021), The Taxation of Household Savings (2018) and The Role and Design of Net Wealth Taxes (2018). The report also complements OECD cross-Directorate work on housing policies as part of the OECD Horizontal Project on Housing.

The report contains three chapters. Chapter 1 provides background on housing market trends and challenges. Chapter 2 examines the distribution of housing assets, largely based on data from the OECD Wealth Distribution Database. Chapter 3 provides an overview of the different types of taxes that are levied on housing in OECD countries and assesses their efficiency, equity and revenue effects. It also evaluates the role of specific tax policy instruments in addressing current housing challenges. Based on the assessment, the report outlines a number of reform options that governments could consider to enhance the design and functioning of their housing tax policies. The Annex provides detailed country-specific information.

Acknowledgements

This study was produced by the Tax Policy and Statistics Division of the OECD Centre for Tax Policy and Administration. The report was supervised by Sarah Perret. Chapter 1 was led by Sarah Perret and jointly authored by Sarah Perret and Antonia Ramm of the OECD Centre for Tax Policy and Administration and Boris Cournède and Volker Ziemann of the OECD Economics Department. Chapter 2 was led by Bethany Millar-Powell and written by Andrew Lonsdale and Bethany Millar-Powell. Chapter 3 was led by Sarah Perret and written by Andrew Lonsdale, Bethany Millar-Powell, Sarah Perret and Antonia Ramm.

The authors would like to thank David Bradbury for his guidance and feedback throughout the project. The report benefited from very helpful comments from Séverine Baranger, Bert Brys and Luisa Dressler (Centre for Tax Policy and Administration), Boris Cournède and Orsetta Causa (Economics Department), Marissa Plouin (Directorate for Employment, Labour and Social Affairs), Carlotta Balestra (Centre on Well-being, Inclusion, Sustainability and Equal Opportunity), Sean Dougherty (Fiscal Network) and Rudiger Ahrend, Jaebeum Cho and Matteo Schleicher (Centre for Entrepreneurship, SMEs, Regions and Cities). The authors would also like to thank Carlotta Balestra for providing the underlying data (OECD Wealth Distribution Database) used in Chapter 2. The authors are also very grateful to Carrie Tyler and Natalie Lagorce for their support with communications, and to Violet Sochay for her assistance with administrative matters. In addition to OECD colleagues, the authors would like to extend a special thanks to Professor John Muellbauer (University of Oxford) for very helpful feedback on an initial draft of the report.

The authors would like to acknowledge the involvement of the delegates of Working Party No.2 on Tax Policy Analysis and Tax Statistics (WP2) who provided feedback throughout the project and provided updated information on countries' tax treatment of housing.

This report was approved by WP2 delegates and by the delegates of the Committee on Fiscal Affairs (CFA). The report was prepared for publication by the OECD Secretariat.

This report uses data from the Eurosystem Household Finance and Consumption Survey.

Table of contents

FIGURES

TABLES

BOXES

Executive Summary

Housing plays a central role in our lives. Access to shelter is a basic human need and a key determinant of individual welfare. Access to well-located, quality housing shapes people's social lives as well as their access to health care, education, job opportunities and recreational activities. Housing also affects well-being on a daily basis as the home is the centre of family life and increasingly of professional life, with the widespread adoption of teleworking during the COVID-19 pandemic. In OECD countries, housing is on average the single-largest expenditure item across all income groups and has accounted for an ever-larger share of total household expenditure in recent years.

Housing also constitutes households' largest lifetime investment and the majority of their wealth, though its significance varies across countries. Housing is a key vehicle for wealth accumulation and is a particularly important asset for middle-class households. In OECD countries, owner-occupied housing accounts on average for 50% of total household wealth across all households and for more than 60% of middle-class wealth. However, the importance of housing varies widely across countries. For instance, homeownership rates range from 44% (Germany) to 93% (Lithuania), while housing wealth (including both owner-occupied and secondary housing) accounts for at least 80% of total household wealth in Chile, Latvia, Lithuania, and Greece, but less than 40% in the United States and New Zealand.

While more equally distributed than financial assets, housing wealth remains concentrated among high-income, high-wealth and older households. High-wealth households, and to a lesser extent high-income households, own a disproportionately large share of owner-occupied housing wealth and own the majority of secondary housing wealth. High-income households also hold a disproportionate share of housing debt, although lower-income households with mortgages generally face higher relative debt burdens. Homeownership and housing wealth are also strongly associated with age, with older households holding more housing wealth and representing a far greater proportion of homeowners.

Recent decades have seen unprecedented growth in house prices, making housing market access increasingly difficult for younger generations. Despite some fluctuations, house prices have seen a strong and continuous growth over the past century, with a rapid acceleration in house price increases in the last 30 years and even sharper growth during the COVID-19 pandemic. House price growth has been uneven across regions, however, with much more significant rises in large metropolitan areas. House price inflation, particularly in urban areas, has been driven by a combination of factors constraining housing supply (e.g. limited space in highly urbanised areas, land use and zoning regulations, rising construction costs) and stimulating demand (e.g. demographic changes, low interest rates, globalisation). Declining housing affordability poses a particular challenge to younger households, with evidence that homeownership rates have been declining for younger cohorts over time, particularly among those with lower income and wealth.

Housing also has wide-ranging environmental impacts. The residential sector has a significant carbon footprint, accounting for around 22% of global final energy consumption and 17% of energy-related CO_2 emissions, with the bulk of the housing sector's energy consumption originating from heating. Housing is also a significant source of fine particulate matter. Housing has wider environmental impacts on land use and biodiversity, for instance through the loss of rural lands and the fragmentation of natural habitats, as well as on transport and water consumption.

Housing taxes are of growing importance given the pressure on governments to raise revenues, improve the functioning of housing markets, and combat inequality. As they emerge from the COVID-19 pandemic, many countries are looking to restore public finances by raising tax revenues while supporting the economic recovery. Many governments are also under increasing pressure to address rising inequality and declining housing affordability, which is more acutely affecting low-income and young households. In addition, in the context of growing international mobility of both capital and people, governments may aim to raise more revenues from less mobile tax bases, in particular real estate. This increased attention on housing taxes reinforces the need to design them effectively and fairly.

Housing taxation already plays an important role in the OECD, with countries levying a wide range of taxes on immovable property. All OECD countries (though not all sub-central governments) levy recurrent taxes on immovable property. Owners of rental properties are taxed on their rental income and, in a minority of countries, owner-occupiers are taxed on imputed rent. Transaction taxes are also commonly levied upon housing purchases and capital gains taxes are levied on the disposal of housing, although many countries exempt capital gains on the sales of main residences. Inheritance and gift taxes may also be levied when immovable property is transferred to heirs.

Nevertheless, the report finds that the way housing taxes are designed often reduces their efficiency, equity and revenue potential. Many countries still levy recurrent property taxes on outdated property values, which significantly reduces their revenue potential (as revenues have not risen in line with property values), their equity (as households whose properties have increased in value may not be paying more tax), as well as their economic efficiency (as property taxes levied on outdated values provide incentives for people to remain in housing that is subject to a lower outdated valuation, even if it no longer suits their needs). Reliance on transaction taxes is high, despite the potential for these taxes to reduce residential, and to some extent, labour mobility. The majority of countries fully exempt capital gains on main residences, and while there may be justification for such an approach, an uncapped exemption provides vastly greater benefits to the wealthiest households and further distorts the allocation of savings in favour of owner-occupied housing. Other forms of tax relief for owner-occupied housing, in particular mortgage interest relief, have been found to be regressive and ineffective at raising homeownership rates. In some countries, features of rental income taxation and inheritance tax rules applying to housing also reduce progressivity and revenue potential. The assessment also shows that, while housing taxes are viewed as harder to avoid and evade than other taxes, tax systems often leave room for such behaviours, reducing the efficiency, fairness and revenues of housing taxes.

This report also finds that some housing tax policies may help address current housing market challenges, although tax policies may not always be the most effective tools. Tax policies may be used to address specific housing market challenges, such as significantly reducing the carbon footprint of housing, encouraging a more efficient use of land and housing, and boosting the supply of affordable housing. However, tax policies may sometimes be a blunt tool and may even be counterproductive under certain circumstances. In particular, where tax relief is intended to encourage homeownership, it can sometimes contribute to raising house prices and redistributing wealth to current homeowners if housing supply is fixed. Even where tax policies can play a positive role (e.g. vacant home taxes, tax incentives for energy-efficient housing renovations), they may not necessarily be as effective as alternative policy instruments (e.g. regulations) and will generally need to be complemented by other policy measures.

The report identifies a number of reform options that countries could consider to simultaneously enhance the efficiency, equity and revenue potential of housing taxes. The report discusses a wide range of reform options that could help enhance the design, functioning and impact of housing taxes, which includes the following:

- Strengthening the role of recurrent taxes on immovable property, in particular by ensuring that they are levied on regularly updated property values, while lowering housing transaction taxes would increase efficiency in the housing market and improve vertical and horizontal equity.
- Considering capping the capital gains tax exemption on the sale of main residences to ensure that the highest-value gains are taxed would strengthen progressivity and reduce some of the upward pressure on house prices, while continuing to exempt capital gains on the main residence for the majority of households.
- Gradually removing or capping mortgage interest relief for owner-occupied housing would also have positive impacts on progressivity, tax revenues and house price affordability.
- Tax incentives for energy efficient housing renovations could be better targeted to ensure that they reach low-income households. This could contribute to greater emissions reductions and enhance the equity of tax incentive schemes.
- Caution should be exercised when considering tax incentives to encourage homeownership; in most cases, encouraging the supply of housing and promoting the more efficient use of existing housing stock through both tax and non-tax measures is likely to have a greater impact on housing affordability.
- Strengthened reporting requirements, including third-party reporting to the tax authority and international exchanges of information for tax purposes, are also key to ensuring that housing taxes are enforced properly.

Any assessment of housing tax policies should take a holistic view of their interactions with other tax and non-tax policies and with housing market conditions. Interactions between different housing tax policies should be carefully assessed. For instance, residential mobility will be affected directly by both transaction taxes and capital gains taxes, and indirectly by the design of recurrent taxes on immovable property. Reforms aimed at enhancing mobility should therefore consider all three taxes. Carefully assessing interactions between taxes may also help identify cases where, before introducing new tax instruments, countries could consider reforming the design of existing housing taxes. For instance, there may be less need for special taxes to reduce speculation where short-term capital gains are adequately taxed. Similarly, a recurrent tax on immovable property based on regularly updated market values may reduce the need for tax instruments (e.g. infrastructure levies) aimed at capturing property value increases resulting from local public investments. Interactions between tax and non-tax policies are also key. There may be cases where non-tax policies may provide a more effective and equitable alternative to tax measures, especially when the goal is to promote housing affordability. There may also be cases where the success of tax measures depends on other policy settings or housing market conditions.

Housing tax reforms require careful timing and consideration for their impact across different households. Housing tax reforms can have a sizeable impact on house prices, with potentially significant distributional effects as well as wider financial and economic repercussions. A gradual implementation of reforms can help prevent negative macroeconomic shocks while also alleviating the adverse effects of reforms on specific groups of individuals, at least in the short run. Accompanying housing tax reforms with other tax or transfer measures may also help mitigate the impacts of some reforms on more vulnerable people and enhance the public acceptability and political feasibility of policy changes. Governments considering housing tax reforms should also be mindful of the evolution in the macroeconomic environment, in particular changes in interest rates and their potential impact on housing markets and households.

1 Housing market trends and challenges

The chapter examines current trends and challenges in OECD housing markets, providing background for the subsequent policy analysis in the report. It covers trends in house prices and affordability, housing supply and demand dynamics, the role of housing in the economy, its equity implications and the impact of housing on the environment. The chapter also briefly discusses the longer-term trends that are likely to shape the future of housing.

1.1. Introduction

Housing plays a central role in our lives. Access to shelter is a basic human need and a key determinant of individual welfare (OECD, 2021[1]). Access to well-located, quality housing shapes people's social lives as well as their access to health care, education, job opportunities and recreational activities (OECD, 2021[1]). Housing also affects well-being on a daily basis as the home is the centre of family life and increasingly of professional life, with the widespread adoption of teleworking during the COVID-19 pandemic.

Housing combines the characteristics of both a consumption and an investment good. In OECD countries, housing is on average the single-largest expenditure item across all income groups and has accounted for an ever-larger share of total household expenditure in recent years (OECD, 2021[2]). For most households, housing also constitutes their largest lifetime investment, commonly financed with debt, and the majority of their wealth. Housing accounts for 50% of total household wealth on average across OECD countries; a figure that rises to more than 60% for middle-income households (see Chapter 2). The fact that housing combines the characteristics of both a consumption and an investment good has significant implications for public policy, in particular for its tax treatment (Mirrlees et al., 2011[3]).

Promoting homeownership has long been a goal of many OECD countries. Homeownership is an ambition for many households for various reasons, including wealth accumulation and a sense of financial security, which is why widespread homeownership has been an enduring objective of governments. Support for homeownership has also been justified by the positive socio-economic outcomes (e.g. better maintenance of the housing stock, greater civic participation) associated with homeownership (Glaeser and Shapiro, 2003[4]; DiPasquale and Glaeser, 1999[5]), though similar outcomes could potentially be achieved by other forms of tenure such as stable long term renting (Acolin, 2022[6]; OECD, 2021[1]). Widespread homeownership can also have some negative effects, including reduced residential mobility (Causa and Pichelmann, 2020[7]), incentives for homeowners to restrict the local housing supply (Glaeser and Shapiro, 2003[4]) and potential negative externalities such as increased energy consumption, land sealing and traffic congestion where homeownership is associated with specific property structures (e.g. detached houses) (Glaeser, 2011[8]).

Housing has become one of the most pressing policy challenges of our time. The concentration of demand in supply-constrained areas has pushed up house prices and deteriorated housing affordability across many OECD countries. Unprecedented house price growth has been making it harder for younger generations to become homeowners and build up housing wealth. The current context of rising inflation and potentially tighter monetary policy could have mixed impacts on borrowers and prospective buyers. The functioning of housing markets also has wider social, economic and environmental implications, including for social cohesion, financial resilience, residential and intergenerational mobility and the transition to a low-carbon economy. The interconnected challenges of housing market inclusiveness, efficiency and environmental sustainability will require a range of policy reforms, which take into account complementarities and trade-offs between different policy tools and objectives.

This chapter outlines trends and challenges in housing markets, providing background to the policy analysis developed in the rest of the report. First, the chapter analyses house price developments and their impact on housing affordability in recent decades. Second, it examines supply and demand dynamics, including trends in housing finance. Third, it looks at the role of the housing sector in the economy, its impact on residential mobility as well as its wider equity implications. The chapter also examines the environmental footprint of the housing sector and its role in transitioning to a climate and environmentally friendly society, before discussing how longer-term trends, including for instance digitalisation and population ageing, may affect housing markets in the future.

1.2. Housing affordability has decreased significantly in both property and rental markets

Real house prices have experienced a sustained and significant increase over the past century, with a particularly strong growth since the mid-1990s. Figure 1.1 shows the average real house price index for 14 developed economies between 1921 and 2012 based on house price data by Knoll, Schularick and Steger (2017[9]) and from 1970 until 2021 based on the OECD Analytical House Price Database.[1] While there have been some fluctuations, the graph shows a strong and continuous growth in real house prices, with the index increasing six-fold over the past century. There has been a significant acceleration in house price growth from the mid-1990s onwards, only briefly interrupted by a temporary house price decline following the global financial crisis.

Figure 1.1. Real house price index, average 14 countries, 1921-2021

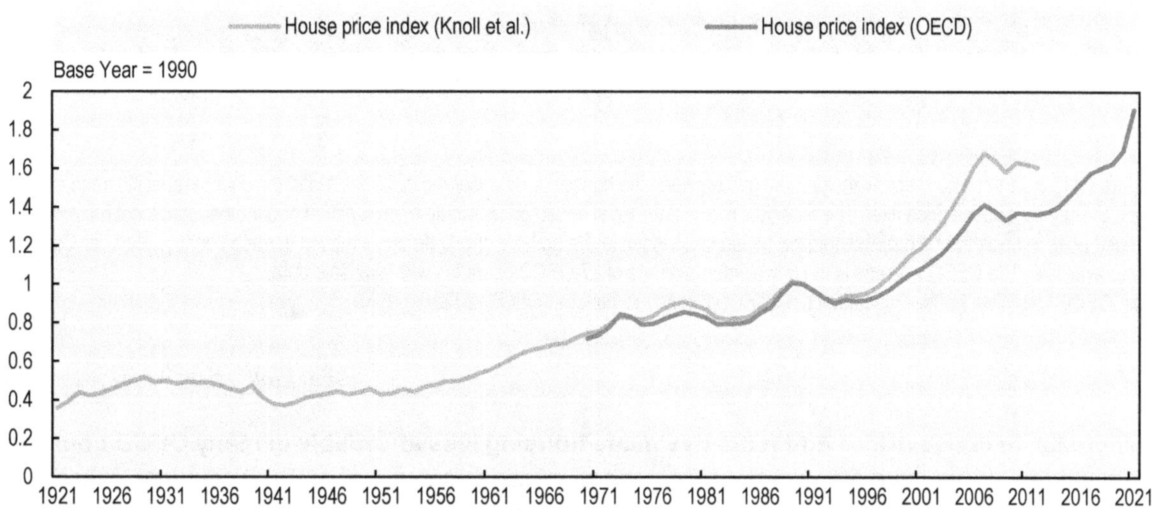

Note: Average of Australia, Belgium, Canada, Denmark, Finland, France, Germany, Japan, the Netherlands, Norway, Sweden, Switzerland, the United Kingdom, the United States. House prices are CPI-adjusted.
Source: Knoll, Schularick and Steger (2017[9]); OECD Analytical House Price database (2022[10])

StatLink https://stat.link/bpokih

Strong house price growth during the COVID-19 pandemic has pushed up housing prices further. Real house prices experienced rapid growth during the pandemic, rising by 13% on average (unweighted) across OECD countries between late 2019 and late 2021 (Figure 1.2). House prices increased in every OECD country but with variation in the rate of growth; 11 countries saw increases of more than 15%, while six countries saw increases of less than 5%. House price growth was above the underlying pre-pandemic trend in nearly every country, which indicates that real house prices are now higher than they would likely have been had the pandemic not occurred. While house prices have historically increased much faster in urban areas, increased demand for living space and the rise of teleworking drove up prices in the peripheral areas around large cities (Ahrend et al., 2022[11]).

Figure 1.2. Real house price growth and real house price gap, 37 OECD countries

Real house price growth: Q4 2019 to Q3 2021; Real house price gap: Q3 2021

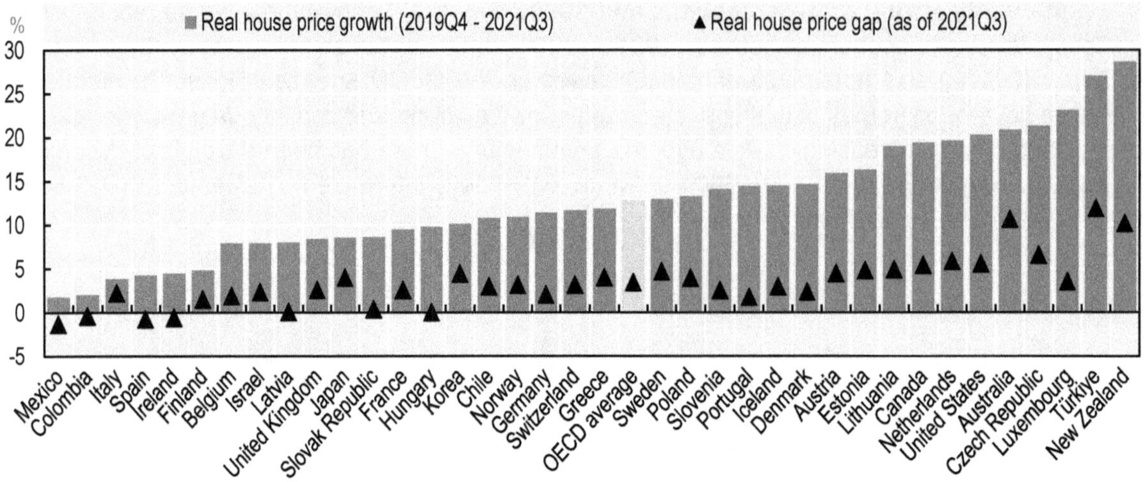

Note: The real house price gap reports the percent gap between the house prices observed in Q3 2021 and the country-specific trend estimated for each country by a house price filter. The latter is a proxy of the level house prices would have reached had the pandemic not happened. The real house price index is the ratio of the nominal house price index to the deflator of private consumption in each country. Data for Costa Rica were not available. The OECD average is the unweighted average of 37 OECD countries with available data.
Source: OECD Analytical House Price database; OECD Economic Outlook (OECD, 2022[12]).

StatLink https://stat.link/ftz685

The increase in house prices and rents has made housing less affordable in many OECD countries. House and rent prices have grown faster than general inflation across many OECD countries over the last 20 years (Figure 1.3). Generally, trends in house prices and rents are expected to follow broadly similar patterns. However, recent increases in price-to-rent ratios may suggest overvaluations in the housing market (OECD, 2021[13]). Importantly, increases in real house prices and rents over the past two decades have varied considerably across countries. For instance, real house prices nearly tripled in New Zealand between 2000 and 2020, while Japan witnessed a decrease in real house prices over the same period (Figure 1.3). Real rent prices have increased more moderately over the last 20 years. The majority of countries have seen real rent price increases of less than 20%, but renters in Iceland have faced real rent increases in excess of 60%. In nine countries, real rent prices decreased over the observed period. It should be noted that house prices and rents have evolved differently within countries, with particularly strong house price and rent growth in urban areas, where demand pressure is high and housing supply is constrained (Bétin and Ziemann, 2019[14]).

Figure 1.3. Percentage changes in real house prices and rents, 2000-2020

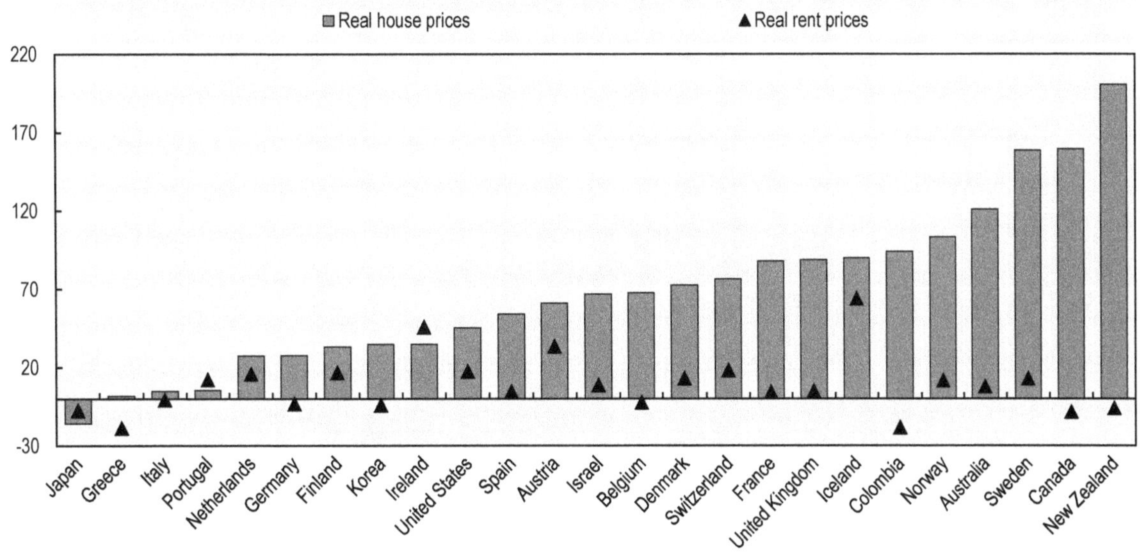

Source: OECD Analytical House Price database (OECD, 2022[10])

StatLink https://stat.link/1dg6mx

Income spent on housing has increased. Housing makes up the largest spending item within household budgets, absorbing more than a third of total household expenditure for households in the bottom quintile and a quarter of household budgets in the top quintile (OECD, 2021[2]). Between 2005 and 2015, the share of middle-income housing expenditure (i.e. expenditure by households earning between 75% and 200% of median incomes) within the total household budget increased on average by 5 percentage points across 23 OECD countries (Figure 1.4). The share of some other household spending items, including health care and transportation, also grew over the same period, though at a much lower rate. Housing costs in the form of rents and mortgage payments often represent a considerable financial burden for households, particularly at the lower end of the income distribution. In 2019, on average across OECD countries, the median mortgage burden including both repayment of the principal and interest payments faced by owner-occupiers (outright owners are not considered as they do not face mortgage costs) was 15% of their disposable income while the median rent burden was 22% (OECD, 2022[10]).

Figure 1.4. Changes in middle-income households' spending shares, 2005-15 average

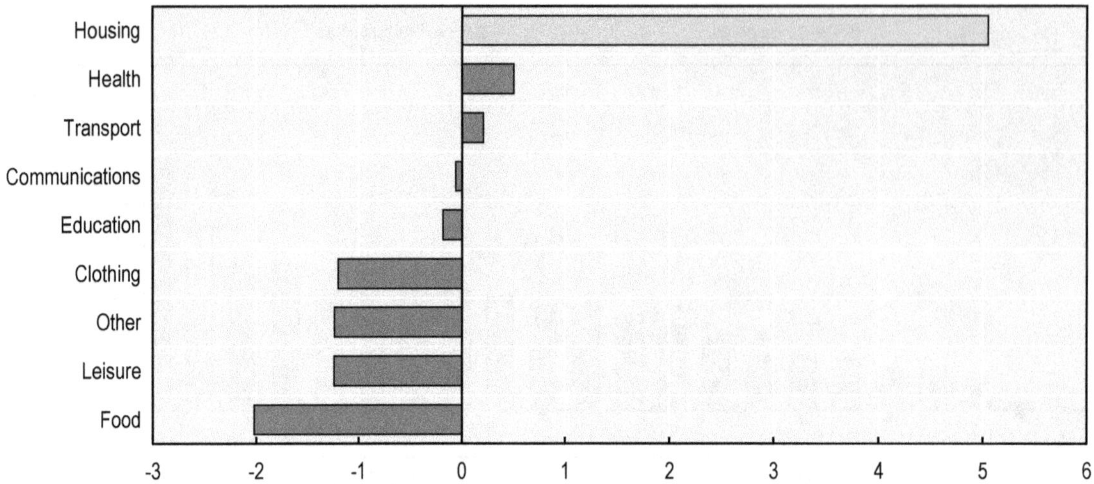

Note: Housing-related expenditures include actual rentals for housing, imputed rentals for owner-occupied housing, maintenance and repair, water supply and miscellaneous services, electricity, gas and other fuels. Unweighted average of 23 OECD countries (Austria, Belgium, Chile, Czech Republic, Germany, Finland, Greece, Hungary, Ireland, Lithuania, Luxembourg, Latvia, Mexico, Netherlands, Norway, Poland, Portugal, Slovak Republic, Slovenia, Spain, Türkiye, United Kingdom and United States). Data refers to middle-income households (75% to 200% of median earnings).
Source: Under Pressure: The Squeezed Middle Class (OECD, 2019[15])

StatLink https://stat.link/xwd5mh

1.3. Supply-side constraints have contributed to decreasing housing affordability

The level of house prices and rents results from the interplay between local housing demand and supply, with supply tending to be less responsive in the short run. Housing supply depends on new residential constructions, as well as the renovation and upgrading of the existing housing stock. Supply tends to adjust more slowly than demand as it takes time to plan and build new structures, which allows price pressures to build up. Slower supply responsiveness also results in more volatile prices and boom-and-bust periods.

Natural and human-made obstacles to construction as well as housing policy choices have contributed to low supply responsiveness, exacerbating the price effects of rising housing demand. Natural geographical constraints as well as regulatory restrictions including those related to land-use and zoning provisions contribute to slowing the responsiveness of housing supply to growing demand (Bétin and Ziemann, 2019[14]). These constraints are particularly binding in already highly urbanised metropolitan areas, where population density is high and housing market regulations are more prevalent (OECD, 2021[1]).

Other supply-side factors contributing to growing house price pressures include higher construction costs and lower public investment in housing developments. Rising construction costs have contributed to declining housing affordability in many countries. Between 2000 and 2019, construction costs for new residential housing increased by more than 70% in the OECD-EU area (OECD, 2021[1]). Increasingly stringent energy efficiency and environmental regulations also contribute to construction cost increases. At the same time, governments have invested less in housing construction. Over the last two decades, governmental capital transfers (i.e. public transfers to organisations outside government) for housing developments decreased by more than 50% on average across OECD countries to a level of 0.06% of GDP in 2018, while direct government investments in housing developments decreased by 80%, accounting for 0.01% of GDP in 2018 (OECD, 2021[1]). These trends are also reflected in the declining share of social housing in the total housing stock across OECD countries, which has contributed to lowering housing affordability in particular for low-income households (OECD, 2021[1]).

The responsiveness of supply to changes in housing demand varies considerably between and within countries. Several studies estimate national (Caldera Sánchez and Johansson, 2011[16]; Cavalleri, Cournède and Özsöğüt, 2019[17]) and regional (Bétin and Ziemann, 2019[14]) housing supply elasticities and analyse their underlying drivers. Across a subset of OECD countries, Bétin and Ziemann (2019[14]) find that housing supply in metropolitan areas is most elastic in the United States and Sweden with supply elasticities mostly above two, though there is wide within-country variation across metropolitan regions (Figure 1.5). Housing supply responsiveness is particularly low in the Netherlands, France and Switzerland, where elasticities range between 0.4 and 0.8. The within-country variation in housing supply elasticities is particularly high in some countries, ranging from 0.8 to 4.7 in the United States and from 0.4 to 2.6 in Denmark. This underscores the importance of spatially aligning supply with demand, meaning that construction should occur where the demand is highest. Mismatches can also relate to housing type with profitable high-end dwellings being abundantly supplied while more affordable and typically more urgently needed flats tend to be undersupplied.

Figure 1.5. Housing supply elasticities across metropolitan regions in a sample of OECD countries, 2019

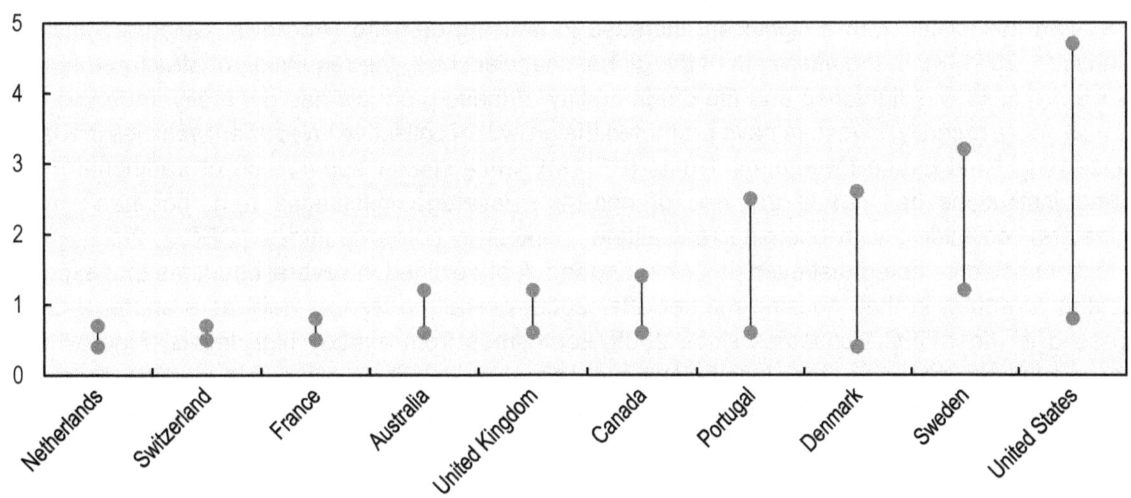

Note: House price elasticities are calculated by regressing changes in real house prices on changes in residential construction using an instrumental variable approach to address potential endogeneity between construction and house prices. A supply elasticity of 1 (unity) indicates that any house price changes leads to a proportional change in housing construction. A larger supply elasticity means that, for a given change in house prices, homebuilding expands by a greater amount.
Source: Bétin and Ziemann, (2019[14])

StatLink https://stat.link/mw4pjh

1.4. At the same time, housing demand has been pushed up by various structural, economic and political factors

Housing demand is affected by accessibility of homeownership as well as structural factors determining housing preferences. The underlying drivers of demand can fall under different categories: those that structurally change the characteristics and location of housing demand, including demographic shifts and urbanisation, and those that make housing more or less accessible to broader segments of the population, such as lower interest rates and the increased availability of housing finance.

Favourable macroeconomic conditions have made housing more accessible in recent decades. A key driver of stark house price increases in the past two decades has been the historical decline in real interest rates (OECD, 2021[18]), which has been reinforced by expansionary monetary policies in the aftermath of the global financial crisis (OECD, 2021[1]). Low interest rates have not only reduced housing debt financing costs for households, but they have also encouraged real estate investments by institutional investors and high-net-worth individuals in search of higher returns (OECD, 2021[18]). Besides, growth in household disposable income tends to push up housing demand and has been one of the main factors behind rising homeownership rates in some OECD countries, including Denmark, Finland, Spain and the United Kingdom (Andrews, Caldera Sánchez and Johansson, 2011[19]).

Developments in housing finance markets have made housing more accessible, though some of these innovations may undermine the resilience of the financial system. Financial deregulation including the relaxation of borrowing conditions and novel housing finance products have promoted the development of mortgage markets in many OECD countries over the past 50 years (OECD, 2021[1]). These trends have made housing finance more accessible for a wide set of credit-constrained households and have been associated with a significant increase in housing demand (Andrews, Caldera Sánchez and Johansson, 2011[19]). In the aftermath of the global financial crisis, the regulation of structured real estate finance products was tightened and the credit quality of these products has generally improved (OECD, 2021[18]). More recently, investors have promoted the growth of collective investment vehicles in real estate finance (e.g. Real Estate Investment Trusts (REITs)), while stricter supervision of traditional mortgage lending institutions has led to the rise of non-bank leverage institutions (e.g. non-bank mortgage originators), coinciding with booming real estate markets in some countries (OECD, 2021[18]). In this context, it should be noted that even though mortgage debt declined in several countries that experienced a severe downturn in their housing market after 2008, overall household debt as a share of GDP has increased in most OECD countries since 2008, sometimes from already high levels (Figure 1.6). This highlights the fact that while these innovations might promote liquidity in real estate markets, there is a risk of inflating house prices and reducing financial resilience (OECD, 2021[18]).

Figure 1.6. Household and mortgage debt to GDP across OECD countries in 2008 and 2018

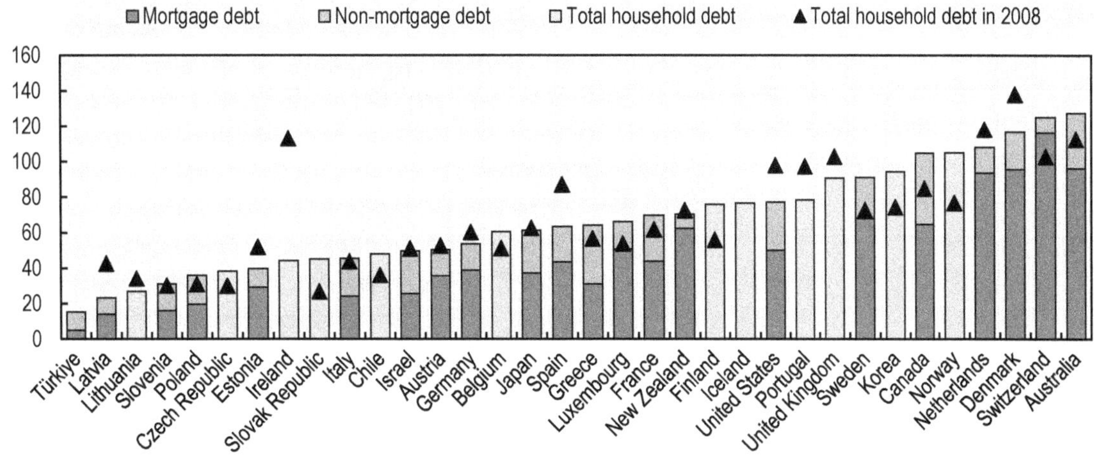

Note: Household debt for Iceland and Türkiye in 2008 was not available
Source: Van Hoenselaar et al. (2021[20])

StatLink https://stat.link/m7ifa5

Policy support for homeownership, while aimed at increasing housing market accessibility, has contributed to the increase in housing demand. In many countries, governments have offered sustained policy support for homeownership, for instance through mortgage interest deductibility (see Chapter 3). However, where housing supply is inelastic, these types of support measures have fuelled house price increases (Andrews, Caldera Sánchez and Johansson, 2011[19]; OECD, 2021[1]).

Urbanisation has affected the geography and concentration of housing demand and has put additional pressure on already supply-constrained areas. The transition from industrial to increasingly service-driven economies has led to a concentration of economic activity in urban areas, accompanied by an agglomeration of professional and educational opportunities (van Doorn, Arnold and Rapoport, 2019[21]). Globalisation contributes to the attractiveness of large metropolitan areas as their superior infrastructure network connects them with the rest of the world while the concentration of cultural, social and recreational activities has enhanced the appeal of urban lifestyles (van Doorn, Arnold and Rapoport, 2019[21]). House prices in large cities have also been inflated by the globalisation of housing investments, which has promoted the rise of institutional investors and high-net worth individuals investing in property abroad in search of high yield (Ahir and Loungani, 2019[22]; Katagiri and Raddatz, 2018[23]).

Demographic changes have both increased overall housing demand and structurally changed demand patterns in terms of property characteristics and geographical location. Demographic factors including migration and population ageing as well as changes in marriage and divorce rates have resulted in more numerous and smaller households (OECD, 2021[1]). This trend has been accompanied by an increase in the average floor space per person (OECD, 2021[1]), partly because fewer people share the same living space and the existing housing stock takes time to adjust.

1.5. Housing market developments have a significant impact on the economy

Housing plays a central role in the economy. Construction accounts on average for 6% of GDP across OECD countries, while housing investments make up around 20% of gross fixed capital accumulation (OECD, 2021[1]). Changes in the housing market affect the real economy through several channels. Housing market developments including changes in house prices, rents or mortgage interest rates, have an impact on household income, wealth and living costs (Cournède, Sakha and Ziemann, 2019[24]). Fluctuations in the housing market can therefore influence aggregated demand, inflation and residential investment (Cournède, Sakha and Ziemann, 2019[24]). Evidence shows that the business cycle is tightly linked to fluctuations in housing-related activities and house prices. In fact, variations in house prices tend to occur before business cycle fluctuations (Figure 1.7), which makes them important indicators to forecast changes in economic activity (Cournède, Sakha and Ziemann, 2019[24]).

Figure 1.7. Annual percentage change in house prices and GDP, 1971-2019

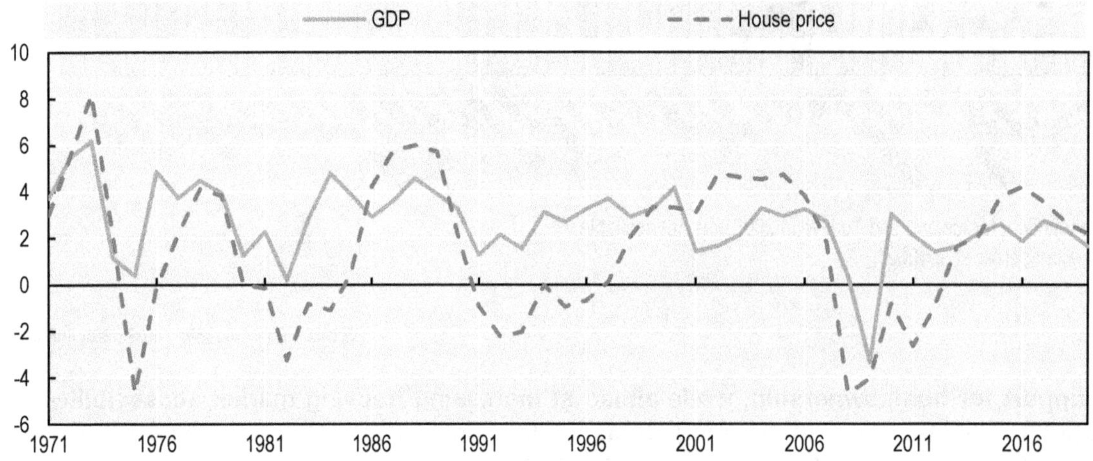

Source: OECD Economic Outlook database and OECD Analytical House Price database (OECD, 2022[10])

StatLink https://stat.link/9b210y

Access to housing finance also has wider impacts on the economy. Well-functioning mortgage markets play a key role in providing access to housing by allowing the smoothing of housing consumption over time. However, they can also confront households with serious financial problems when they run into repayment difficulties or negative home equity. High levels of mortgage debt can also increase economic volatility by aggravating downturns and hamper economic performance. Significant downward pressure on house prices often has substantial adverse effects on economic activity via wealth effects that decrease consumption (Caldera Sánchez and Johansson, 2011[16]). Depressed housing markets deteriorate bank balance sheets, with repercussions on lending activity. These effects are particularly detrimental when high amounts of debt are involved (Jordà, Schularick and Taylor, 2015[25]). Earlier OECD work has also shown that rapid growth in household debt is an early warning indicator of economic downturns (Hermansen and Röhn, 2017[26]).

The smooth functioning of housing markets is also key to labour market efficiency and an economy's ability to cope with structural changes. Residential mobility is crucial to the efficient allocation of human capital in the job-matching process. Particularly during periods of structural economic change that require a geographical or sectoral reallocation of resources (e.g. from industry to services), high residential mobility increases the speed of economic adjustments and thereby limits the adverse effects on overall economic performance (Caldera Sánchez and Johansson, 2011[16]). Empirical evidence shows that residential mobility is closely linked to dynamics in housing markets, including public policies affecting market conditions (Andrews, Caldera Sánchez and Johansson, 2011[19]). In particular, residential mobility is higher in countries with a more flexible housing supply, lower transaction costs, lower rent controls and less binding credit constraints (Caldera Sánchez and Andrews, 2011[27]; Causa and Pichelmann, 2020[7]).

1.6. Recent housing market developments risk reinforcing pre-existing inequalities

Declining housing affordability has led to economic and social challenges that disproportionately affect poorer and younger households. Real house and rental prices have risen faster than inflation (Figure 1.3) and incomes (Figure 1.8) in recent decades, and while the reduction in real interest rates has lowered mortgage repayment costs, this has only partly cushioned the impact of higher house prices. The mean share of housing-related expenditures in overall household expenditures has therefore increased across the OECD during this period (Figure 1.4). These developments have stronger effects on low-income and younger households, who, as discussed in Chapter 2, generally report low levels of homeownership and are thus more likely to bear the adverse impacts of rising house prices. Poorer households, in particular, are also more likely to live in low quality dwellings than their higher-income counterparts (OECD, 2021[2]), and rising housing costs make it more difficult for this population to afford necessary housing maintenance or move to better-quality housing. Empirically, low-quality housing has been associated with poor access to health care, education, digital infrastructure and labour market opportunities, all of which have long lasting effects on income and will further put low-income households at a socioeconomic disadvantage (OECD, 2021[1]).

Rising house prices contribute to a growing economic divide between households that own property and those that do not. Rising house prices present a major opportunity for wealth accumulation, as property owners benefit from significant investment returns on a major household asset category. Besides direct wealth effects, rising house prices also promote homeowners' access to credit as property may serve as a collateral, for which lending terms improve with rising property values (Andrews, Caldera Sánchez and Johansson, 2011[19]). Homeownership trends across the OECD suggest that these benefits will disproportionately accrue to older and higher-income households, who are more likely to own their residence (see Chapter 2). At the same time, rising property values pose a growing barrier to homeownership by leading to greater up-front buying costs and higher mortgage burdens for new market entrants. For instance, the number of years of disposable income that is equivalent to the price of a 100m^2 dwelling increased almost everywhere in the OECD, and almost doubled in some countries between 2000 and 2020 (Figure 1.8). Housing price inflation, pushing up rental prices, also reduces the disposable income of households renting on the private market, which decreases their economic wellbeing and makes it more difficult to save for homeownership. Households that do not presently own a home (which, as noted above, are more likely to be younger and poorer households) will thus find it increasingly difficult to get on the property ladder and reap the economic advantages of homeownership. In addition to these effects on income and inter-generational equity, housing price inflation may exacerbate intra-generational equity concerns among younger generations by further restricting homeownership to individuals who have received wealth transfers (e.g. gifts, inheritances – see Chapter 2).

Figure 1.8. Number of years over which cumulated average household disposable income equals the average price of a 100m2 dwelling, 2000 and 2020

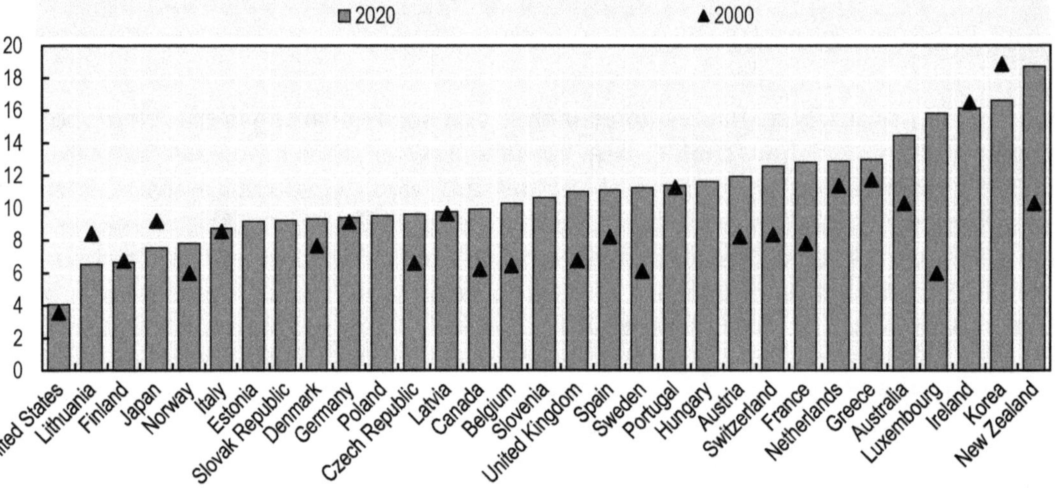

Note: The choice of fixed-size (100m2) dwelling is made to ease cross-country comparisons. Data from 2000 are missing from Estonia, Hungary, Poland, and Slovak Republic

Source: Bricongne, Turrini and Pontuch (2019[28]) and OECD calculations

StatLink https://stat.link/lxkg1v

Housing price inflation can also contribute to spatial segregation, with important implications for household wellbeing, access to public services, and social mobility. House price growth and associated housing cost increases vary considerably across regions, with increasing regional differences in property values constraining the ability of lower-income individuals to live close to where they work, which can lead to long commutes and negatively affect their wellbeing. Rising housing costs may also affect households' ability to relocate to areas that offer better employment and training opportunities or access to higher quality public services, thereby reinforcing existing economic inequalities. In addition, strong geographic discrepancies in housing price inflation raise important concerns linked to the unequal concentration of capital gains on real estate. Households in high-demand areas, who may have already been relatively better off to begin with, will experience disproportional increases in capital gains on housing assets, further reinforcing levels of spatial segregation.

1.7. The housing sector has a sizeable impact on the environment

The housing sector has a sizeable carbon footprint. Overall, the buildings and construction sector accounted for 35% of final energy use and 38% of energy and process-related CO_2 emissions in 2019.). 28% of total global energy-related emissions alone arose from the operations of buildings (UNEP, 2020[29]). The residential sector accounted for around 22% of global final energy consumption and 17% of total energy-related CO_2 emissions in 2019 (Figure 1.9). The bulk of the energy consumption of the residential sector originates from heating, with local temperatures and dwelling sizes being key drivers of energy use (Global Alliance for Buildings and Construction, International Energy Agency and United Nations Environment Programme, 2019[30]). Construction is another major driver of emissions, accounting for 8% of total energy consumption and 10% of energy-related CO_2 emissions (Figure 1.9), mainly attributable to the manufacturing of building materials such as cement, steel and glass (Global Alliance for Buildings and Construction, International Energy Agency and United Nations Environment Programme, 2019[30]). While energy-intensity per square metre has improved in recent decades, total energy-related CO_2 emissions from the building sector rose by 25% globally between 2000 and 2017 due to the increase in floor space (Global Alliance for Buildings and Construction, International Energy Agency and United Nations Environment Programme, 2019[30]).

Figure 1.9. Global share of buildings and construction final energy and emissions, 2019

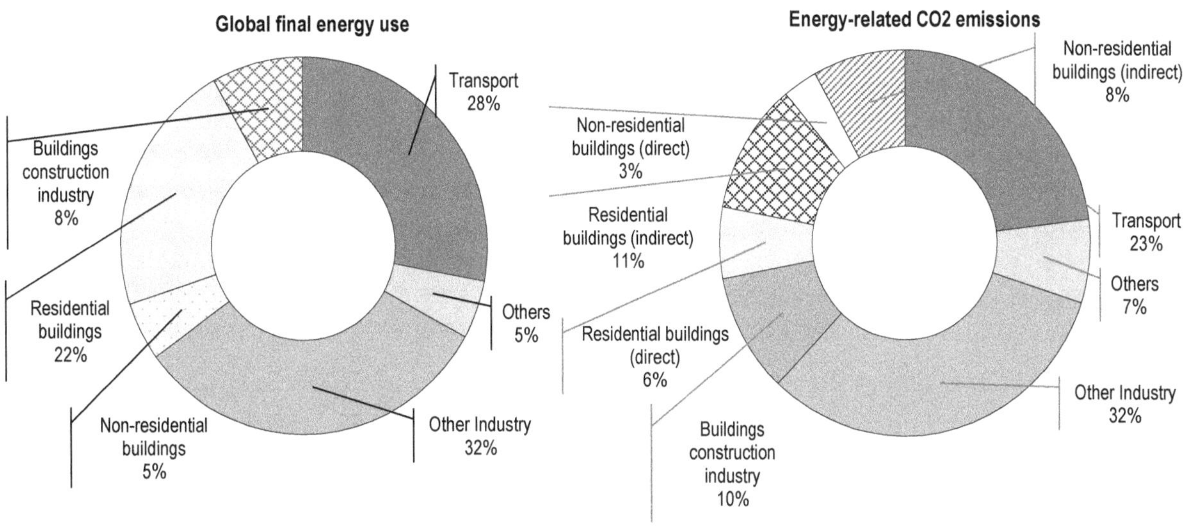

Note: Buildings construction industry is the portion (estimated) of overall industry devoted to manufacturing building construction materials such as steel, cement and glass. Indirect emissions are emissions from power generation for electricity and commercial heat.
Source: United Nations Environment Programme, (2020)

StatLink https://stat.link/vf47z6

Reducing carbon emissions in the residential sector, particularly by encouraging energy-efficiency renovations of the existing housing stock, will be key to achieving climate goals. To comply with the climate goals of the Paris Agreement, average energy use per square metre in buildings would need to be reduced by 30% by 2030 (IEA, 2019[31]). Given the low level of annual construction relative to the existing building stock in OECD countries (for instance, annual constructions as a share of existing buildings amount to 1% in the EU), energy-efficient renovations to reduce carbon emissions from the existing building stock will be key (OECD, 2021[32]). To achieve higher levels of insulation and promote energy saving, the UN Environment and International Energy Agency predicts that the annual rate of energy renovations of the existing building stock has to increase from 1-2% to more than 2-3% by 2025 to comply with the Paris Agreement (UN Environment and International Energy Agency, 2017[33]). To reduce emissions in the construction phase, efforts will have to focus, among other things, on material efficiency, building practices to enhance the life span of buildings and material recycling (IEA, 2019[31]).

Housing is also a significant source of fine particulate matter (PM2.5). PM2.5 is the air pollutant that poses the greatest threat to health, and significant exposure to these particles considerably increases the risk of respiratory and cardiovascular diseases. On average, the residential sector accounts for 37% of PM2.5 emissions globally. PM2.5 emissions from the housing sector are particularly high in countries where reliance on solid fuels, notably wood and coal, remains significant for residential heating (e.g. Central and Eastern European countries) (Karagulian et al., 2015[34]). Exposure to PM2.5 concentration is also positively correlated with the density of urban areas (Borck and Schrauth, 2021[35]). Over the last 30 years, mean exposure to PM2.5 emissions has been decreasing in most OECD countries due to optimised combustion processes (in industry and residential heating), a decrease of coal in the energy mix, and lower emissions from transport and agriculture, but still remains high and above the 10 µg/m3 recommended by the World Health Organization (OECD, 2020[36]).

Housing has an impact on land use, biodiversity, water quality and transport, which may be exacerbated by urban sprawl. Urban sprawl is characterised by low-density, spread-out and discontinuous or scattered urban developments, and has been identified as a common challenge faced by cities in many OECD countries (OECD, 2018[37]). Urban sprawl can have significant environmental consequences through a number of channels, such as the loss of rural or natural land, reduced biodiversity following the fragmentation of natural habitats, and lower water quality due to increased run-off from impervious surfaces (e.g. roads). More spread-out urban developments have also been shown to increase car dependency, which leads to higher greenhouse gas emissions and declining air quality. It is important to note, however, that there can be some positive social and economic benefits associated with urban sprawl. These developments may cater to the preferences of specific households for neighbourhoods with lower levels of noise, congestion, and air pollution, among other factors. They may also contribute to the economic revival of certain rural areas, which find themselves better connected to key economic centres as urban peripheries grow in size. While these benefits should not be overlooked when assessing the desirability of future housing developments, it is important to ensure that residential construction is carried out in a way that limits unnecessary urban sprawl and its adverse environmental consequences.

1.8. Longer-term structural shifts are likely to have profound impacts on housing markets in the future

There are signs that the prolonged period of low inflation and low interest rates may be coming to an end, which will have implications for the housing market. Countries may begin normalising monetary policy in light of recent increases to inflation, raising the possibility that countries will transition out of the era of very low interest rates and inflation (OECD, 2022[12]). In the short term, this creates the risk of rising debt service burdens, although many households would likely be cushioned from interest rate rises by the substantial savings accumulated during 2020-21 and by the high share of fixed interest rate mortgages in many markets (see Box 1.1) (OECD, 2022[12]). Lower-income borrowers, who may have smaller financial reserves and higher debt service-to-income ratios, will be more vulnerable to higher costs of living and borrowing. Higher borrowing costs will also likely affect house prices. They may lead to house prices stabilising and even adjusting downwards, which could improve housing affordability. However, a significant and unexpected drop in house prices could have a significantly negative impact on some households and wider implications for the stability of the financial system.

Box 1.1. Vulnerabilities in the housing sector from rising mortgage rates

House prices, along with household debt, rose steadily throughout the pandemic, even in countries where these were already high. The strong rise in house prices in many countries was due in part to higher demand from exceptionally accommodative monetary conditions, a surge in household savings and unprecedented fiscal support, as well as restricted supply due to mobility restrictions and logistical bottlenecks. With monetary policy now beginning to normalise, mortgage rates are increasing in many OECD countries, raising solvency concerns. Vulnerabilities seem currently contained, due to households' relatively strong balance sheets and the limited use of adjustable-rate mortgages. Still, fragile borrowers could be at risk in economies where adjustable-rate mortgages dominate, debt-service ratios are high and monetary policy is likely to tighten substantially. Countries will need to monitor the situation closely to identify risks and consider any appropriate policy adjustments.

Low debt service ratios, high household savings, and the prevalence of fixed-rate mortgages may reduce vulnerabilities to changes in the monetary landscape. Average debt service ratios remain close to or below long-term norms and significantly below what would be considered a stressed debt service ratio. Average household savings also increased significantly during the pandemic, due in part to restricted consumption options and income support measures. Many households have fixed rates mortgages, which dominate in the largest mortgage markets and are associated with a lower probability of default on mortgages when interest rates rise (Gross et al., 2022[38]). These factors may allay some of the solvency concerns raised by tightening monetary policy.

Figure 1.10. Fixed-rate mortgages and moderate debt service ratios limit risks in housing markets

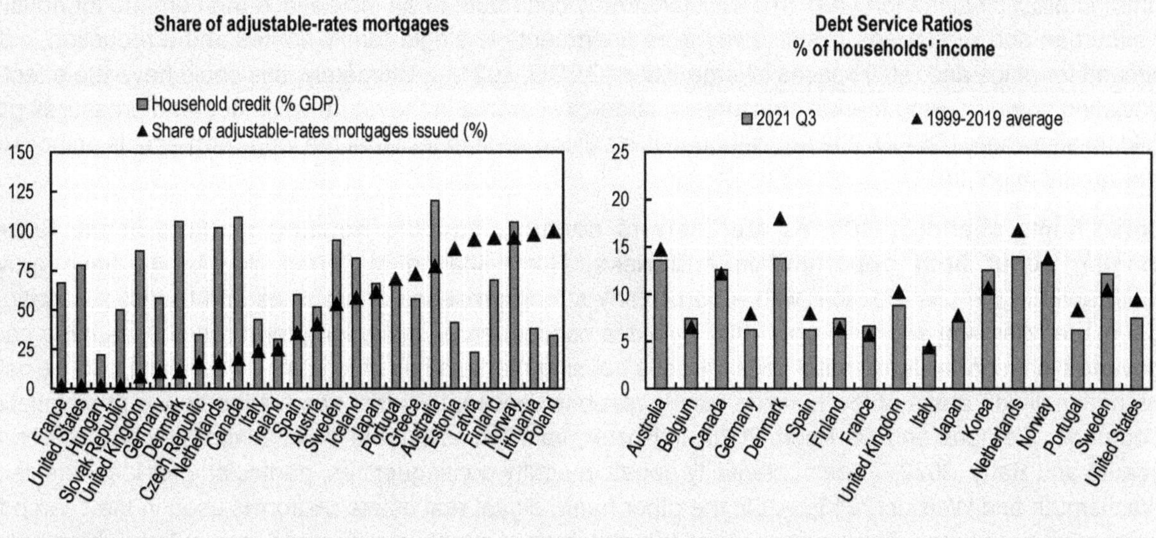

Note: The level of household credit is measured as of 2021 Q3, and the average share of ARM at issuance in 2019 and 2020 is used to proxy for the importance of each type of mortgage in each country

Source: OECD Economic Outlook (OECD, 2022[12]))

StatLink https://stat.link/uly372

However, these aggregate measures conceal important heterogeneity within and across countries. Many lower-income households were unable to build savings during the pandemic, in part due to higher food and energy expenditures and job losses, and some borrowers already facing high debt service ratios are under additional pressures from the withdrawal of pandemic income support measures and higher inflation. In addition, adjustable-rate mortgages are prevalent in some mortgage markets, which raises additional concerns in countries where rising inflation pressures raise the possibility of sharp increases in interest rates.

Given uncertainty regarding future levels of inflation and monetary and fiscal policy responses, it is critical to monitor the situation closely. Monetary and fiscal policy will differ across countries and depend on country-specific factors such as inflation, wage growth and fiscal space. In this uncertain context, countries may need to react quickly to ensure the stability of the housing market and prevent sharp increases in the cost of living. In parallel, countries may consider a range of medium term policies to ease housing pressures, including investment in social housing and reforms to property taxation, rental regulation and land use policies (OECD, 2021[1]).

Source: OECD Economic Outlook (OECD, 2022[12])

Housing supply will also need adapt to structural shifts in housing demand. Buildings have long life spans, which increases the difficulty of adapting to structural shifts in housing markets. In OECD countries, nearly a fifth of the residential building stock was built before 1945, while about half was constructed before 1980 (OECD, 2021[32]). At the same time, digitalisation and technological change, population ageing, climate change, and most recently the COVID-19 pandemic are changing the needs and preferences of private households and businesses. These trends are expected to have significant, although in some cases uncertain, effects on housing markets (OECD, 2021[1]).

The COVID-19 pandemic has triggered changes in work practices and housing preferences with potentially longer lasting effects on the housing market. The widespread adoption of teleworking during the COVID-19 crisis may have lasting effects on demand for housing if remote work remains a common practice in the long run. In particular, it may contribute to an increase in the demand for housing in suburban and rural areas, a shift away from apartments to single-family homes and a reduction in the demand for office and retail spaces in large cities (OECD, 2021[1]). Ultimately, this could have the effect of alleviating some housing market pressures in large city centres in the future while demand pressures may build up elsewhere (OECD, 2021[1]), although it is still too soon to tell what the long-term effects on housing affordability might be.

Digital home sharing platforms are likely to continue shaping housing markets in the future, bringing about both opportunities and risks. Home-sharing platforms like Airbnb have grown significantly in the past decade, with a particularly strong presence in big cities and tourist destinations (Cournède, Ziemann and De Pace, 2020[39]). As a consequence, many long-term rental units have been converted into shorter-term rental housing while housing markets have increasingly opened up to demand internationally. In areas of low housing supply responsiveness, this shift has fuelled house price inflation (Cournède, Ziemann and De Pace, 2020[39]; Koster, van Ommeren and Volkhausen, 2021[40]; Shabrina, Arcaute and Batty, 2022[41]) with potentially negative equity consequences, particularly for local residents (Wachsmuth and Weisler, 2018[42]). On the other hand, digital real estate platforms used in the search for longer-term accommodations may enhance the matching of supply and demand, particularly where online content allows for more effective filtering and online viewings reduce costly in-person visits (OECD, 2021[1]).

E-commerce affects the demand for commercial property, though its effects on residential housing affordability are still uncertain. Online retail trade has grown significantly, with visible shifts away from brick-and-mortar retail to online channels (OECD, 2019[43]). Research shows that the rise in e-commerce is associated with a decline in the demand for commercial real estate (Worzala et al., 2002[44]; Zhang, Zhu and Ye, 2016[45]), accompanied by a stronger polarisation in demand between properties in prime locations and other less attractively located properties (Dixon and Marston, 2002[46]). Lockdown measures during the COVID-19 crisis have accelerated this trend, pushing the share of e-commerce in total sales to an all-time high in 2020 of 16% in the United States, 31% in the United Kingdom and 25% in China (OECD, 2019[43]). Online shopping is likely to persist in the future as convenience is reported as one of the main drivers behind its adoption (OECD, 2020[47]). However, e-commerce trends also show that online and physical stores are considered complements rather than perfect substitutes, which is why physical stores are likely to continue to exist (Jones and Livingstone, 2015[48]; OECD, 2019[43]; Zhang, Zhu and Ye, 2016[45]). The increase in e-commerce also comes with an increasing demand for warehouses, which are located increasingly close to customers and within city boundaries to keep up with the promises of ever shorter delivery times. Besides the shift in commercial real estate demand, the effect of these trends on residential housing affordability will also depend on the flexibility with which commercial property can be converted into residential property (OECD, 2021[1]).

Rapid population ageing around the world will continue to alter household structures and preferences. An ageing population has been associated with decreasing household sizes and more numerous households. Nowadays, people live longer and more commonly on their own or in a two-person household, which is also driven by a significant decline in multigenerational households. These shifts in household composition have put pressure on housing markets, given the slow responsiveness of housing supply. The existing housing stock also has to be adapted to the needs of older tenants, to enhance accessibility for instance, and retrofitting existing properties is costly and may contribute to rising house prices and housing costs. Older households also need to live in close proximity to a range of essential services (OECD, 2021[1]), which could push up housing demand in already popular urban and sub-urban areas and require an adaption of urban infrastructure.

Climate change will increasingly affect housing demand while housing supply will need to adapt to changing weather conditions. Climate change will alter the desirability of different locations, with some regions standing to benefit from milder weather conditions while others will be increasingly at risk of natural disasters and capital depletion due to rising sea levels, desertification and extreme temperatures. These demand changes could alter house price evolutions across and within countries (Atreya and Czajkowski, 2019[49]; Beltrán, Maddison and Elliott, 2018[50]; Li, 2009[51]), though the short- and medium-term impacts on housing markets critically depend on individual beliefs and the risk assessments of both buyers and sellers (Bakkensen and Barrage, 2021[52]; Baldauf, Garlappi and Yannelis, 2020[53]). Housing insurance may also become increasingly costly in areas subject to more extreme weather conditions and climate risks, which could in turn lead to higher overall housing costs. At the same time, construction, including the use of materials and property retrofitting, will need to adapt to changing weather conditions (Global Alliance for Buildings and Construction, International Energy Agency and United Nations Environment Programme, 2019[30]).

References

Acolin, A. (2022), "Owning vs. Renting: the benefits of residential stability?", *Housing Studies*, Vol. 37/4, pp. 644-667, https://doi.org/10.1080/02673037.2020.1823332. [6]

Ahir, H. and P. Loungani (2019), "Managing House Price Booms: Evolution of IMF Surveillance and Policy Advice", in Nijskens, R. et al. (eds.), *Hot Property*, Springer International Publishing, Amsterdam, The Netherlands, https://doi.org/10.1007/978-3-030-11674-3_7. [22]

Ahrend, R. et al. (2022), "Changes in the geography housing demand after the onset of COVID-19: First results from large metropolitan areas in 13 OECD countries", *OECD Economics Department Working Papers*, No. 1713, OECD Publishing, Paris, https://doi.org/10.1787/9a99131f-en. [11]

Andrews, D., A. Caldera Sánchez and Å. Johansson (2011), "Housing Markets and Structural Policies in OECD Countries", *OECD Economics Department Working Papers*, No. 836, OECD Publishing, Paris, https://doi.org/10.1787/5kgk8t2k9vf3-en. [19]

Atreya, A. and J. Czajkowski (2019), "Graduated Flood Risks and Property Prices in Galveston County", *Real Estate Economics*, Vol. 47/3, pp. 807-844, https://doi.org/10.1111/1540-6229.12163. [49]

Bakkensen, L. and L. Barrage (2021), "Flood risk belief heterogeneity and coastal home price dynamics: going under water?", *NBER Working Paper Series*, No. 23854, National Bureau of Economic Research, https://doi.org/10.3386/w23854. [52]

Baldauf, M., L. Garlappi and C. Yannelis (2020), "Does Climate Change Affect Real Estate Prices? Only If You Believe In It", *The Review of Financial Studies*, Vol. 33/3, pp. 1256-1295, https://doi.org/10.1093/rfs/hhz073. [53]

Beltrán, A., D. Maddison and R. Elliott (2018), "Is Flood Risk Capitalised Into Property Values?", *Ecological Economics*, Vol. 146, pp. 668-685, https://doi.org/10.1016/j.ecolecon.2017.12.015. [50]

Bétin, M. and V. Ziemann (2019), "How responsive are housing markets in the OECD? Regional level estimates", *OECD Economics Department Working Papers*, No. 1590, OECD Publishing, Paris, https://doi.org/10.1787/1342258c-en. [14]

Borck, R. and P. Schrauth (2021), "Population density and urban air quality", *Regional Science and Urban Economics*, Vol. 86, p. 103596, https://doi.org/10.1016/j.regsciurbeco.2020.103596. [35]

Bricongne, J., A. Turrini and P. Pontuch (2019), "Assessing House Prices: Insights from "Houselev", a Dataset of Price Level Estimates", *European Economy Discussion Papers*, No. 101, European Commission, Brussels. [28]

Caldera Sánchez, A. and D. Andrews (2011), "To Move or not to Move: What Drives Residential Mobility Rates in the OECD?", *OECD Economics Department Working Papers*, No. 846, OECD Publishing, Paris, https://doi.org/10.1787/5kghtc7kzx21-en. [27]

Caldera Sánchez, A. and Å. Johansson (2011), "The Price Responsiveness of Housing Supply in OECD Countries", *OECD Economics Department Working Papers*, No. 837, OECD Publishing, Paris, https://doi.org/10.1787/5kgk9qhrnn33-en. [16]

Causa, O. and J. Pichelmann (2020), "Should I stay or should I go? Housing and residential mobility across OECD countries", *OECD Economics Department Working Papers*, No. 1626, OECD Publishing, Paris, https://doi.org/10.1787/d91329c2-en. [7]

Cavalleri, M., B. Cournède and E. Özsöğüt (2019), "How responsive are housing markets in the OECD? National level estimates", *OECD Economics Department Working Papers*, No. 1589, OECD Publishing, Paris, https://doi.org/10.1787/4777e29a-en. [17]

Cournède, B., S. Sakha and V. Ziemann (2019), "Empirical links between housing markets and economic resilience", *OECD Economics Department Working Papers*, No. 1562, OECD Publishing, Paris, https://doi.org/10.1787/aa029083-en. [24]

Cournède, B., V. Ziemann and F. De Pace (2020), "The Future of Housing: Policy Scenarios", *OECD Economics Department Working Papers*, No. 1624, OECD Publishing, Paris, https://doi.org/10.1787/0adf02cb-en. [39]

DiPasquale, D. and E. Glaeser (1999), "Incentives and Social Capital: Are Homeowners Better Citizens?", *Journal of Urban Economics*, Vol. 45/2, pp. 354-384, https://doi.org/10.1006/juec.1998.2098. [5]

Dixon, T. and A. Marston (2002), "U.K. Retail Real Estate and the Effects of Online Shopping", *Journal of Urban Technology*, Vol. 9/3, pp. 19-47, https://doi.org/10.1080/1063073022000044279. [46]

Glaeser, E. (2011), "Rethinking the Federal Bias Toward Homeownership", *SSRN Electronic Journal*, https://doi.org/10.2139/ssrn.1914468. [8]

Glaeser, E. and J. Shapiro (2003), "The Benefits of the Home Mortage Interest Deduction", in Porterba, J. (ed.), *Tax Policy and the Economy*, MIT Press, http://www.nber.org/chapters/c11534 (accessed on 2 November 2021). [4]

Global Alliance for Buildings and Construction, International Energy Agency and United Nations Environment Programme (2019), *2019 global status report for buildings and construction: Towards a zero-emission, efficient and resilient buildings and construction sector*, https://www.worldgbc.org/news-media/2019-global-status-report-buildings-and-construction (accessed on 21 February 2022). [30]

Gross, M. et al. (2022), "What Drives Mortgage Default Probabilities In Europe and the United States?", *IMF Working Papers*, No. 065, IMF, https://doi.org/10.5089/9798400205705.001. [38]

Hermansen, M. and O. Röhn (2017), "Economic resilience: The usefulness of early warning indicators in OECD countries", *OECD Journal: Economic Studies*, https://doi.org/10.1787/eco_studies-2016-5jg2ppjrd6r3. [26]

IEA (2019), *Perspectives for the Clean Energy Transition: The Critical Role of Buildings*, International Energy Agency, https://www.iea.org/reports/the-critical-role-of-buildings. [31]

Jones, C. and N. Livingstone (2015), "Emerging implications of online retailing for real estate", *Journal of Corporate Real Estate*, Vol. 17/3, pp. 226-239, https://doi.org/10.1108/JCRE-12-2014-0033. [48]

Jordà, Ò., M. Schularick and A. Taylor (2015), "Leveraged bubbles", *NBER Working Paper Series*, No. 21486, National Bureau of Economic Research, Cambridge, https://doi.org/10.1016/j.jmoneco.2015.08.005. [25]

Karagulian, F. et al. (2015), “Contributions to cities’ ambient particulate matter (PM): A systematic review of local source contributions at global level”, *Atmospheric Environment*, Vol. 120, pp. 475-483, https://doi.org/10.1016/j.atmosenv.2015.08.087. [34]

Katagiri, M. and C. Raddatz (2018), “House Price Synchronization and Financial Openness: A Dynamic Factor Model Approach”, *IMF Working Papers*, IMF, https://doi.org/10.5089/9781484378243.001.A001. [23]

Knoll, K., M. Schularick and T. Steger (2017), “No Price Like Home: Global House Prices, 1870-2012”, *American Economic Review*, Vol. 107/2, p. 353, https://doi.org/10.1257/AER.20150501. [9]

Koster, H., J. van Ommeren and N. Volkhausen (2021), “Short-term rentals and the housing market: Quasi-experimental evidence from Airbnb in Los Angeles”, *Journal of Urban Economics*, Vol. 124, p. 103356, https://doi.org/10.1016/j.jue.2021.103356. [40]

Li, R. (2009), “The Impact of Climate Change on Residential Transactions in Hong Kong”, *SSRN Electronic Journal*, https://doi.org/10.2139/ssrn.1429727. [51]

Mirrlees, J. et al. (2011), “The Taxation of Land and Property”, in *Tax by design*, Oxford University Press, Oxford. [3]

OECD (2022), *Affordable Housing Database*, https://www.oecd.org/housing/data/affordable-housing-database/ (accessed on 21 February 2022). [10]

OECD (2022), *OECD Economic Outlook, Volume 2022 Issue 1*, OECD Publishing, Paris, https://doi.org/10.1787/edfbca02-en. [12]

OECD (2021), *Brick by Brick: Building Better Housing Policies*, OECD Publishing, Paris, https://doi.org/10.1787/b453b043-en. [1]

OECD (2021), *Building for a Better Tomorrow: Policies to Make Housing more Affordable*, OECD Publishing, Paris, https://doi.org/10.1787/5d9127d4-en. [2]

OECD (2021), *Decarbonising Buildings in Cities and Regions: A whole-of-government and multi-level governance approach*, OECD, https://doi.org/10.1787/a48ce566-en. [32]

OECD (2021), *OECD Economic Outlook, Volume 2021 Issue 2*, OECD Publishing, Paris, https://doi.org/10.1787/66c5ac2c-en. [13]

OECD (2021), *The rise of non-bank financial intermediation in real estate finance: Post-COVID-19 trends, vulnerabilities and policy implications*, OECD Publishing, Paris, https://doi.org/10.1787/8123cd42-en. [18]

OECD (2020), “E-commerce in the time of COVID-19”, *OECD Policy Responses to Coronavirus (COVID-19)*, OECD Publishing, Paris, https://doi.org/10.1787/3a2b78e8-en. [47]

OECD (2020), *Environment at a Glance 2020*, OECD Publishing, Paris, https://doi.org/10.1787/4ea7d35f-en. [36]

OECD (2019), *Under Pressure: The Squeezed Middle Class*, OECD Publishing, Paris, https://doi.org/10.1787/689afed1-en. [15]

OECD (2019), *Unpacking E-commerce: Business Models, Trends and Policies*, OECD Publishing, Paris, https://doi.org/10.1787/23561431-en. [43]

OECD (2018), *Rethinking Urban Sprawl: Moving Towards Sustainable Cities*, OECD Publishing, Paris, https://doi.org/10.1787/9789264189881-en. [37]

Shabrina, Z., E. Arcaute and M. Batty (2022), "Airbnb and its potential impact on the London housing market", *Urban Studies*, Vol. 59/1, pp. 197-221. [41]

UN Environment and International Energy Agency (2017), *Towards a zero-emission, efficient, and resilient buildings and construction sector. Global Status Report 2017*, https://www.worldgbc.org/sites/default/files/UNEP%20188_GABC_en%20%28web%29.pdf (accessed on 21 February 2022). [33]

UNEP (2020), *Global Status Report for Buildings and Construction: Towards a Zero-emission, Efficient and Resilient Buildings and Construction Sector*, United Nations Environment Programme, Nairobi. [29]

van Doorn, L., A. Arnold and E. Rapoport (2019), "In the Age of Cities: The Impact of Urbanisation on House Prices and Affordability", in Nijskens, R. et al. (eds.), *Hot Property*, Springer International Publishing, Amsterdam, The Netherlands, https://doi.org/10.1007/978-3-030-11674-3. [21]

van Hoenselaar, F. et al. (2021), "Mortgage finance across OECD countries", *OECD Economics Department Working Papers*, No. 1693, OECD Publishing, Paris, https://doi.org/10.1787/f97d7fe0-en. [20]

Wachsmuth, D. and A. Weisler (2018), "Airbnb and the rent gap: Gentrification through the sharing economy", *Environment and Planning A: Economy and Space*, Vol. 50/6, pp. 1147-1170. [42]

Worzala, E. et al. (2002), "E-commerce and retail property in the UK and USA", *Journal of Property Investment & Finance*, Vol. 20/2, pp. 142-158, https://doi.org/10.1108/14635780210420034. [44]

Zhang, D., P. Zhu and Y. Ye (2016), "The effects of E-commerce on the demand for commercial real estate", *Cities*, Vol. 51, pp. 106-120, https://doi.org/10.1016/j.cities.2015.11.012. [45]

Notes

[1] The OECD House Price Database compiles residential property prices in OECD countries over time, with real house prices commonly referring to the price of newly-constructed and existing properties, adjusted for the consumer expenditure deflator.

2 The distribution of housing assets

The chapter examines how housing wealth and liabilities are distributed across households with different levels of income and wealth and across households of different ages and generations. The chapter also discusses the role of inheritances and gifts in the acquisition of housing. The findings in this chapter inform the policy assessments and reform options outlined in the remainder of the report.

2.1. Introduction

Understanding the distribution of housing wealth is essential for the design of effective and equitable housing tax policies. Accounting for the distribution of housing wealth and housing debt can help policy makers anticipate the impacts of housing taxes. This chapter presents key indicators of the distribution of housing assets and liabilities across OECD countries (Box 2.1). In particular, it documents how the allocation of housing wealth and debt varies across the income and wealth distributions and across the lifecycle. It also examines how homeownership has changed over generations and touches on the role of inheritances in the acquisition of housing. The findings in this section hold significant relevance for the design of housing taxes, and help to inform the policy assessment and options for reform outlined in the remainder of the report.

Housing is a key component of household wealth, especially for the middle class, although it tends to be concentrated among older, high-wealth, and high-income households. Housing is a key vehicle for wealth accumulation and is a particularly important asset for middle-class households. Homeownership rates vary widely across countries, but they rise with income in nearly all countries. Housing wealth (both owner-occupied housing and secondary real estate) is highly concentrated among high-wealth households, and to a lesser extent among top income earners. High-income households hold a disproportionately large share of housing debt but lower-income households with mortgages generally face higher debt burdens, which has implications for tax relief on mortgage interest. Homeownership and housing wealth are strongly associated with age. Older households tend to have high levels of housing wealth but low levels of income, raising potential liquidity concerns linked to the taxation of housing. Evidence also shows that homeownership rates have been declining for younger generations, particularly lower-income and lower-wealth households. In addition, those who receive inheritances are much more likely to become homeowners in some countries. The distributional impact of housing taxation policies will depend on whether policy makers measure their effects along the income distribution or the wealth distribution and will differ in absolute and relative terms, given the concentration of housing wealth at the top yet the importance of housing for the middle class.

2.2. Household wealth and homeownership

Housing is the main asset category for most households and accounts for the bulk of household wealth for the middle class. Owner-occupied housing wealth ranges from 28% of total gross household wealth in the United States to 65% in the Slovak Republic, but accounts for 50% of total household wealth on average across the 29 OECD countries with available data and comprises over half of total household wealth in 17 countries (Figure 2.1). Secondary real estate[1] also makes up a significant component of gross household wealth in many OECD countries, where it is generally the second or third largest household asset class. Owner-occupied housing is particularly important for households in the middle of the wealth distribution (i.e. the second, third, and fourth quintiles), where it accounts for roughly 65% of household wealth on average (Figure 2.2). This share is significantly smaller at the top of the wealth distribution, where households hold a large portion of their wealth as financial assets; for example, owner-occupied housing comprises on average just 21% of household wealth for the top 1%. Owner-occupied housing is also relatively less important among the lowest wealth quintile, where it comprises 52% of household assets on average, as other real assets (e.g. vehicles, valuables, and other non-housing goods) play a comparatively larger role in household wealth. Several factors contribute to the predominance of housing within middle class wealth. For example, owner-occupied housing is both a consumption and investment good that is typically heavily tax-favoured compared to most other savings vehicles (OECD, 2018[1]). Housing is also often perceived as a safe investment and allows people to live on lower incomes once their mortgage debt is repaid (i.e. in retirement). The availability of housing-related debt finance has also allowed lower-wealth households to accumulate substantial levels of net housing wealth over their lifetimes (Causa, Woloszko and Leite, 2019[2]).

Figure 2.1. Average decomposition of household assets, 29 OECD countries

2019 or latest available year

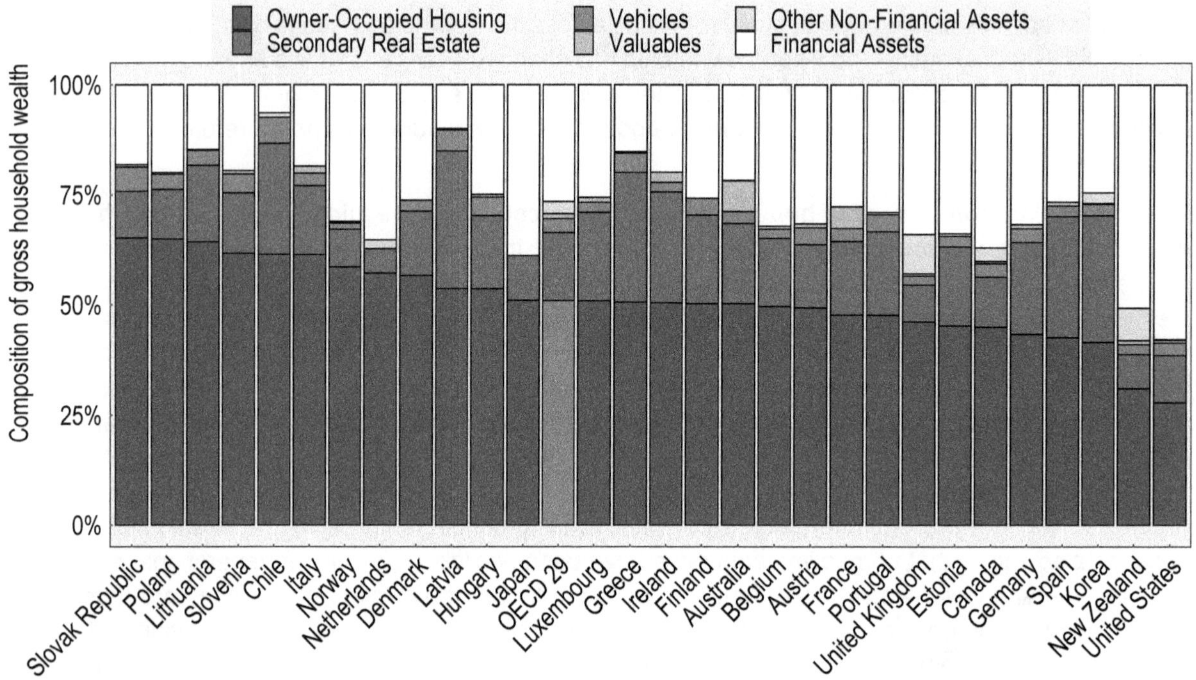

Source: OECD Wealth Distribution Database, oe.cd/wealth.

StatLink https://stat.link/z6oj0i

Figure 2.2. Composition of household assets by wealth quintile, unweighted average, 29 OECD countries

2019 or latest available year

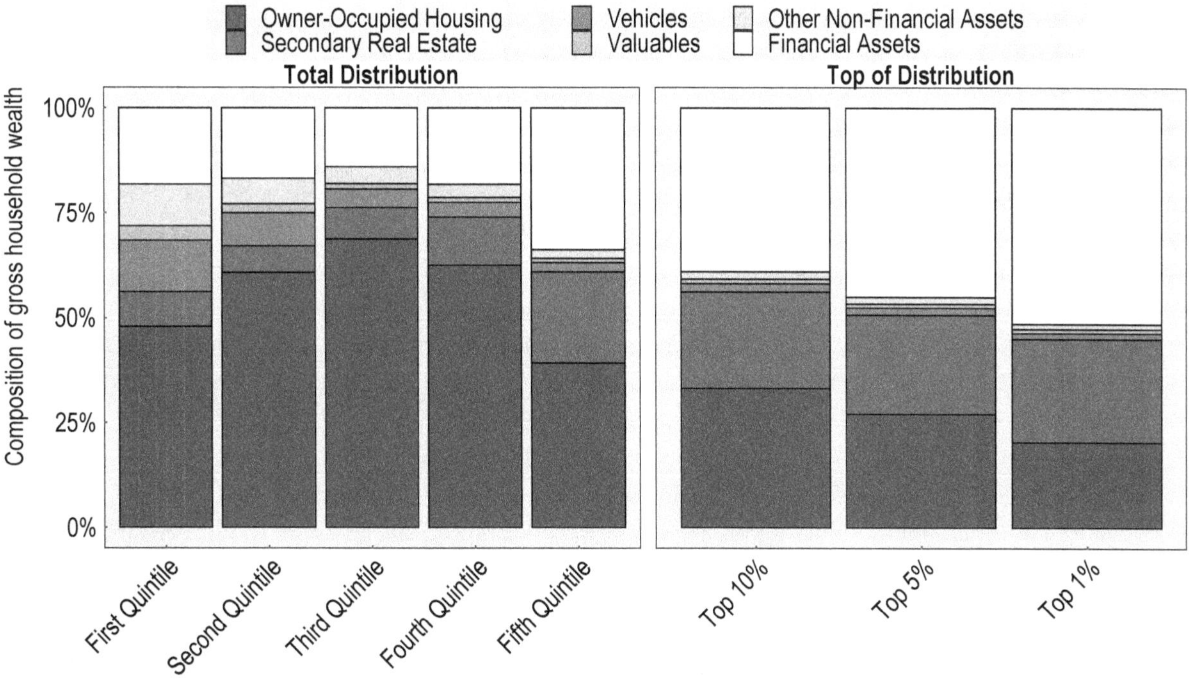

Note: Quintiles range from first (lowest) to fifth (highest). See Box 2.1 for a description of how quintiles are calculated. Average of Australia, Austria, Belgium, Canada, Chile, Germany, Denmark, Estonia, Finland, France, Greece, Hungary, Ireland, Italy, Japan, Korea, Lithuania, Luxembourg, Latvia, Netherlands, Norway, New Zealand, Poland, Portugal, Slovak Republic, Slovenia, Spain, United Kingdom, United States. Missing observations were removed.

Source: OECD Wealth Distribution Database, oe.cd/wealth.

StatLink https://stat.link/hkt52o

Box 2.1. Measuring household wealth

Data sources

This chapter draws extensively on the OECD's Wealth Distribution Database (WDD), which includes data on 29 OECD countries, and the European Central Bank's Household Finance and Consumption Survey (HFCS), which includes data on 19 European OECD countries. Data are available in both datasets for Austria, Belgium, Estonia, Finland, France, Germany, Greece, Hungary, Ireland, Italy, Latvia, Lithuania, Luxembourg, Netherlands, Poland, Portugal, Slovak Republic, Slovenia, and Spain. Data are available only in the WDD for Australia, Canada, Chile, Denmark, Japan, Korea, New Zealand, Norway, the United Kingdom (limited to Great Britain) and the United States.

Both sources provide micro-level data that is largely comparable across participating countries. The HFCS draws on household surveys whose questionnaires are harmonised across participating countries. The WDD relies on tax and administrative data for three countries (Denmark, the Netherlands, and Norway), while estimates for the remaining countries are based on household surveys, which includes the HFCS for participating countries.

Indicators

The chapter examines non-equivalised household wealth; that is, without adjusting for household size. Gross wealth is the sum of the total assets of households, while net wealth is the difference between the total assets and the total liabilities of households (this means net wealth may be negative). Note that household wealth does not include public or occupational pensions. Throughout this chapter, net wealth is generally used to examine overall wealth levels, as it better reflects the wealth that households have at their disposal. Gross wealth is generally used for compositional analysis, which avoids the possible problem of negative wealth.

The chapter examines how wealth is distributed across the income and wealth distributions. Income quintiles are calculated on household non-equivalised disposable income for Australia, Canada, Chile, Denmark, Finland, Italy, Japan, Korea, New Zealand, the Netherlands, Norway, the United Kingdom and the United States, and are based on household non-equivalised gross income for the remaining countries. While this reduces comparability across countries with different measures, the impact is expected to be minor as households typically occupy a similar relative position in the distribution of gross and disposable income. Wealth quintiles are calculated on household non-equivalised net wealth for all countries.

It is important to be cautious when interpreting the results contained in this chapter. As no adjustment is made for household size and because higher income and higher wealth households are less likely to be single-person households, the top 10% and top 1% may represent more than 10% and 1% of the population, respectively. Adjusting for household size could reduce the income and wealth share of the top households, although the extent of the reduction would depend on the country. In addition, across countries, different factors influence the levels and distribution of housing wealth, and the drivers behind trends in housing wealth will have changed over time. The enduring impact of past public policies, changing demographics, the development of mortgage markets and many other factors increase the complexity of the analysis.

Source: Wealth Distribution Database: https://www.oecd.org/social/WDD-Metadata.pdf. Household Finance and Consumption Survey https://www.ecb.europa.eu/pub/economic-research/research-networks/html/researcher_hfcn.en.html

The proportion of homeowners and renters varies substantially across OECD countries. The proportion of households that own their home (with or without a mortgage) is lowest in Germany (44%), followed by Austria (46%) and Denmark (46%), with the remainder renting or living in other forms of tenure (Figure 2.3). On the other hand, 93% of households in Lithuania own their primary residence, with particularly high levels also found in the Slovak Republic (89%) and Poland (84%). Homeownership patterns vary across regions, with lower homeownership rates in Northern and Western European countries, compared to particularly high levels in Central and Eastern Europe. In general, homeownership rates in Anglophone countries (e.g. Australia (66%), Canada (64%), the United States (65%)) and Southern European countries (e.g. Greece (72%), Italy (68%)) fall between these two groups. Among homeowners, the tendency to hold a mortgage also differs considerably across countries. In the Netherlands, for example, only 9% of households are outright owners of their primary residence and 47% of households own their residence with a mortgage. In contrast, just 8% of households in Slovenia own their primary residence with a mortgage, while 68% own their home outright. The role of debt finance in the acquisition of owner-occupied housing wealth appears to play a far greater role in some OECD countries than in others (see Figure 2.14).

Figure 2.3. Share of households that are renters, owners with a mortgage, or outright owners, 28 OECD countries

2019 or latest available year

Note: A breakdown between outright owners and owners with a mortgage was not available for Norway.
Source: OECD Wealth Distribution Database, oe.cd/wealth.

StatLink https://stat.link/kfq1ve

Homeownership rates are highest at the top of the income distribution in nearly all OECD countries, but there are substantial differences in homeownership for lower- and middle-income households. Figure 2.4 shows that homeownership rates are generally highest for households in the top income quintile; more than three-quarters of top income households are homeowners in 26 of the 29 OECD countries with available data. However, there is considerable cross-country variation for households with lower incomes. In several Central and Eastern European countries (e.g. Hungary, Lithuania, the Slovak Republic), homeownership is widespread along the income distribution with marginal differences across income quintiles. Other countries, such as Japan and Poland, have larger differences between quintiles but still exhibit high rates of homeownership across the board. Germany, the Netherlands, and Canada have low levels of homeownership among the bottom quintile and considerable disparities between successive income groups, while countries such as Chile and New Zealand display comparable but low levels of homeownership across the distribution. These cross-country differences in homeownership rates along the income distribution align with the country differences in housing tenure types displayed in Figure 2.3. In countries with a low proportion of renters, homeownership appears to be broadly accessible across the income distribution. Where renting is widespread, however, homeownership is more dependent on household income.

Figure 2.4. Homeownership rate by income quintile, 29 OECD countries

2019 or latest available year

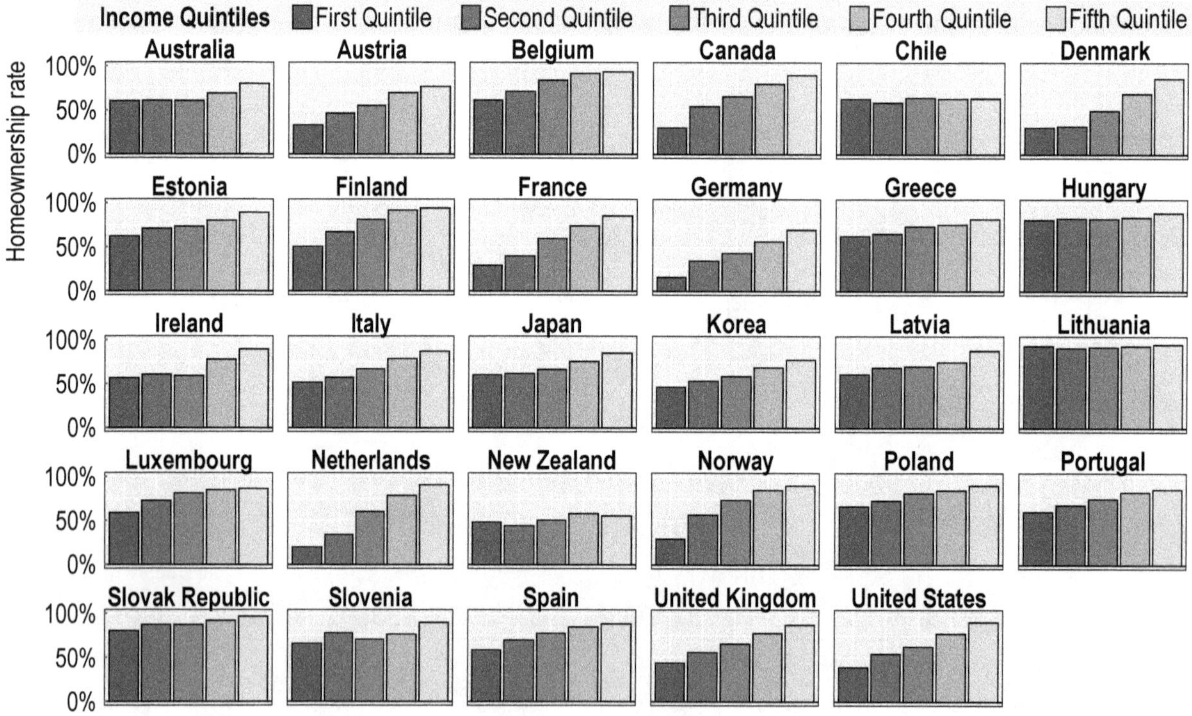

Note: Quintiles range from first (lowest) to fifth (highest). See Box 2.1 for a description of how quintiles are calculated. This indicator only refers to the ownership of households' primary residences, and does not account for homeowners who may rent their primary residence and own secondary property.
Source: OECD Wealth Distribution Database, oe.cd/wealth.

StatLink https://stat.link/ce8si2

Despite marked differences in homeownership patterns across OECD countries, there are striking similarities in the relationship between housing tenure and households' relative levels of income and wealth. Figure 2.5 examines renters, outright owners, and owners with a mortgage, comparing their income and wealth to that of the total population in each of the 27 OECD countries with available data. The figure measures the ratio of each group's mean net wealth to the mean net wealth of the total population (on the y-axis) and the ratio of each group's mean pre-tax income to the mean pre-tax income of the total population (on the x-axis) in each country. In all countries, levels of income and wealth among renting households are significantly lower than the population average. This reflects the key role of owner-occupied housing in household wealth, as well as the importance of income to service mortgage debt and save for a down payment. As young households are highly concentrated among renters (Causa, Woloszko and Leite, 2019[2]), access to quality jobs, mortgage finance, and affordable housing are key for this group to build wealth over their lifecycle. Owners with mortgages, on the other hand, tend to have higher incomes while holding average levels of net wealth. This group is largely comprised of people in the middle of their careers (Causa, Woloszko and Leite, 2019[2]), who have substantial debt relative to their total wealth but earn sufficiently high incomes to service their mortgage. Lastly, outright owners possess above-average net wealth with average levels of income. This group contains a large number of elderly households (Causa, Woloszko and Leite, 2019[2]), who have finished repaying their mortgages and no longer earn substantial income.

Figure 2.5. Net wealth and gross income relative to population average by housing tenure type, 27 OECD countries

2019 or latest available year

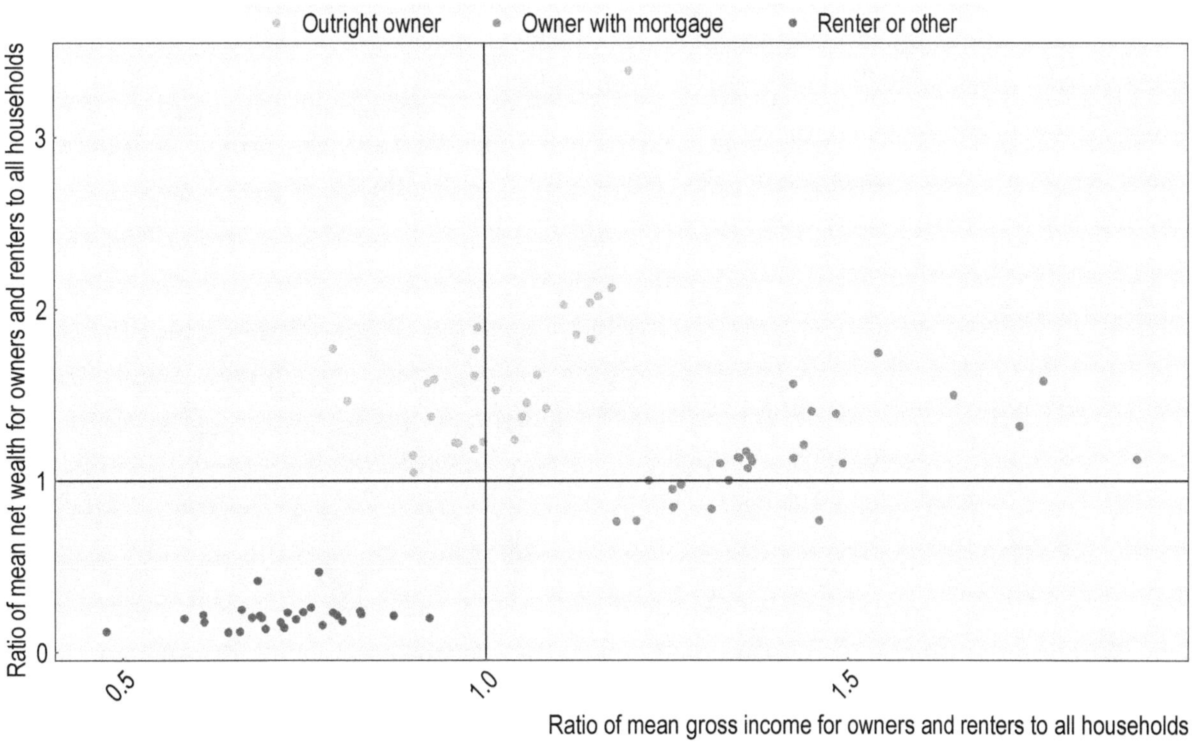

Note: Each dot corresponds to a single country. These indicators were calculated by taking the average value of gross income and net wealth for each group in a particular country and dividing by the average values found among all households in that country. On each axis, the value of 1 is equal to the population average. Countries included are Australia, Austria, Belgium, Canada, Chile, Germany, Denmark, Spain, Estonia, Finland, France, Greece, Hungary, Ireland, Italy, Japan, Korea, Lithuania, Luxembourg, Latvia, New Zealand, Poland, Portugal, Slovak Republic, Slovenia, United Kingdom, United States. Gross income data were not available for the Netherlands and a breakdown between outright owners and owners with a mortgage was not available for Norway.
Source: OECD Wealth Distribution Database, oe.cd/wealth.

StatLink https://stat.link/gd2as7

2.3. Housing assets and liabilities across the income and wealth distributions

Mean owner-occupied housing wealth varies substantially across countries, though it is systematically higher for top income households and lower for those at the bottom. The upper panel in Figure 2.6 shows that mean gross owner-occupied housing wealth for all households is USD 164 500 on average across OECD countries, and ranges from USD 28 500 in Latvia to USD 582 000 in

Luxembourg. It is interesting to note that countries with the highest mean gross housing wealth often have average homeownership rates, while Central and Eastern European countries with particularly high homeownership rates have relatively low mean housing wealth (Figure 2.3, Figure 2.6). As overall housing wealth follows from homeownership levels and housing values, this reflects low housing asset values in Eastern Europe. Figure 2.6 also reports average owner-occupied housing wealth for households in the top and bottom income quintiles. In all countries, households at the top of the income distribution have the highest average housing wealth and households at the bottom of the income distribution have the lowest. Average owner-occupied housing wealth for households in the top income quintile (USD 309 500) is almost twice that of the population average (USD 164 500) and more than three and a half times higher than the average among the bottom quintile (USD 79 500).

The level of secondary real estate wealth is lower than the level of owner-occupied housing wealth, but it is much more concentrated at the top of the income distribution (Figure 2.6). Mean gross secondary real estate wealth amounts to USD 157 000 on average across countries and is lower than mean owner-occupied housing wealth in every country, ranging from USD 11 500 in Poland to USD 229 000 in Luxembourg. These assets are also significantly more concentrated among the top income quintile. Average gross secondary real estate wealth for households at the top of the income distribution (USD 157 000) is roughly three times that of the population average (USD 53 000) and almost nine times higher than the average among the bottom quintile (USD 18 000).

Figure 2.6. Mean gross wealth in owner-occupied housing and secondary real estate, all households and top and bottom income quintiles, 29 OECD countries

2019 or latest available year

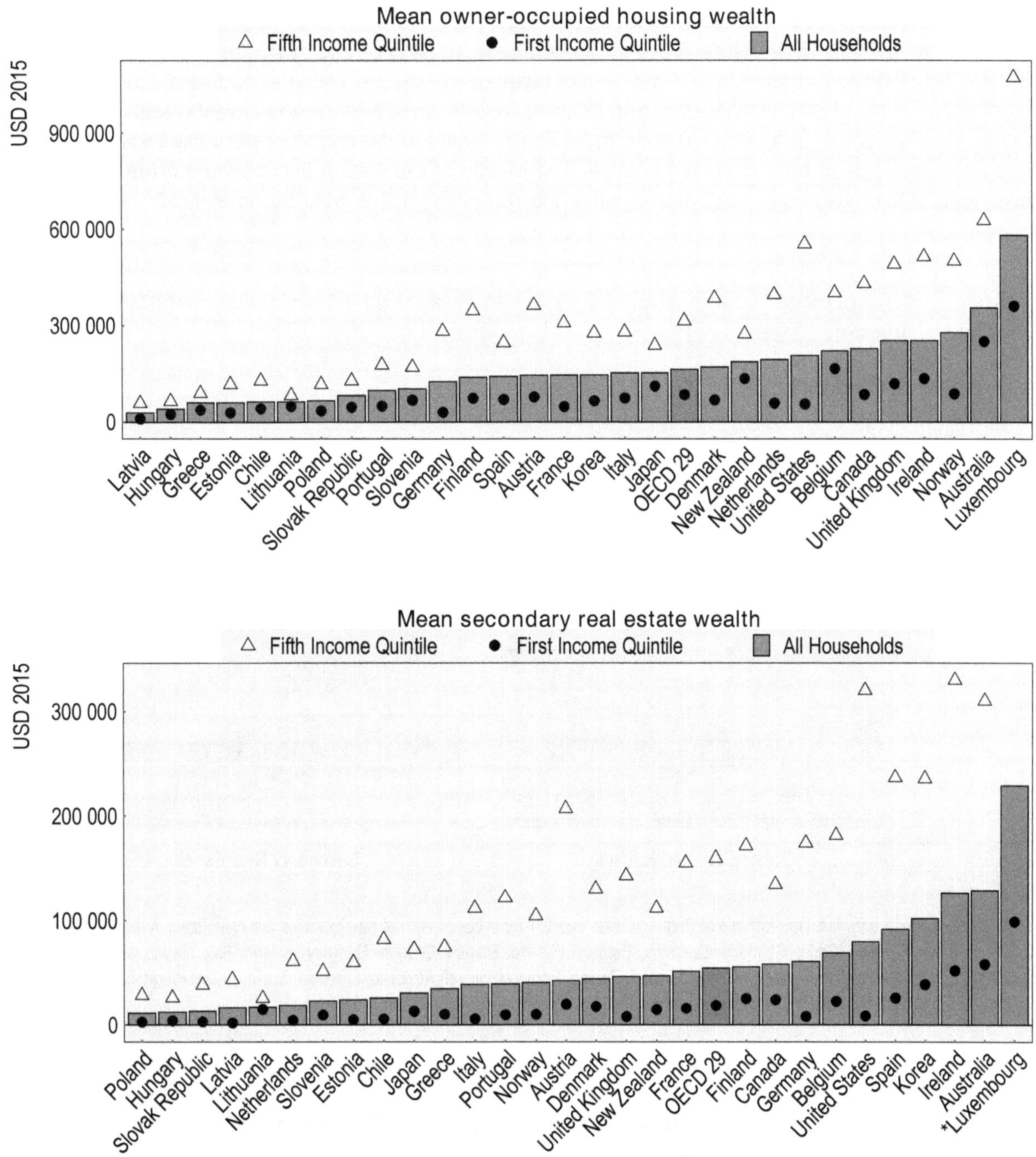

Note: Quintiles range from first (lowest) to fifth (highest). See Box 2.1 for a description of how quintiles are calculated. Wealth values are expressed in 2015 USD by, first, expressing values in prices of the same year (2015) through consumer price indices and, second, by converting national values into PPP USD.

*The mean level of secondary real estate wealth for the top income quintile in Luxembourg is USD 889 500. This observation was removed for readability.

Source: OECD Wealth Distribution Database, oe.cd/wealth.

StatLink https://stat.link/k49onw

The wealthiest households hold a disproportionately large share of housing wealth and own the majority of secondary real estate wealth. Figure 2.7 looks across the wealth distribution and complements the analysis above on the income distribution, as income and wealth are not strongly correlated in OECD countries (OECD (2020[3])). Figure 2.7 shows that on average across 29 OECD countries, nearly half (46%) of total gross owner-occupied housing is held by households in the top wealth quintile. Households in the middle of the wealth distribution (i.e. the second, third, and fourth quintiles) together hold 51% of gross owner-occupied housing wealth, while those in the lowest wealth quintile own roughly 3%. Secondary real estate is even more concentrated at the top, where roughly 75% of wealth is held by households in the top wealth quintile. The middle of the wealth distribution, on the other hand, owns just 24% of secondary real estate, while the remaining 1% is held by households in the bottom quintile.

Figure 2.7. Share of owner-occupied housing and secondary real estate by wealth quintile, unweighted average, 29 OECD countries

2019 or latest available year

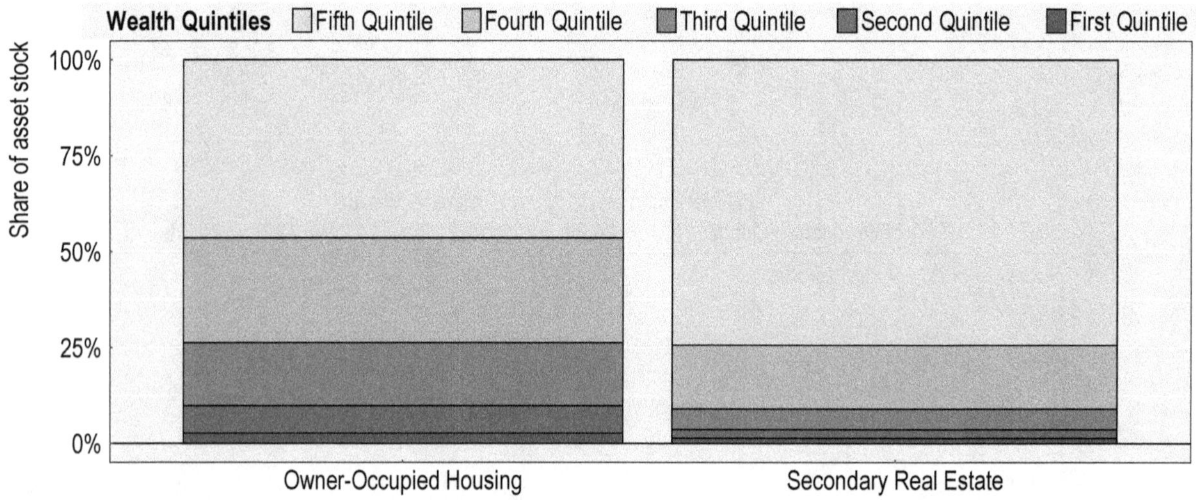

Note: Quintiles range from first (lowest) to fifth (highest). See Box 2.1 for a description of how quintiles are calculated. Average of Australia, Austria, Belgium, Canada, Chile, Germany, Denmark, Estonia, Finland, France, Greece, Hungary, Ireland, Italy, Japan, Korea, Lithuania, Luxembourg, Latvia, Netherlands, Norway, New Zealand, Poland, Portugal, Slovak Republic, Slovenia, Spain, United Kingdom, United States.
Source: OECD Wealth Distribution Database, oe.cd/wealth.

StatLink https://stat.link/ltir3n

Housing debt tends to be disproportionately concentrated in the top income quintile, while low-income households hold relatively little mortgage debt. Across 28 OECD countries, households in the top 20% of the income distribution typically own the largest share of total owner-occupied housing debt, ranging from 68% in Estonia to 16% in Luxembourg (Figure 2.8). Households in the middle of the income distribution (i.e. the second, third, and fourth income quintiles) hold 76% (Belgium) to 32% (Estonia) of owner-occupied housing debt, while the share of debt among households in the lowest income quintile ranges from 14% in Greece to 0.4% in Estonia. The distribution of secondary real estate debt is even more concentrated among households in the upper income quintile, who own 57% of all secondary real estate debt on average, compared with 45% of owner-occupied housing debt. The share of secondary real estate debt held by the top income quintile ranges from 88% (United States) to 24% (Belgium), which is a significantly larger share than that held by households in the bottom quintile (highest in Hungary at 8.7% and lowest in Estonia at 0.09%). Differences between countries in the share of mortgage debt held across the income distribution may reflect factors such as housing affordability, the degree of concentration of income, and access to mortgage finance for households outside the top income quintile. For example, among countries where the share of owner-occupied mortgage debt is more evenly spread across the income distribution, households in the lowest four quintiles tend to make up a greater proportion of owner-occupied mortgage holders than in countries where holding a mortgage is more dependent on household income, suggesting that the volume of mortgages is an important factor in the distribution of mortgage debt. Cross-country differences may also reflect limited mortgage interest relief for high-income households, which reduces the incentive to hold large mortgages. The concentration of mortgage debt at the top has important distributional implications, as mortgage interest relief is widely available in OECD countries and is typically not capped for high earners (see Chapter 3).

Figure 2.8. Share of owner-occupied and secondary real estate debt by income quintile, 28 OECD countries

2019 or latest available year

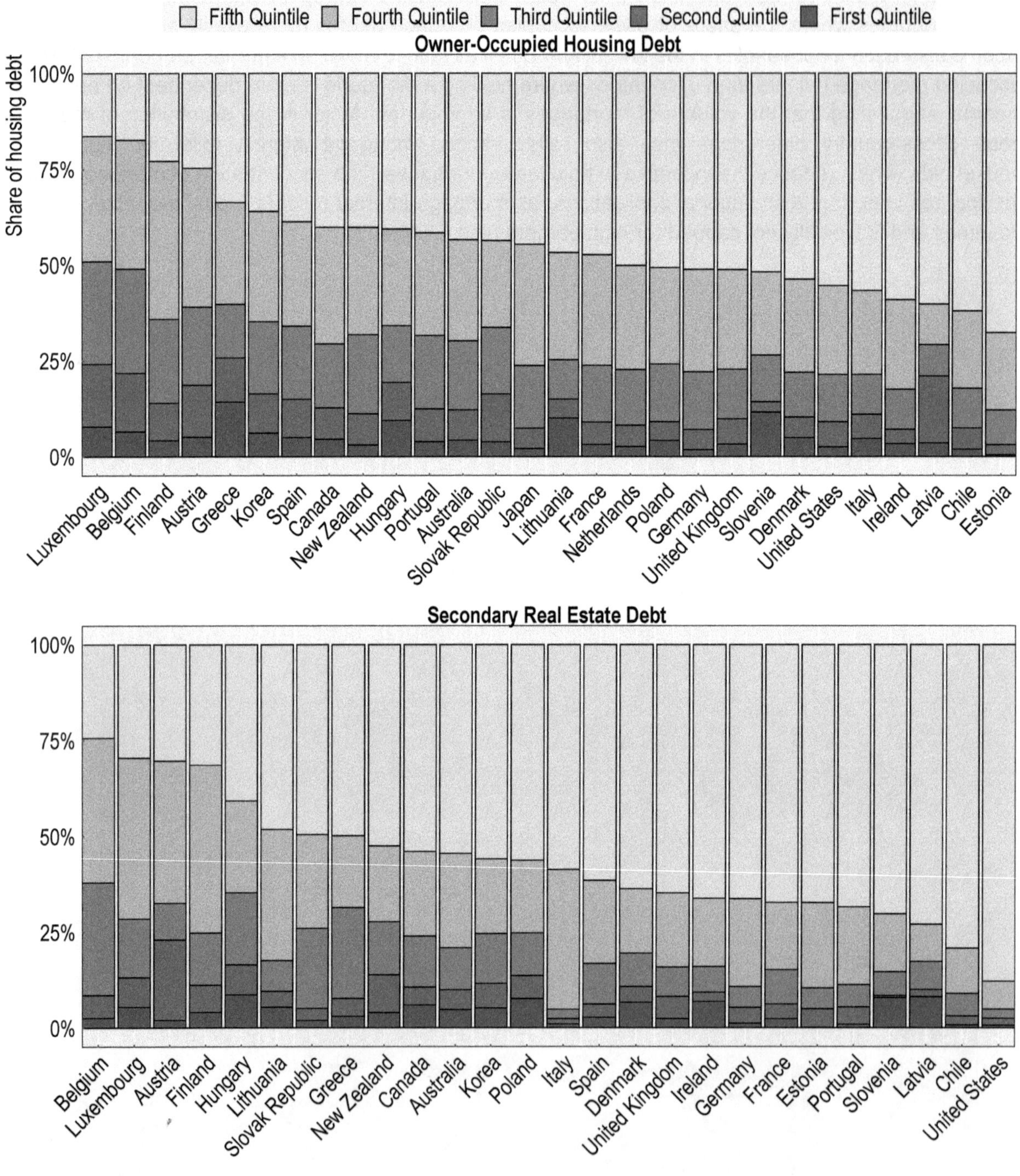

Note: Quintiles range from first (lowest) to fifth (highest). See Box 2.1 for a description of how quintiles are calculated. Data on owner-occupied housing debt were not available for Norway. Data on secondary real estate debt were not available for Norway, Japan and the Netherlands.
Source: OECD Wealth Distribution Database, oe.cd/wealth.

StatLink https://stat.link/v95uho

Mortgage debt is highly concentrated among top income households, while it is more equally distributed along wealth quintiles. Households in the top income quintile hold the highest absolute levels of mortgage debt, compared to both lower-income households and all wealth quintiles (Figure 2.9). In contrast, mortgage debt is particularly low for households at the bottom of the income distribution, driven in part by low-income retirees who have finished paying off their mortgages, and by other households whose incomes are simply too low to obtain a mortgage. On the other hand, households at the bottom of the wealth distribution have much larger debt relative to household wealth than households at the top, and mortgage debt is more evenly distributed across the wealth distribution in general. The differences in the composition of income and wealth quintiles suggest that the distributional effects of housing tax policies will differ considerably depending on whether the income or the wealth distribution is considered.

Figure 2.9. Mean value of owner-occupied housing assets and liabilities by income and wealth quintiles, unweighted average, 28 OECD countries

2019 or latest available year

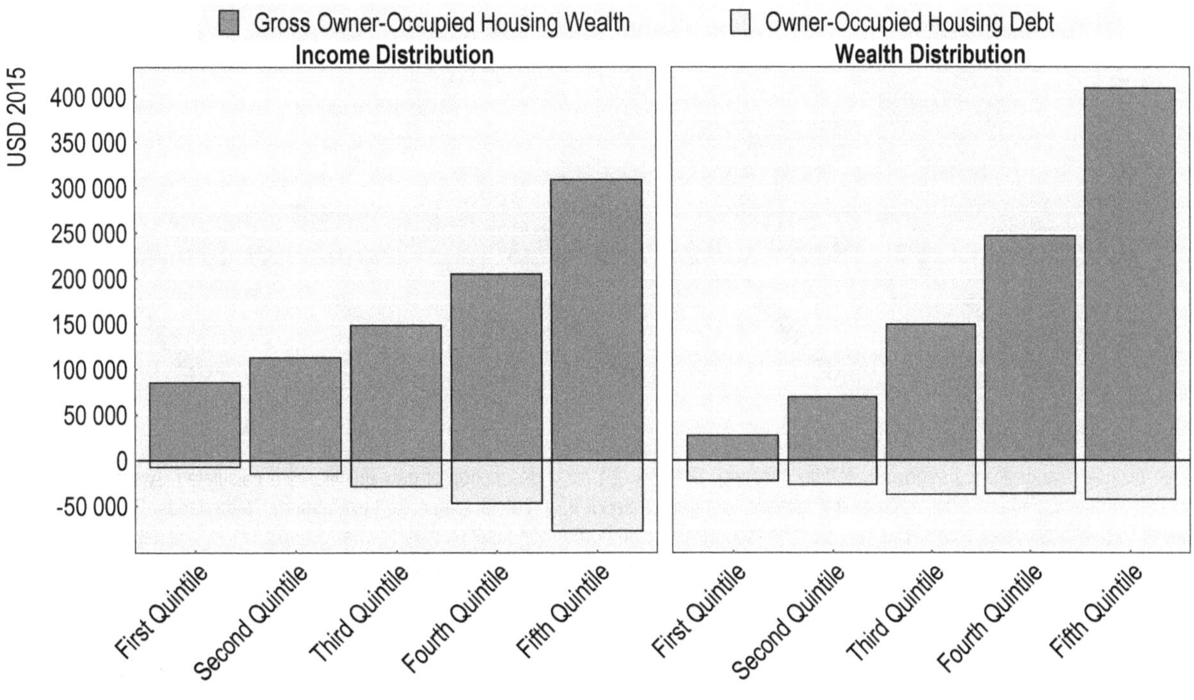

Note: Quintiles range from first (lowest) to fifth (highest). See Box 2.1 for a description of how quintiles are calculated. Average of Australia, Austria, Belgium, Canada, Chile, Germany, Denmark, Estonia, Finland, France, Greece, Hungary, Ireland, Italy, Japan, Korea, Lithuania, Luxembourg, Latvia, Netherlands, New Zealand, Poland, Portugal, Slovak Republic, Slovenia, Spain, United Kingdom, United States. Data on owner-occupied housing debt were not available for Norway. Wealth values are expressed in 2015 USD by, first, expressing values in prices of the same year (2015) through consumer price indices and, second, by converting national values into PPP USD.
Source: OECD Wealth Distribution Database, oe.cd/wealth.

StatLink https://stat.link/g6czns

While owner-occupied housing debt is disproportionately concentrated at the top of the income distribution, low-income households with mortgages tend to face larger relative debt burdens than their high-income counterparts. Figure 2.10, drawing on the level of owner-occupied housing debt relative to gross income on average for 19 OECD countries, finds that two-thirds of mortgage-bearing households[2] in the bottom income quintile face a mortgage debt-to-income ratio greater than three. This percentage declines with each successive income quintile and is less than 10% for mortgage-bearing households in the top income quintile. Conditional on holding a mortgage, lower-income households therefore have larger debt burdens and may be more likely to face difficulties in servicing their housing debt. Policy initiatives aimed at supporting households with mortgage debt (such as mortgage interest relief) may have a larger relative impact on lower-income households, despite their small share of the overall stock of housing liabilities.

Figure 2.10. Proportion of mortgage-bearing households with owner-occupied mortgage debt equal to at least 3 times gross income, unweighted average, 19 OECD countries

2017 or closest available year

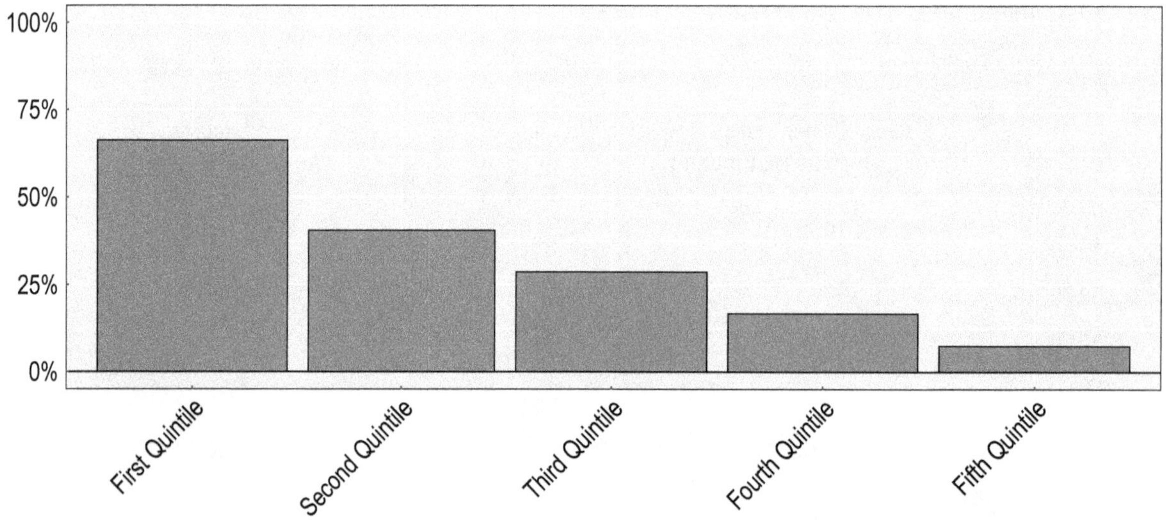

Note: Quintiles range from first (lowest) to fifth (highest). See Box 2.1 for a description of how quintiles are calculated. Average of Austria, Belgium, Estonia, Finland, France, Germany, Greece, Hungary, Ireland, Italy, Latvia, Lithuania, Luxembourg, Netherlands, Poland, Portugal, Slovak Republic, Slovenia, Spain. This indicator corresponds to the proportion of households with owner-occupied mortgage debt in each income quintile whose outstanding mortgage debt is 3 or more times larger than their gross annual household income.
Source: Eurosystem Household Finance and Consumption Survey.

StatLink https://stat.link/23im0x

From a static perspective, higher rates of homeownership have been associated with lower levels of wealth inequality. Causa, Woloszko and Leite (2019[2]) find a negative cross-country association between homeownership and wealth inequality. Compared to financial assets, which make up the second largest share of household wealth on average (Figure 2.1), owner-occupied housing is more equally distributed across the income and wealth distributions. Causa, Woloszko and Leite (2019[2]) also find that the Gini index of total net wealth is lower than the Gini index of financial and non-housing real wealth (i.e. removing housing from overall net wealth), suggesting that housing tends to equalise the distribution of wealth from a static perspective.

From a dynamic perspective, the links between homeownership rates, house price increases and wealth inequality are more difficult to predict. High levels of homeownership can, in theory, moderate rising wealth inequality over time by ensuring that a large share of the population has access to an important vehicle for wealth accumulation. Under these circumstances, rising housing prices could bring greater relative benefits to the property-owning middle class (who, as noted above, hold the majority of their assets in the form of owner-occupied housing) than to the top of the wealth distribution (Alvaredo et al., 2018[4]). However, rising housing prices are not free from distributional concerns. High-wealth households may derive greater absolute benefit from asset price inflation, while housing market access will inevitably decline for households who do not own property. High house prices can also raise household indebtedness, which is already high for low-income households. Rising house prices could thus exacerbate wealth inequality between households that own their residence and those that do not, and between households that can afford to service a mortgage and those that cannot. As discussed in Chapter 1, younger and poorer households are more likely to bear the adverse impacts of declining housing affordability. Younger generations will likely not be able to rely on housing as a vehicle for wealth accumulation in the same way that previous generations have done.

2.4. Housing across age groups

Homeownership and housing wealth vary across age groups, which reflects a combination of lifecycle and generational effects. Differences in homeownership and housing wealth across age groups may reflect the fact that these vary along stages of the lifecycle. For instance, as people age, they may be more likely to become homeowners and accumulate housing wealth. These differences may also reflect changing access to homeownership between different generations. For example, homeownership rates at a given age may be different for households born at different times. This section looks at homeownership and housing wealth across age groups by looking at both cross-sectional data (i.e. at a fixed point in time), which capture a combination of lifecycle and generational effects, and panel data focusing on generational effects in a few countries.

Housing wealth rises steadily with age on average across OECD countries, while mortgage debt is highest as households enter a period of the lifecycle characterised by relatively high earnings. Figure 2.11 displays mean gross and net owner-occupied and secondary housing wealth and mean debt on owner-occupied and secondary housing across household age groups, according to the age of the household head.[3] Gross owner-occupied housing wealth increases with age from the 16-34 age group up to the 45-54 age group, before it stabilises for households aged between 45 and 74 and then declines for households aged over 75. Net owner-occupied housing wealth, however, rises steadily until the 65-74 age bracket, after which it falls slightly for the oldest group. This indicates a key role of mortgage debt in facilitating the accumulation of housing wealth; gross wealth jumps as households enter the housing market but net wealth rises slowly as households pay down their mortgage. Indeed, the graph shows a substantial increase in mean owner-occupied mortgage debt in the 35-44 age group, suggesting that households are most likely to take out a mortgage and begin accumulating housing wealth as they enter a period of the lifecycle characterised by relatively high and stable incomes. Mean owner-occupied housing liabilities then drop substantially with age after peaking for 35-44 year olds, as households gradually repay this debt over the course of their working lives. Secondary housing wealth is much lower than owner-occupied wealth but follows a similar pattern over the lifecycle. Secondary housing wealth (both gross and net) rises steadily with age and peaks for households aged 55-64 years, after which households may begin drawing down their secondary housing wealth as they enter retirement. Debt peaks slightly later for secondary housing (45-54 age group) compared to owner-occupied housing (35-44), suggesting households may prioritise acquiring housing for their personal use before acquiring other housing.

Figure 2.11. Mean value of owner-occupied and secondary housing assets and liabilities by age group of household head, unweighted average, 26 OECD countries

2019 or latest available year

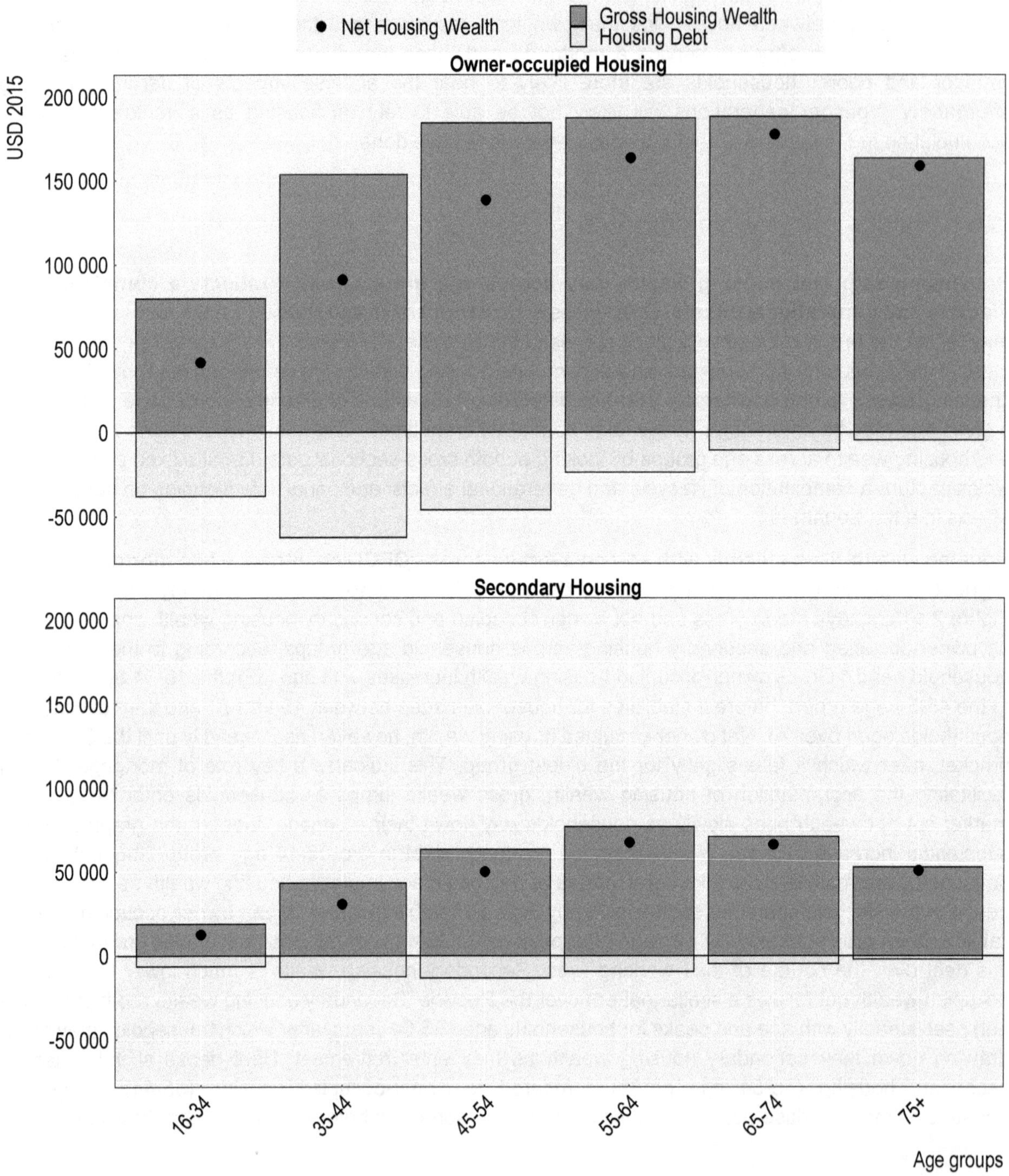

Note: Average of Australia, Austria, Belgium, Canada, Chile, Germany, Denmark, Estonia, Finland, France, Greece, Hungary, Ireland, Italy, Korea, Lithuania, Luxembourg, Latvia, New Zealand, Poland, Portugal, Slovak Republic, Slovenia, Spain, United Kingdom, United States. Data on the breakdown of debt were not available for Norway. Data on secondary housing debt were not available for Japan and Netherlands. Wealth values are expressed in 2015 USD by, first, expressing values in prices of the same year (2015) through consumer price indices and, second, by converting national values into PPP USD.

Source: OECD Wealth Distribution Database, oe.cd/wealth.

StatLin https://stat.link/hcz0oy

There are remarkable similarities in the division of housing debt between different types of households, as mortgage debt is highly concentrated among two-adult working-aged households. Figure 2.12 shows that the majority of mortgage debt in every country is held by working-age households with two or more adults. It is particularly concentrated in two-adult working age households with children, whose share of the debt stock ranges from 42% in Denmark to 74% in Latvia. On the other hand, single working-age household heads (either with or without children) hold less than 20% of housing debt in nearly all cases, with the exception of Lithuania (33%) and Italy (21%). Retirement-age households also account for a particularly low share of mortgage debt, holding under 5% of mortgage debt in 21 of 28 OECD countries. This illustrates that the acquisition of housing debt is strongly linked to lifecycle factors, such as co-habitating with a partner and having children. The prevalence and age at which individuals in a given country will typically enter these stages will depend on a mixture of cultural and economic factors (e.g. cultural norms around families, access to the housing and labour markets, household income, the level of government support for families, etc.).

Figure 2.12. Share of owner-occupied housing debt by household composition, 28 OECD countries

2019 or latest available year

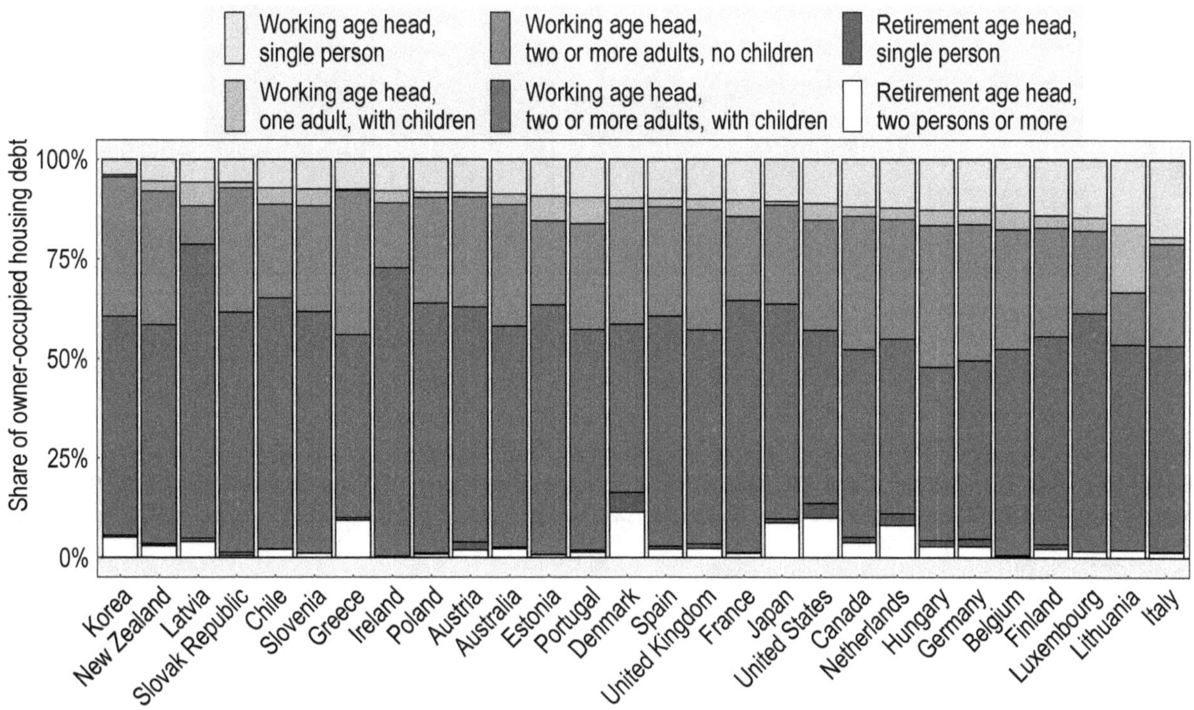

Note: Data on owner-occupied housing debt were not available for Norway.
Source: OECD Wealth Distribution Database, oe.cd/wealth.

StatLink https://stat.link/yu7s32

While older households generally have lower incomes and debt, they possess sizeable net housing wealth. Older populations comprise a large share of retirees, who generally have lower incomes compared to the rest of the population. However, older households possess high average levels of owner-occupied housing wealth and have limited outstanding mortgage debt (Figure 2.11). Figure 2.13 depicts the ratio of mean owner-occupied housing wealth to mean gross household income for different age groups, on average across 26 OECD countries. The ratio increases steadily with the age of the household head and is highest for the 75+ year old category. When considered alongside Figure 2.11, the clear differences in this ratio across age groups seem to be driven by rising wealth for younger age groups and by declining income for older age groups. This points to the existence of a substantial group of relatively income-poor but asset-rich retirees in OECD countries. These findings suggests that housing taxation policies need to be designed with both income and wealth in mind and incorporate measures such as deferral, as older populations hold sizeable levels of housing wealth but might lack the necessary income and asset liquidity to meet their tax obligations.

Figure 2.13. Ratio of mean gross owner-occupied housing wealth to mean gross income by age of household head, unweighted average, 26 OECD countries

2019 or latest available year

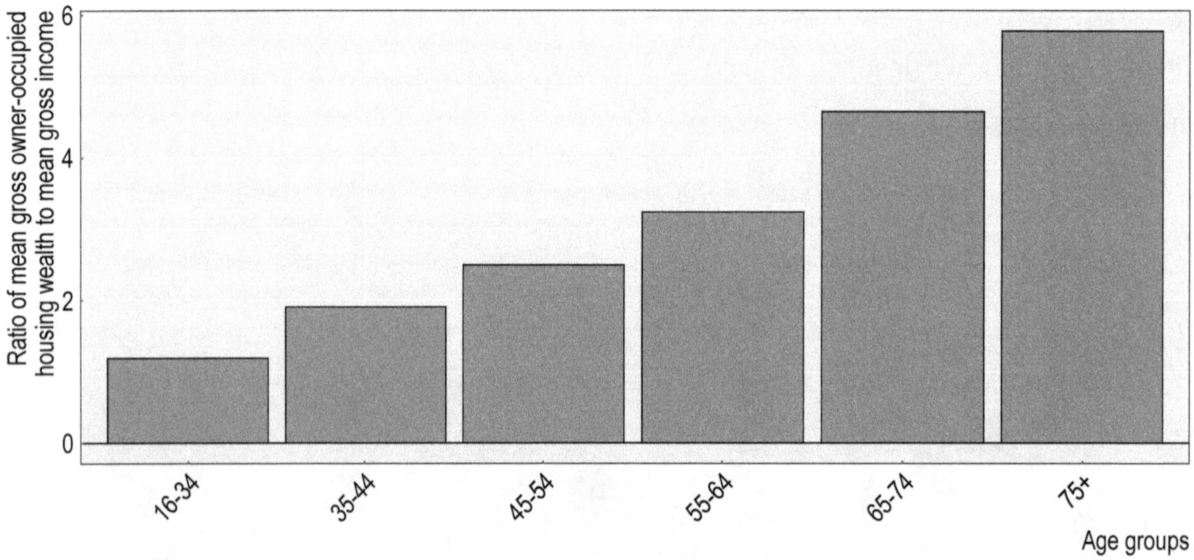

Note: Average of Australia, Austria, Belgium, Canada, Germany, Denmark, Spain, Estonia, Finland, France, Greece, Hungary, Ireland, Italy, Japan, Korea, Lithuania, Luxembourg, Latvia, New Zealand, Poland, Portugal, Slovak Republic, Slovenia, United Kingdom, United States. Data on gross household income were not available for the Netherlands. Data on owner-occupied housing debt were not available for Norway. Chile was removed due to extremely low values.
Source: OECD Wealth Distribution Database, oe.cd/wealth.

StatLink https://stat.link/5tlm07

Homeownership rates are generally higher for middle-aged and older households, although there are significant cross-country differences in the evolution of homeownership across age groups. While there are some similarities in homeownership rates for each age group, the typical timeline of housing wealth acquisition varies significantly across countries (Figure 2.14). Households led by 16-34 year olds have the lowest levels of homeownership in each of their respective countries. Homeownership rates then rise steadily with age in some countries, while in others homeownership rates rise for middle aged households before either stabilising or falling for the oldest households. In countries such as Australia and the United States, homeownership rates gradually increase with age, which suggests that some younger households are unable to access the property market or prefer not to become homeowners. In countries such as Belgium, Poland, and Portugal, homeownership largely plateaus at relatively high levels from the 35-44 year old age group onwards, suggesting relatively widespread housing market accessibility for younger people. In countries such as Germany, Korea, and the Netherlands, there is a clear drop in homeownership rates for households of retirement age, which may be more reflective of differences in cohorts than in age. These differing patterns in homeownership across age groups reflect a range of cross-country differences, encompassing housing price affordability, the availability of finance (both mortgages and family contributions), historical homeownership rates and attitudes towards homeownership.

The importance of mortgage debt in facilitating homeownership and the age at which households pay off their mortgage differ considerably across countries. Figure 2.14 shows the proportion of households that hold a mortgage on their principal residence, by age of the household head. In many countries, nearly all young homeowners have mortgage debt, which suggests a crucial role of debt finance in enabling younger households to access homeownership (e.g. Australia, France, New Zealand). In countries such as Chile, Greece, and Lithuania, however, the share of young households with mortgage debt is far below the homeownership rates of younger households. This may suggest that mortgage finance is less accessible, that homeownership is affordable or that financial support from family plays a significant role in the acquisition of housing wealth for young households. As households age, the prevalence of mortgage debt declines across the board, as mortgage-bearing households progressively pay off their debt. In countries where few young households have mortgage debt, most homeowners appear to have paid off their mortgage by the time they reach 45 years of age (e.g. Hungary, Latvia, Lithuania, Poland). In addition to low initial debt levels and fewer households taking out mortgage debt, this may reflect shorter average loan terms and increasing access to mortgage finance for younger generations. In countries that have a closer link between homeownership and mortgage debt, mortgages tend to be repaid closer to retirement age (e.g. Australia, Japan, and New Zealand). In Denmark and the Netherlands, the proportion of households with mortgage debt peaks within the 45-54 year old age bracket and only diminish slightly over time, remaining relatively high into the 75+ year old age group. These cross-country differences in mortgage prevalence depend on a number of factors, such as housing affordability, access to credit and the tax treatment of housing and mortgage debt.

Figure 2.14. Proportion of households that own their principal residence and proportion of households that hold principal residence mortgage debt, by age group of household head, 29 OECD countries

2019 or latest available year

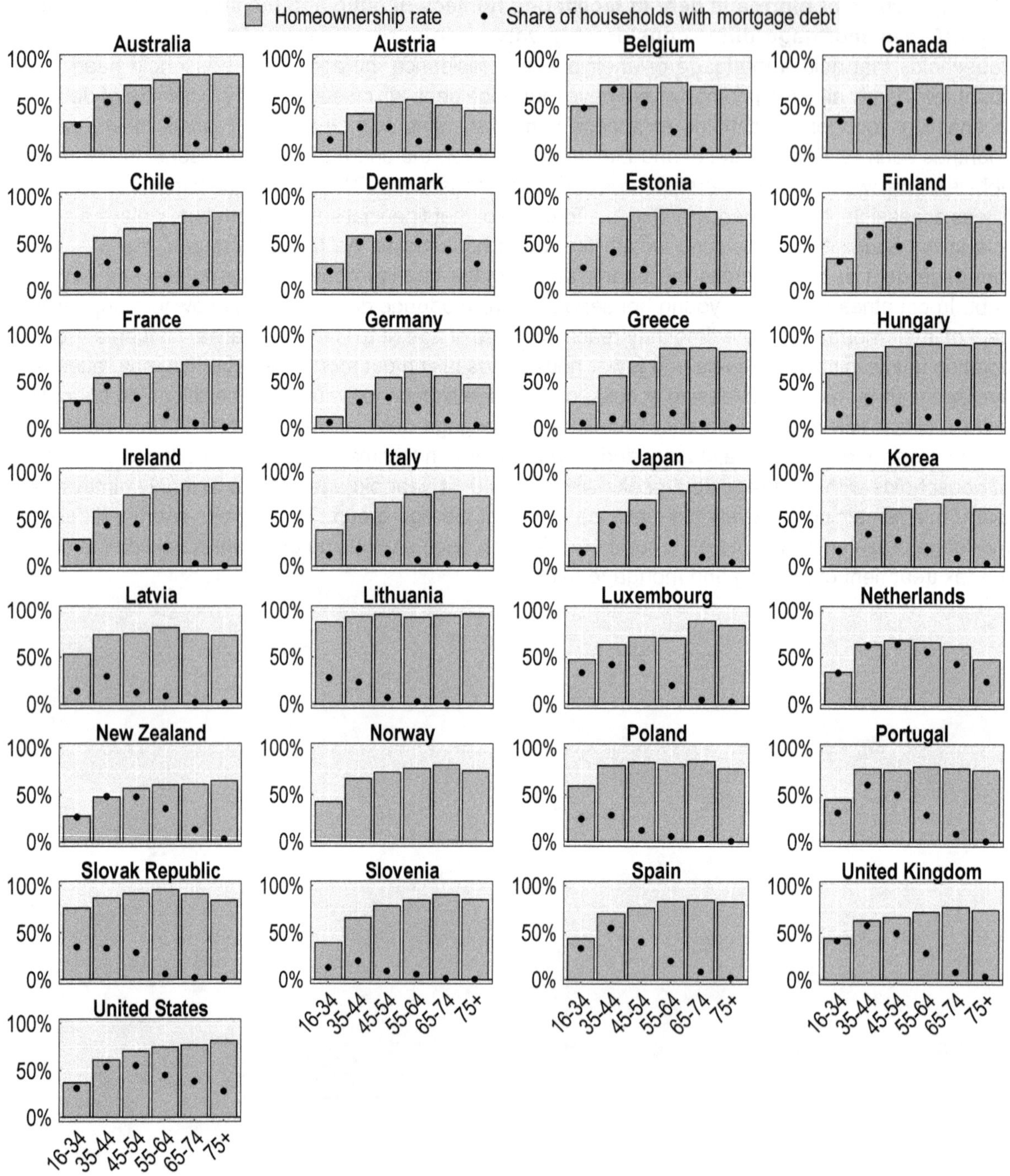

Note: Data on owner-occupied housing debt were not available for Norway.
Source: OECD Wealth Distribution Database, oe.cd/wealth.

StatLink https://stat.link/typj5m

Homeownership trends have changed over generations. While the cross-sectional data discussed above show significant differences in homeownership and housing wealth across age groups, these reflect both lifecycle effects (i.e. individuals being in different stages of their lives) and cohort effects (i.e. individuals being born at a particular time and living under different circumstances). Cross-sectional analyses therefore do not capture how homeownership rates may evolve for each group over their lives. In contrast, panel data can show, for example, how changes in homeownership rates between 30 and 40 years old may be different for households born in the 1960s compared to households born in the 1980s. Figure 2.15 and Figure 2.16 follow several cohorts over the lifecycle for a selection of countries for which data are available. The figures reveal that homeownership is declining and becoming less egalitarian for successive generations, as housing becomes more difficult to obtain and less accessible as a vehicle for wealth accumulation. Given the complex nature of the topic and the few countries with available data, caution should be exercised in generalising these trends and attributing them to potential drivers, including changing public policies, demographic shifts, and evolving access to mortgage credit, among others.

Homeownership rates have declined steadily over successive generations in a number of countries. Figure 2.15 and Figure 2.16 examines homeownership rates for several cohorts over their lifecycle in Australia, Southern Europe, the United Kingdom, and the United States, showing that each generation in these countries is generally less likely to own their homes at a given age than the previous generation. In Australia, for instance, average homeownership rates have decreased with each successive post-war generation. The differences between generational cohorts are greatest for households under 40 years of age, indicating a particularly large drop in access to housing for young people in this country. In the United Kingdom the homeownership rate at 25 years of age was 34% for those born in 1970-74, but fell to 16% for those born in 1985-89. In the United States, 69% of households born in 1940 owned their home at age 35, compared to 61% of those born in 1980. In the United Kingdom and the United States, homeownership rates have begun levelling off at lower levels than they have in the past, suggesting lower homeownership rates for younger generations in these countries may not be made up at later stages in their lifecycle. In Southern Europe, successive generations have lower homeownership rates than the previous generation, but given they are rising at a faster rate for the youngest generation, homeownership rates for the youngest cohort may still reach those of previous cohorts. The results show that a simple focus on average homeownership rates is misleading, as continued high levels of homeownership are partly due to property-owning older cohorts who are living longer.

Figure 2.15. Homeownership rates over the lifecycle for successive birth cohorts in Australia, Southern Europe, the United Kingdom and the United States

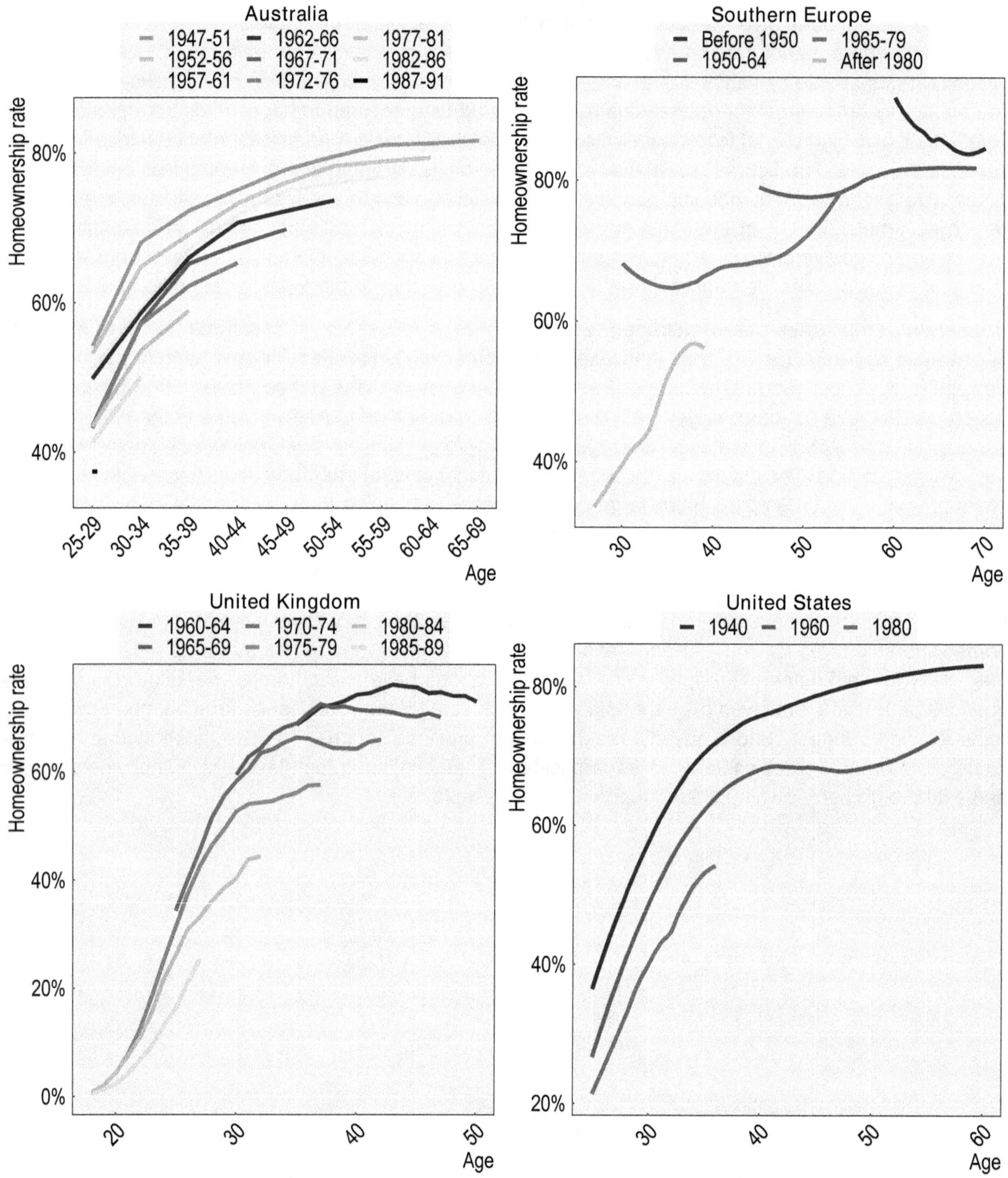

Note: The years in the legend refer to the birth years of each cohort. Southern Europe corresponds to a population-weighted average of Cyprus,[4], [5] Greece, Italy, Malta, Portugal, and Spain.

Source: The figure for Australia is taken from AIHW (2021[5]). The figures for Southern Europe and the United States are taken from Paz-Paredo (2022[6]). The figure for the United Kingdom is taken from Cribb, Hood, and Hoyle (2018[7]).

StatLink https://stat.link/bnekt5

The chance of becoming a homeowner may be increasingly dictated by household income and wealth in some countries. In France in 1973, homeownership rates were very similar for young households (aged 25 to 34) in the first three wealth quartiles. However, over the decades between 1973 and 2013, the gap between the top and bottom wealth quartiles of young households widened substantially (Figure 2.16), with the wealthiest households experiencing a significant increase in homeownership rates and the least wealthy experiencing a sharp decline. In Australia, the decline in homeownership rates between generations has been significantly more pronounced for bottom income households than for top income households (Figure 2.16). Between 1981 and 2016, homeownership rates for households aged 25-34 dropped by 40 percentage points for households in the first income quintile, compared to 7 percentage points for households in the top income quintile. Although the decrease in homeownership rates is smaller for older age groups, the size of the drop across generations remains much larger for households in the bottom income quintile compared to households in the top. For example, for 55-64 year old households, homeownership rates dropped by 16 percentage points in the first quintile and by 1 percentage point in the fifth quintile.

Figure 2.16. Evolution of homeownership rates among young households in France and working-age households in Australia, by income or wealth

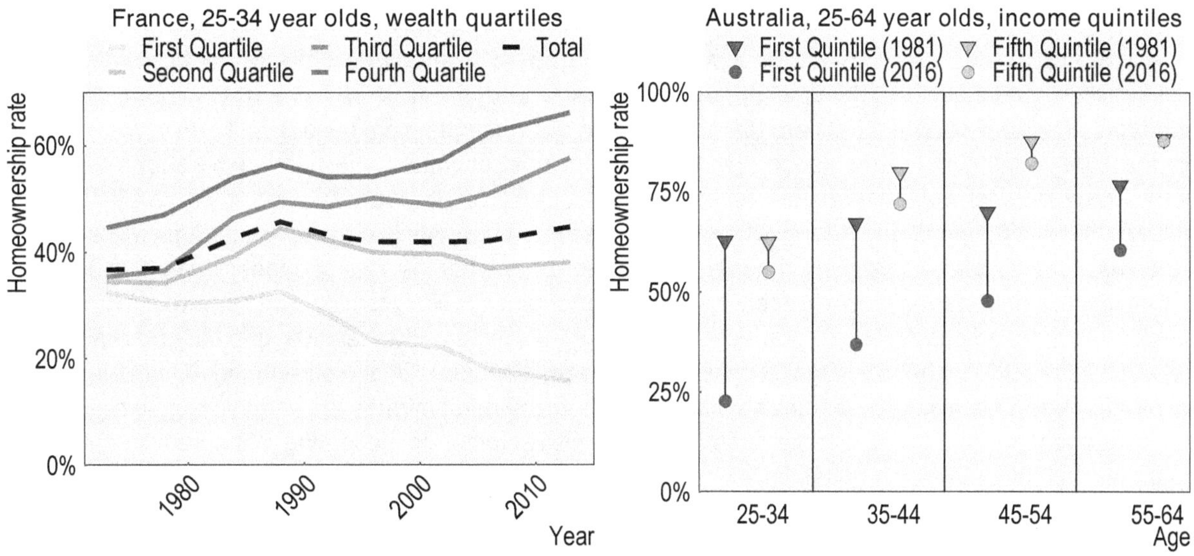

Note: The data for France are broken down by household wealth quartile, while the data for Australia are broken down into the top and bottom equivalised household income quintiles.
Source: The figure for France is taken from Bonnet, Garbinti, and Grobon (2018[8]). The figure for Australia is taken from Daley, Coates, and Wiltshire (2018[9]).

StatLink https://stat.link/uya82n

These figures illustrate growing concerns about the homeownership prospects of younger generations in OECD countries, as homeownership rates decline and become increasingly reliant on income, wealth, and inheritances. These trends are in part driven by rising house prices and decreasing housing affordability (see Chapter 1), as well as by urbanisation and changing family structures. For example, Bonnet, Garbinti and Grobon (2018[8]) find fewer young households living in rural areas (where housing is generally more affordable) and fewer young low-wealth households with children (these households may have different preferences regarding homeownership or may be delaying having children until they can buy a home). The growing wealth and income divide among young people may be driven by rising mortgage debt, which requires high incomes to service, and by the growing importance of financial assistance from families, which is concentrated among wealthy heirs (OECD (2021[10]), Bonnet, Garbinti and Grobon (2018[8])). While future generations are therefore likely to see continued drops in homeownership rates over time, households with high income, high wealth, and/or access to significant family resources may instead see rising homeownership rates or at least smaller declines. These findings are relevant for countries experiencing changing demography and rising house prices, but it is important to exercise caution in drawing lessons for other countries due to the limited sample of countries with available data.

2.5. Inheritances and housing

Gifts and inheritances likely play a key role in facilitating homeownership for some households, particularly among younger beneficiaries. Wealth transfers, in the form of either gifts received during the donor's life or inheritances after their death, can facilitate access to homeownership for some younger households, kick-starting wealth accumulation for the young people that benefit from these transfers. While wealth transfers may help young households put together a down payment, some households will instead inherit housing assets directly. Understanding the role of inheritances and gifts in accessing homeownership is important from an equity perspective and has important tax policy implications, in particular for the taxation of intergenerational wealth transfers.

In many OECD countries, there is a significant gap in homeownership rates between young households that have received a gift or inheritance and those that have not. Among 18 OECD countries, households aged 16-34 are far more likely to own their principal residence if they have benefited from a substantial gift[6] or inheritance (Figure 2.17). In most countries, the homeownership rate among young recipients of wealth transfers is roughly twice that of non-beneficiaries. The relative gap in homeownership is largest in Greece, where the homeownership rates for these two groups are 94% and 13%, respectively, and smallest in Lithuania, where the homeownership rate of beneficiaries (97%) is close to that of non-beneficiaries (83%). Receiving a gift or inheritance is likely to play a decisive role in facilitating homeownership among younger generations in countries where the relative gap in homeownership between heirs and non-heirs is large (e.g. Austria, Greece, Slovenia). On the other hand, Finland, Lithuania and the Slovak Republic have a much smaller gap in homeownership rates between young heirs and non-heirs, suggesting that these transfers are not a decisive factor in becoming a homeowner in these countries. In the future, rising house prices may make it more difficult for younger people to acquire housing without receiving external support, which could widen the homeownership gap between young households that have benefited from gifts or inheritances and those that have not, and increase intra-generational wealth inequality.

Figure 2.17. Homeownership rates for 16-34 year old households, recipients and non-recipients of a substantial gift or inheritance, 18 OECD countries

2017 or closest available year

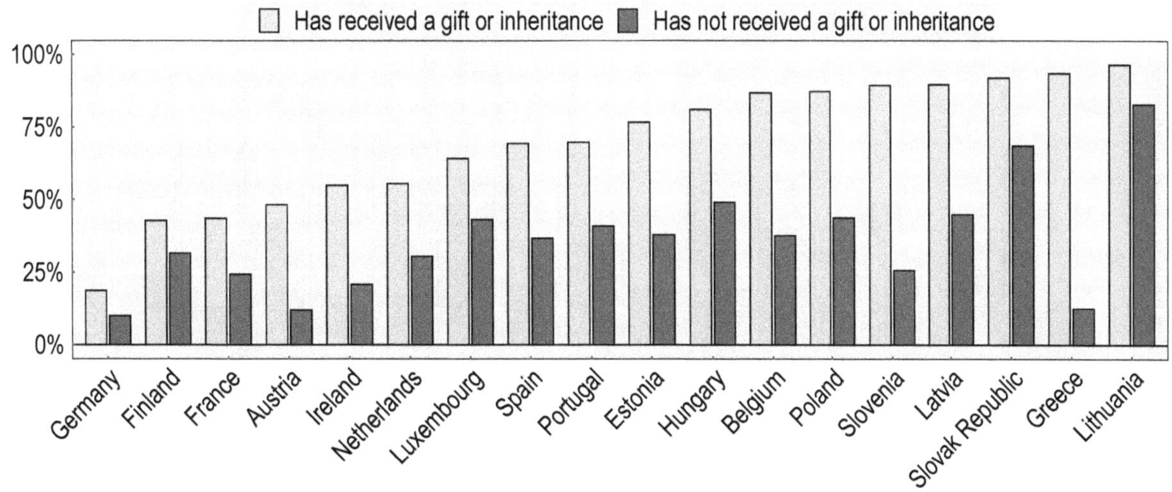

Note: The population-weighted average of each pair of bars is equal to the homeownership rate for 16-34 year old households in each country. Data on the prevalence of gifts and inheritances were not available for Italy.
Source: Eurosystem Household Finance and Consumption Survey.

StatLink https://stat.link/udb9ni

A majority of households that have received a gift or inheritance have received housing wealth, and many continue to live in that housing. Among recipients of wealth transfers, the share of households that received housing assets varies from 19% (the Netherlands) to 94% (Greece), and is higher than 50% in all but five countries (Figure 2.18). There are strong regional patterns, with high rates of housing transfers among beneficiaries in Eastern European countries and relatively low rates in Western Europe. The relatively high prevalence of housing transfers among recipients of gifts and inheritances reflects the key importance of housing in household wealth portfolios. In particular, given the high rates of homeownership among older populations, it follows that these households will frequently pass on housing assets to their descendants. Once housing is received as a gift or inheritance, households may sell or keep the asset, and those keeping it may choose to live in the residence or use it for other purposes. In countries such as Greece, Lithuania, and Slovenia, the vast majority of households that received inherited or gifted housing use it as their principal residence. In contrast, most beneficiaries of housing transfers in Belgium, France and Luxembourg use their inherited or gifted housing as a secondary residence or dispose of the housing. These differences may be partly due to mobility patterns across generations, as households may inherit housing that is far from their jobs in urban centres and that they are not able to use as a principal residence. Cross-country variations in family composition may also play a role, as inherited property will be more likely to have multiple recipients when families have several children and may therefore be sold to divide the value among recipients.

Figure 2.18. Share of wealth transfer recipients reporting inherited or gifted housing, 17 OECD countries

2017 or closest available year

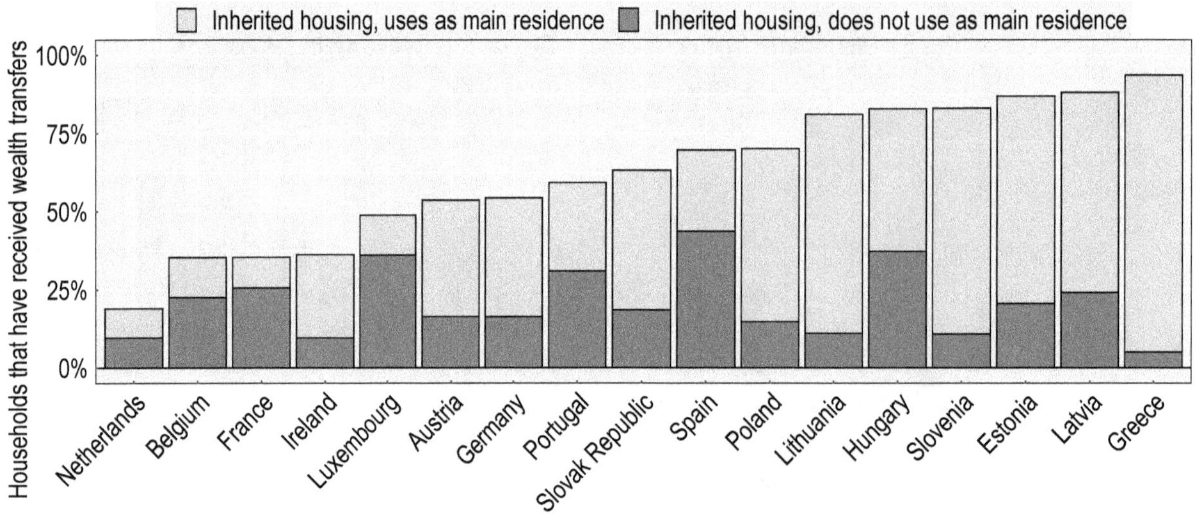

Note: Households that do not use inherited or gifted housing as their main residence may use it for other purposes or may have disposed of it. Data on inherited or gifted non-primary housing assets were not available for Finland. Data on the prevalence of gifts and inheritances were not available for Italy.
Source: Eurosystem Household Finance and Consumption Survey.

StatLink https://stat.link/vs8nu1

Housing assets are usually inherited rather than gifted. On average in 19 OECD countries, roughly 75% of housing wealth transfers take the form of an inheritance, while roughly 25% take the form of a gift during the donor's life (Figure 2.19, left panel). This could reflect the fact that the donors intending to bequeath their primary residence will often maintain ownership of these assets until the end of their lives, but may also reflect more preferential taxation of inherited, compared to gifted, homes in some countries (OECD, 2021[10]). Gifts of housing assets may also be more limited to individuals who own secondary property or who use strategies such as trusts and the separation of bare ownership and usufruct to gift their main residence during their life.

Inherited owner-occupied housing wealth is highly concentrated among households at the top of the wealth distribution. On average among households that have inherited their principal residence,[7] over half of inherited owner-occupied housing wealth belongs to the top wealth quintile (Figure 2.19, right panel). In contrast, only 1% of inherited main residence housing wealth is held by households in the bottom 20% of the wealth distribution. This suggests that the tax treatment of inherited housing assets will have the largest impact on wealthy households and minimal consequences for households at the bottom of the wealth distribution. It is important to note, however, that this figure may underestimate inherited housing wealth as it does not account for households that do not live in or have sold inherited housing prior to the survey, and may overestimate inherited housing wealth where the value of the housing has increased since it was first received. In addition, households' position in the wealth distribution may have changed since they received the housing assets, as the data measure household wealth at the time of the survey and include the value of the gift or inheritance. These figures hold particular relevance for discussions on the tax treatment of inherited housing and can help to contextualise the distributional impacts of such policies.

Figure 2.19. Share of housing wealth by gift or inheritance and across net wealth quintiles, unweighted average, select OECD countries

2017 or closest available year

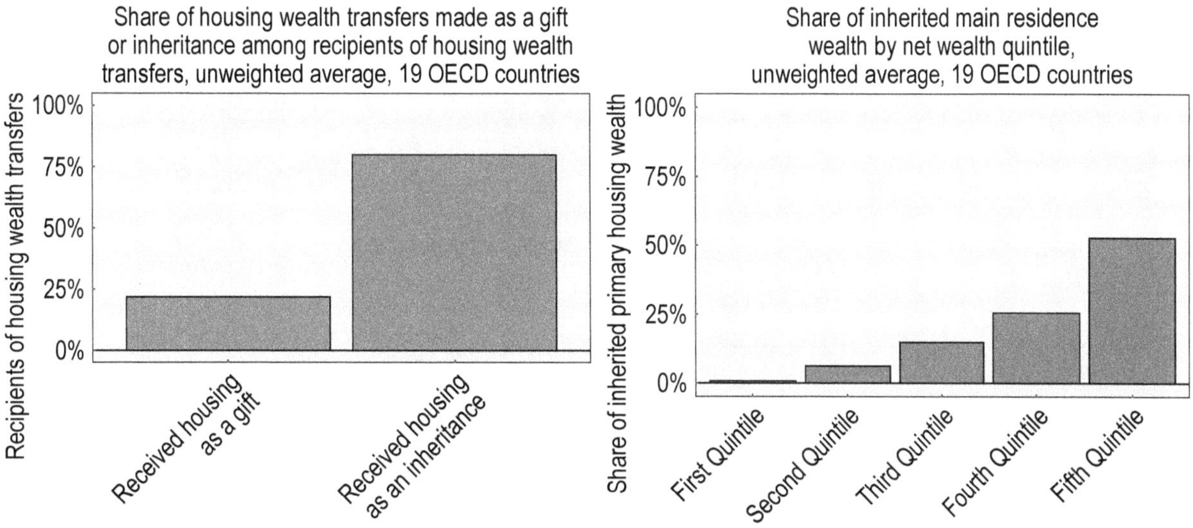

Note: Average of Austria, Belgium, Germany, Estonia, Finland, France, Greece, Hungary, Ireland, Italy, Lithuania, Luxembourg, Latvia, Netherlands, Poland, Portugal, Slovenia, Slovak Republic, Spain. Left panel: Households who have received both inherited and gifted housing were counted in both categories; therefore, the two bars in this figure add up to slightly more than 100%. Right panel: Quintiles range from first (lowest) to fifth (highest). See Box 2.1 for a description of how quintiles are calculated.
Source: Eurosystem Household Finance and Consumption Survey.

StatLink https://stat.link/7lwcxm

References

Advani, A., E. Chamberlain and A. Summers (2020), *Is it time for a UK wealth tax?*, https://www.ukwealth.tax/wealth-in-the-uk (accessed on 2 November 2021). [55]

Ahuja, A. and M. Nabar (2011), "Safeguarding Banks and Containing Property Booms: Cross-Country Evidence on Macroprudential Policies and Lessons From Hong Kong SAR", *IMF Working Papers*, No. WP/11/284, International Monetary Fund, https://ideas.repec.org/p/imf/imfwpa/2011-284.html (accessed on 2 November 2021). [42]

AIHW (2021), *Home ownership and housing tenure*, Australian Institute of Health and Welfare, https://www.aihw.gov.au/reports/australias-welfare/home-ownership-and-housing-tenure. [5]

Alpanda, S. and S. Zubairy (2016), "Housing and Tax Policy", *Journal of Money, Credit and Banking*, Vol. 48/2-3, pp. 485-512, https://doi.org/10.1111/JMCB.12307. [74]

Alsaïdi, I. et al. (2021), "Factors associated with SARS-CoV2 infection and care pathways among the most vulnerable populations living in Marseille: a case control study", *BMC Public Health*, Vol. 21/1704, pp. 1-14, https://doi.org/10.1186/S12889-021-11716-6. [17]

Alvaredo, F. et al. (2018), *World Inequality Report*, World Inequality Lab, Paris, France, http://www.wid.world/team. [4]

Andrews, D., A. Caldera Sánchez and Å. Johansson (2011), "Housing Markets and Structural Policies in OECD Countries", *OECD Economics Department Working Papers*, No. 836, OECD Publishing, Paris, https://doi.org/10.1787/5kgk8t2k9vf3-en. [112]

Andriopoulou, E. et al. (2020), "The distributional impact of recurrent immovable property taxation in Greece", pp. 506-526, https://doi.org/10.3326/pse.44.4.4. [24]

Arnold, J. et al. (2011), "Tax Policy for Economic Recovery and Growth", *The Economic Journal*, Vol. 121/550, pp. 59-80, https://doi.org/10.1111/J.1468-0297.2010.02415.X. [52]

Aroul, R., J. Hansz and J. Yang (2021), ""Fix it with Green:" The Valuation Impact of Green Retrofits on Residential Transaction Price", *Journal of Housing Research*, https://doi.org/10.1080/10527001.2021.1984755. [95]

Aroul, R., J. Hansz and J. Yang (2021), ""Fix it with Green:" The Valuation Impact of Green Retrofits on Residential Transaction Price", *Journal of Housing Research*, https://doi.org/10.1080/10527001.2021.1984755. [104]

Banzhaf, H. and N. Lavery (2010), "Can the land tax help curb urban sprawl? Evidence from growth patterns in Pennsylvania", *Journal of Urban Economics*, Vol. 67/2, pp. 169-179, https://doi.org/10.1016/j.jue.2009.08.005. [101]

Barakova, I. et al. (2003), "Does credit quality matter for homeownership?", *Journal of Housing Economics*, Vol. 12/4, pp. 318-336, https://doi.org/10.1016/J.JHE.2003.09.002. [61]

Barker, N. (2020), *The housing pandemic: four graphs showing the link between COVID-19 deaths and the housing crisis*, https://www.insidehousing.co.uk/insight/the-housing-pandemic-four-graphs-showing-the-link-between-covid-19-deaths-and-the-housing-crisis-66562?utm_source=Ocean%20Media%20Group&utm_medium=email&utm_campaign=11575108_IH-THE-FRIDAY-LONG-READ-29-5-2020-GR&dm_i=1HH2,6W3ES,WM2OTO,ROCH0,1 (accessed on 3 November 2021). [18]

Baum-Snow, N. and J. Marion (2009), "The effects of low income housing tax credit developments on neighborhoods", *Journal of Public Economics*, Vol. 93/5-6, pp. 654-666, https://doi.org/10.1016/j.jpubeco.2009.01.001. [84]

Berger, T. et al. (2000), "The Capitalization of Interest Subsidies: Evidence from Sweden", *Journal of Money, Credit and Banking*, Vol. 32/2, p. 217, https://doi.org/10.2307/2601239. [66]

Besley, T., N. Meads and P. Surico (2014), "The incidence of transaction taxes: Evidence from a stamp duty holiday", *Journal of Public Economics*, Vol. 119, pp. 61-70, https://doi.org/10.1016/J.JPUBECO.2014.07.005. [33]

Best, M. and H. Kleven (2018), "Housing Market Responses to Transaction Taxes: Evidence From Notches and Stimulus in the U.K.", *The Review of Economic Studies*, Vol. 85/1, pp. 157-193, https://doi.org/10.1093/RESTUD/RDX032. [34]

Bonnet, C., B. Garbinti and S. Grobon (2018), "Rising inequalities in access to home ownership among young households in France, 1973-2013", *Economie et Statistique / Economics and Statistics* 500-501-502, pp. 117-138, https://doi.org/10.24187/ecostat.2018.500t.1948. [8]

Borbely, D. (2021), "Limiting the distortionary effects of transaction taxes: Scottish stamp duty after the Mirrlees Review", *Fiscal Studies*, Vol. 42/2, pp. 265-290, https://doi.org/10.1111/1475-5890.12270. [46]

Borenstein, S. and L. Davis (2016), "The Distributional Effects of US Clean Energy Tax Credits", *Tax Policy and the Economy*, Vol. 30/1, pp. 191-234, https://doi.org/10.1086/685597. [91]

Bourassa, S. et al. (2013), "Mortgage Interest Deductions and Homeownership: An International Survey", *Swiss Finance Institute Research Papers*, No. 12-06, Swiss Finance Institute, https://doi.org/10.2139/SSRN.2002865. [68]

Bowman, J. and M. Bell (2004), "Implications of a Split-Rate Real Property Tax: An Initial Look at Three Virginia Local Government Areas", Lincoln Institute of Land Policy, https://www.lincolninst.edu/sites/default/files/pubfiles/905_BowmanBell_PDF.pdf. [130]

Brown, J. and D. Phillips (2010), "Tax and Benefit Reforms Under Labour", *2010 Election Briefing Note*, Institute for Fiscal Studies, https://doi.org/10.1920/bn.ifs.2010.0088. [127]

Brys, B. et al. (2016), "Tax Design for Inclusive Economic Growth", *OECD Taxation Working Papers*, No. 26, OECD Publishing, Paris, https://doi.org/10.1787/5jlv74ggk0g7-en. [117]

Caldera Sánchez, A. and D. Andrews (2011), "To Move or not to Move: What Drives Residential Mobility Rates in the OECD?", *OECD Economics Department Working Papers*, No. 846, OECD Publishing, Paris, https://doi.org/10.1787/5kghtc7kzx21-en. [113]

Carasso, A., C. Steuerle and E. Bell (2005), "How to Better Encourage Homeownership", *Tax Policy Issues and Options*, No. 12, Urban Brookings Tax Policy Center, http://www.taxpolicycenter.org/TaxModel/income.cfm. (accessed on 3 November 2021). [70]

Carozzi, F., C. Hilber and X. Yu (2020), "On the economic impacts of mortgage credit expansion policies: evidence from help to buy", *CEP Discussion Papers*, No. 1681, Centre for Economic Performance, LSE, https://ideas.repec.org/p/cep/cepdps/dp1681.html (accessed on 3 November 2021). [81]

Causa, O. and J. Pichelmann (2020), *Should I stay or should I go? Housing and residential mobility across OECD countries*, OECD Publishing, Paris, https://doi.org/10.1787/acf95e90-en. [108]

Causa, O., N. Woloszko and D. Leite (2019), "Housing, wealth accumulation and wealth distribution: Evidence and stylized facts", *OECD Economics Department Working Papers*, No. 1588, OECD Publishing, Paris, https://doi.org/10.1787/86954c10-en. [2]

Chapelle, G., B. Vignolles and C. Wolf (2018), "Impact of a housing tax credit on local housing markets: Evidence from France", *Annals of Economics and Statistics* 130, pp. 101-131, https://doi.org/10.15609/annaeconstat2009.130.0101. [83]

Charlier, D., A. Risch and C. Salmon (2018), "Energy Burden Alleviation and Greenhouse Gas Emissions Reduction: Can We Reach Two Objectives With One Policy?", *Ecological Economics*, Vol. 143, pp. 294-313, https://doi.org/10.1016/j.ecolecon.2017.07.002. [92]

Chawla, R. and W. Ted (2003), *Property taxes*, Statistics Canada, https://www150.statcan.gc.ca/n1/en/catalogue/75-001-X200310713094 (accessed on 2 November 2021). [23]

Clerc, M., A. Mauroux and V. Marcus (2010), *Le recours au crédit d'impôt en faveur du développement durable*, Insee Première, Paris, France. [93]

Cohen, J. and C. Coughlin (2005), "An Introduction to Two-Rate Taxation of Land and Buildings", *Federal Reserve Bank of St. Louis Review*, Vol. 87/3, pp. 359-374, https://doi.org/10.20955/r.87.359-374. [126]

Cribb, J. and P. Simpson (2018), "Barriers to homeownership for young adults", in Emmerson, C., C. Farquharson and P. Johnson (eds.), *The IFS Green Budget 2021*, Institute for Fiscal Studies, London, https://ifs.org.uk/green-budget/2018 (accessed on 3 November 2021). [63]

Crowe, C. et al. (2011), "How to Deal with Real Estate Booms: Lessons from Country Experiences", *IMF Working Paper*, No. WP/11/91, International Monetary Fund, https://doi.org/10.5089/9781455253302.001.A001. [44]

Cunningham, C. and G. Engelhardt (2008), "Housing capital-gains taxation and homeowner mobility: Evidence from the Taxpayer Relief Act of 1997", *Journal of Urban Economics*, Vol. 63/3, pp. 803-815, https://doi.org/10.1016/J.JUE.2007.05.002. [49]

Dachis, B., G. Duranton and M. Turner (2012), "The effects of land transfer taxes on real estate markets: evidence from a natural experiment in Toronto", *Journal of Economic Geography*, Vol. 12, pp. 327-354, https://doi.org/10.1093/jeg/lbr007. [35]

Daley, J., B. Coates and T. Wiltshire (2018), *Housing affordability: re-imagining the Australian dream*, Grattan Institute. [9]

Dam, N. et al. (2011), "The Housing Bubble that Burst: Can House Prices be Explained? And Can Their Fluctuations be Dampened?", *Monetary Review*, Nationalbank Denmark, Copenhagen. [28]

Davis, C. et al. (2009), "Who Pays? A Distributional Analysis of the Tax Systems in All 50 States 3rd Edition Institute on Taxation and Economic Policy", Institute on Taxation and Economic Policy, http://www.itepnet.org (accessed on 2 November 2021). [22]

Davis, M. (2019), "The Distributional Impact of Mortgage Interest Subsidies: Evidence from Variation in State Tax Policies", *Job Market Paper*, The Wharton School, University of Pennsylvania. [69]

Deniau, F. et al. (2019), *Évaluation du dispositif d'aide fiscale à l'investissement locatif Pinel*, Inspection générale des finances, Paris, France. [87]

Di Maggio, M. and A. Kermani (2016), "Credit-Induced Boom and Bust", *The Review of Financial Studies*, https://doi.org/10.2139/SSRN.2463516. [78]

Diamond, P. and J. Mirrlees (1971), "Optimal Taxation and Public Production I: Production Efficiency", *The American Economic Review*, Vol. 61/1, pp. 8-27, https://www.jstor.org/stable/1910538?seq=1#metadata_info_tab_contents (accessed on 2 November 2021). [32]

Duca, J., J. Muellbauer and A. Murphy (2011), "House Prices and Credit Constraints: Making Sense of the US Experience", *The Economic Journal*, Vol. 121/552, pp. 533-551, https://doi.org/10.1111/J.1468-0297.2011.02424.X. [77]

Economidou, M. et al. (2020), "Review of 50 years of EU energy efficiency policies for buildings", *Energy and Buildings*, Vol. 225, https://doi.org/10.1016/j.enbuild.2020.110322. [89]

Eriksen, M. and S. Rosenthal (2010), "Crowd out effects of place-based subsidized rental housing: New evidence from the LIHTC program", *Journal of Public Economics*, Vol. 94/11-12, https://doi.org/10.1016/j.jpubeco.2010.07.002. [82]

European Commission (2012), "Possible reforms of real estate taxation: Criteria for successful policies", *Occasional Papers*, No. 119, European Commission, Brussels, https://doi.org/10.2765/24556. [27]

Fatica, S. (2015), "Housing taxation: from micro design to macro impact", *Quaterly Report on the Euro Area*, No. 14(1), Directorate General Economic and Financial Affairs - European Commission, https://ideas.repec.org/a/euf/qreuro/0141-03.html (accessed on 3 November 2021). [72]

Fatica, S. and D. Prammer (2017), "Housing and the tax system: how large are the distortions in the euro area?", *ECB Working Paper*, No. 2087, European Central Bank, https://doi.org/10.2866/456421. [51]

Favara, G. and J. Imbs (2015), "Credit Supply and the Price of Housing", *American Economic Review*, Vol. 105/3, pp. 958-92, https://doi.org/10.1257/AER.20121416. [80]

Fitzgerald, K. (2020), *Speculative Vacancies 10: A Persistent Puzzle*, Prosper Australia, Melbourne, Victoria, https://www.prosper.org.au/2020/12/the-persistent-puzzle-speculative-vacancies-10/. [128]

Floetotto, M., M. Kirker and J. Stroebel (2016), "Government intervention in the housing market: Who wins, who loses?", *Journal of Monetary Economics*, Vol. 80, pp. 106-123, https://doi.org/10.1016/J.JMONECO.2016.04.005. [75]

Gabriel, S. and S. Rosenthal (1991), "Credit rationing, race, and the mortgage market", *Journal of Urban Economics*, Vol. 29/3, pp. 371-379, https://doi.org/10.1016/0094-1190(91)90007-T. [62]

Gale, W., J. Gruber and S. Stephens-Davidowitz (2007), "Encouraging Homeownership Through the Tax Code", *Tax Notes*, No. Vol.115, No.12, https://papers.ssrn.com/sol3/papers.cfm?abstract_id=1758888 (accessed on 3 November 2021). [60]

Gbohoui, W., W. Lam and V. Lledo (2019), "The Great Divide: Regional Inequality and Fiscal Policy by William Gbohoui, W. Raphael Lam, Victor Lledo", *88*, No. 19, IMF, https://ssrn.com/abstract=3417725 (accessed on 2 November 2021). [16]

Giraudet, L., C. Bourgeois and P. Quirion (2021), "Policies for low-carbon and affordable home heating: A French outlook", *Energy Policy*, Vol. 151, https://doi.org/10.1016/j.enpol.2021.112140. [94]

Glaeser, E. and J. Gyourko (2002), "The Impact of Zoning on Housing Affordability", No. w8835, National Bureau of Economic Research, Cambridge, MA, https://doi.org/10.3386/w8835. [88]

Glaeser, E. and J. Shapiro (2003), "The Benefits of the Home Mortage Interest Deduction", in Porterba, J. (ed.), *Tax Policy and the Economy*, MIT Press, http://www.nber.org/chapters/c11534 (accessed on 2 November 2021). [13]

Goldstein, D. et al. (2012), *A Retrospective Look at Federal Energy Efficiency Tax Incentives: How Do Cost and Performance-Based Incentives Compare in Their Ability to Transform Markets?*, ACEEE Summer Study on Energy Efficiency in Buildings. [97]

Goode, R. (1960), "Imputed rent of owner-occupied dwellings under income tax", *The Journal of Finance*, Vol. 15/4, pp. 504-530, https://doi.org/10.1111/J.1540-6261.1960.TB02766.X. [58]

Goodman, L. and C. Mayer (2018), "Homeownership and the American Dream", *Journal of Economic Perspectives*, Vol. 32/1, pp. 31-58, https://doi.org/10.1257/JEP.32.1.31. [11]

Green, R., P. Hendershott and D. Capozza (1996), "Taxes, Mortgage Borrowing and House Prices", *Wisconsin-Madison CULER working papers*, No. 96-06, Center for Urban Land Economic Research, Wisconsin, https://ideas.repec.org/p/wop/wisule/96-06.html (accessed on 3 November 2021). [59]

Gruber, J., A. Jensen and H. Kleven (2021), "Do People Respond to the Mortgage Interest Deduction? Quasi-experimental Evidence from Denmark", *American Economic Journal: Economic Policy*, Vol. 13/2, pp. 273-303, https://doi.org/10.1257/POL.20170366. [64]

Grudnoff, M. (2016), "CGT main residence exemption Why removing the tax concession for homes over $2 million is good for the budget, the economy and fairness", The Australia Institute, https://www.tai.org.au (accessed on 2 November 2021). [54]

Haider, M., A. Anwar and C. Holmes (2016), "Did the Land Transfer Tax Reduce Housing Sales in Toronto?", *IMFG Papers*, No. 28, Institute on Municipal Finance & Governance, http://munkschool.utoronto.ca/imfg/ (accessed on 2 November 2021). [37]

Harris, B. (2010), *The Effect of Proposed Tax Reforms on Metropolitan Housing Prices*, Tax Policy Center - Urban Institute and Brookings Institute. [67]

Harris, B. and L. Parker (2014), *The Mortgage Interest Deduction Across Zip Codes*, Brookings, https://www.brookings.edu/research/the-mortgage-interest-deduction-across-zip-codes/ (accessed on 3 November 2021). [71]

Hartzok, A. (1997), "Pennsylvania's Success with Local Property Tax Reform", *American Journal of Economics and Sociology*, Vol. 56/2, https://doi.org/10.1111/j.1536-7150.1997.tb03461.x. [102]

Hilber, C. and T. Lyytikäinen (2017), "Transfer taxes and household mobility: Distortion on the housing or labor market?", *Journal of Urban Economics*, Vol. 101, https://doi.org/10.1016/j.jue.2017.06.002. [38]

Hilber, C. and T. Turner (2014), "The mortgage interest deduction and its impact on homeownership decisions", *Review of Economics and Statistics*, Vol. 96/4, pp. 618-637, https://doi.org/10.1162/REST_A_00427. [65]

Hodge, T. et al. (2017), "Assessment Inequity in a Declining Housing Market: The Case of Detroit", *Real Estate Economics*, Vol. 45/2, pp. 237-258, https://doi.org/10.1111/1540-6229.12126. [25]

Hood, A., J. Hoyle and J. Cribb (2018), *The decline of homeownership among young adults*, Institute for Fiscal Studies, https://doi.org/10.1920/BN.IFS.2018.BN0224. [7]

Housing Vancouver (2020), *Empty Homes Tax Annual Report*, City of Vancouver, Vancouver, British Colombia, https://vancouver.ca/files/cov/vancouver-2021-empty-homes-tax-annual-report.pdf. [129]

Hui, E., J. Zhong and K. Yu (2017), "Property prices, housing policies for collateral and resale constraints", *International Journal of Strategic Property Management*, Vol. 21/2, pp. 115-128, https://doi.org/10.3846/1648715X.2016.1249984. [41]

Hungerford, T. (2011), *Changes in the Distribution of Income Among Tax Filers Between 1996 and 2006: The Role of Labor Income, Capital Income, and Tax Policy*, Congressional Research Service, http://www.crs.gov (accessed on 2 November 2021). [53]

Johansson, Å. et al. (2008), "Taxation and Economic Growth", *OECD Economics Department Working Papers*, No. 620, OECD Publishing, Paris, https://doi.org/10.1787/241216205486. [111]

Joumard, I., M. Pisu and D. Bloch (2012), "Tackling income inequality: The role of taxes and transfers", *OECD Journal: Economic Studies*, https://doi.org/10.1787/eco_studies-2012-5k95xd6l65lt. [119]

Karlman, M., K. Kinnerud and K. Kragh-Sørensen (2021), "Costly reversals of bad policies: The case of the mortgage interest deduction", *Review of Economic Dynamics*, Vol. 40, pp. 85-107, https://doi.org/10.1016/J.RED.2020.08.003. [76]

Katagiri, M. and C. Raddatz (2018), "House Price Synchronization and Financial Openness: A Dynamic Factor Model Approach", *IMF Working Papers*, IMF, https://doi.org/10.5089/9781484378243.001.A001. [15]

Kim, K. and P. Lambert (2008), "Redistributive Effect of U.S. Taxes and Public Transfers, 1994-2004:", *http://dx.doi.org/10.1177/1091142108324423*, Vol. 37/1, pp. 3-26, https://doi.org/10.1177/1091142108324423. [21]

Knoll, K., M. Schularick and T. Steger (2017), "No Price Like Home: Global House Prices, 1870-2012", *American Economic Review*, Vol. 107/2, p. 353, https://doi.org/10.1257/AER.20150501. [14]

Kuttner, K. and I. Shim (2013), "Can Non-Interest Rate Policies Stabilize Housing Markets? Evidence from a Panel of 57 Economies", *NBER Working Paper Series*, No. 19723, National Bureau of Economic Research, Cambridge, MA, https://doi.org/10.3386/W19723. [47]

Kwak, S. and J. Mak (2011), "Political Economy of Property Tax Reform: Hawaii's Experiment with Split-Rate Property Taxation", *American Journal of Economics and Sociology*, Vol. 70/1, https://doi.org/10.1111/j.1536-7150.2010.00761.x. [103]

Malakellis, M. and M. Warlters (2021), "The economic costs of transfer duty: a literature review", *Treasury Technical Research Paper Series*, No. 21-08, NSW Government. [45]

Matsaganis, M. and M. Flevotomou (2007), "The impact of mortgage interest tax relief in the Netherlands, Sweden, Finland, Italy and Greece", *EUROMOD Working Papers*, No. EM2/07, Institute for Social and Economic Research, https://ideas.repec.org/p/ese/emodwp/em2-07.html (accessed on 3 November 2021). [73]

McClure, K. (2019), "What Should Be the Future of the Low-Income Housing Tax Credit Program?", *Housing Policy Debate*, Vol. 29/1, pp. 65-81, https://doi.org/10.1080/10511482.2018.1469526. [86]

McMillen, D. and R. Singh (2020), "Assessment Regressivity and Property Taxation", *Journal of Real Estate Finance and Economics*, Vol. 60/1-2, pp. 155-169, https://doi.org/10.1007/S11146-019-09715-X. [26]

Mecca, U. et al. (2020), "How Energy Retrofit Maintenance Affects Residential Buildings Market Value?", *Sustainability*, Vol. 12/12, https://doi.org/10.3390/su12125213. [96]

Mian, A. and A. Sufi (2009), "The Consequences of Mortgage Credit Expansion: Evidence from the U.S. Mortgage Default Crisis", *The Quarterly Journal of Economics*, Vol. 124/4, pp. 1449-1496, https://doi.org/10.1162/QJEC.2009.124.4.1449. [79]

Mirrlees, J. et al. (2011), "The Taxation of Land and Property", in *Tax by design*, Oxford University Press, Oxford. [12]

New Zealand Treasury (2021), *Tax, Housing and RBNZ Information Release*, New Zealand Treasury, https://treasury.govt.nz/publications/information-release/tax-and-housing. [100]

Norregaard, J., V. Perry and M. Keen (2013), *Taxing Immovable Property Revenue Potential and Implementation Challenges; by John Norregaard; IMF Working Paper 13/129; May 1, 2013.* [31]

O'Connor, B. et al. (2015), "Searching for the inclusive growth tax grail: The distributional impact of growth enhancing tax reform in Ireland", *OECD Economics Department Working Papers*, No. 1270, OECD Publishing, Paris, https://doi.org/10.1787/5jrqc6vk3n30-en. [116]

OECD (2021), *Brick by Brick: Building Better Housing Policies*, OECD Publishing, Paris, https://doi.org/10.1787/b453b043-en. [109]

OECD (2021), *Building for a Better Tomorrow: Policies to Make Housing more Affordable*, OECD Publishing, Paris, https://doi.org/10.1787/5d9127d4-en. [105]

OECD (2021), *Inheritance Taxation in OECD Countries*, OECD Tax Policy Studies, No. 28, OECD Publishing, Paris, https://doi.org/10.1787/e2879a7d-en. [10]

OECD (2021), *Making Property Tax Reform in China Happen: A Review on Best Practices in Property Tax Design and Reforms in OECD Countries*, OECD Publishing (forthcoming), Paris. [19]

OECD (2021), "Measuring effective taxation of housing: Building the foundations for policy reform", *OECD Tax Policy Analysis and Tax Statistics (forthcoming)*, OECD, Paris. [40]

OECD (2021), *OECD Economic Surveys: Netherlands 2021*, OECD Publishing, Paris, https://doi.org/10.1787/dd476bd3-en. [110]

OECD (2021), *OECD Secretary-General Tax Report to G20 Finance Ministers and Central Bank Governors, Italy*, OECD, Paris, http://www.oecd.org/tax/oecd-secretary-general-tax-report-g20-finance-ministers-october-2021.pdf (accessed on 3 November 2021). [20]

OECD (2021), "Tax relief for homeownership", *OECD Affordable Housing Database*, No. PH2.2, OECD, Paris, https://www.google.com/url?sa=t&rct=j&q=&esrc=s&source=web&cd=&cad=rja&uact=8&ved=2ahUKEwi3pr2s9fzzAhWKxlUKHV6LBj0QFnoECBAQAQ&url=https%3A%2F%2Fwww.oecd.org%2Fels%2Ffamily%2FPH2-1-Public-spending-support-to-home-buyers.pdf&usg=AOvVaw1UZS7T07XlzewV6VjtDA6p (accessed on 3 November 2021). [56]

OECD (2020), *How's Life? 2020: Measuring Well-being*, OECD Publishing, Paris, https://doi.org/10.1787/9870c393-en. [3]

OECD (2020), *Revenue Statistics 2020*, OECD Publishing, Paris, https://doi.org/10.1787/8625f8e5-en. [107]

OECD (2019), *OECD Economic Surveys: Denmark 2019*, OECD Publishing, Paris, https://doi.org/10.1787/eco_surveys-dnk-2019-en. [125]

OECD (2018), *OECD Tax Policy Studies*, OECD Publishing, Paris, https://doi.org/10.1787/19900538. [1]

OECD (2018), *Rethinking Urban Sprawl: Moving Towards Sustainable Cities*, OECD Publishing, Paris, https://doi.org/10.1787/9789264189881-en. [123]

OECD (2018), *Taxation of Household Savings*, OECD Tax Policy Studies, No. 25, OECD Publishing, Paris, https://doi.org/10.1787/9789264289536-en. [124]

OECD (2016), *OECD Economic Surveys: Netherlands 2016*, OECD Publishing, Paris, https://doi.org/10.1787/eco_surveys-nld-2016-en. [122]

OECD (2014), *OECD Economic Surveys: Australia 2014*, OECD Publishing, Paris, https://doi.org/10.1787/eco_surveys-aus-2014-en. [121]

OECD (2014), *OECD Economic Surveys: Netherlands 2014*, OECD Publishing, Paris, https://doi.org/10.1787/eco_surveys-nld-2014-en. [120]

Palameta, B. and I. Macredie (2005), "Property taxes relative to income", *Perspectives*, No. 75-001-XIE, Statistics Canada, https://www150.statcan.gc.ca/n1/en/pub/75-001-x/10305/7796-eng.pdf?st=PNhrj3nA (accessed on 2 November 2021). [132]

Paz-Pardo, G. (2022), *Younger generations and the lost dream of home ownership*, European Central Bank, https://www.ecb.europa.eu/pub/economic-research/resbull/2022/html/ecb.rb220126~4542d3cea0.en.html#:~:text=Decreasing%20home ownership%20rates&text=Among%20households%20headed%20up%20by,millennials%E2%80%9D%20born%20in%20the%201980s. [6]

Petkova, K. and A. Weichenrieder (2017), "Price and Quantity Effects of the German Real Estate Transfer Tax", *WU International Taxation Research Paper Series*, No. 2, https://papers.ssrn.com/sol3/papers.cfm?abstract_id=2988888 (accessed on 2 November 2021). [39]

Poghosyan, T. (2016), "Can Property Taxes Reduce House Price Volatility? Evidence from U.S. Regions", *IMF Working Paper*, No. WP/16/216, International Monetary Fund, https://doi.org/10.5089/9781475552799.001. [43]

Poterba, J., S. Venti and D. Wise (2011), "The Composition and Draw-down of Wealth in Retirement", *NBER Working Paper Series*, No. 17536, National Bureau for Economic Research, https://doi.org/10.3386/W17536. [48]

Risch, A. (2020), "Are environmental fiscal incentives effective in inducing energy-saving renovations? An econometric evaluation of the French energy tax credit", *Energy Economics*, Vol. 90, https://doi.org/10.1016/j.eneco.2020.104831. [90]

Segú, M. (2020), "The impact of taxing vacancy on housing markets: Evidence from France", *Journal of Public Economics*, Vol. 185, p. 104079, https://doi.org/10.1016/j.jpubeco.2019.104079. [99]

Shan, H. (2011), "The Effect of Capital Gains Taxation on Home Sales: Evidence from the Taxpayer Relief Act of 1997", *Journal of Public Economics*, Vol. 95, p. 188, https://doi.org/10.1016/J.JPUBECO.2010.10.006. [50]

Sinai, T. and J. Waldfogel (2005), "Do low-income housing subsidies increase the occupied housing stock?", *Journal of Public Economics*, Vol. 89/11-12, pp. 2137-2164, https://doi.org/10.1016/j.jpubeco.2004.06.015. [85]

Slack, E. and R. Bird (2015), "How to Reform the Property Tax: Lessons from around the World", *IMFG Papers*, No. 21, Institute of Municipal Finance and Governance, http://munkschool.utoronto.ca/imfg/ (accessed on 2 November 2021). [30]

Slack, E. and R. Bird (2014), "The Political Economy of Property Tax Reform", *OECD Working Papers on Fiscal Federalism*, No. 18, OECD Publishing, Paris, https://doi.org/10.1787/5jz5pzvzv6r7-en. [115]

Slemrod, J., C. Weber and H. Shan (2017), "The behavioral response to housing transfer taxes: Evidence from a notched change in D.C. policy", *Journal of Urban Economics*, Vol. 100, pp. 137-153, https://doi.org/10.1016/J.JUE.2017.05.005. [36]

Smidova, Z. (2016), "Betting the house in Denmark", *OECD Economics Department Working Papers*, No. 1337, OECD Publishing, Paris, https://doi.org/10.1787/5jln042vd3kk-en. [118]

Sommer, K. and P. Sullivan (2018), "Implications of US Tax Policy for House Prices, Rents, and Homeownership", *American Economic Review*, Vol. 108/2, p. 274, https://doi.org/10.1257/AER.20141751. [57]

Sutherland, D. and P. Hoeller (2012), "Debt and Macroeconomic Stability: An Overview of the Literature and Some Empirics", *OECD Economics Department Working Papers*, No. 1006, OECD Publishing, Paris, https://doi.org/10.1787/5k8xb75txzf5-en. [114]

Thomas, A. (2021), "Reforming the taxation of housing in Israel", *OECD Taxation Working Papers*, No. 53, OECD Publishing, Paris, https://doi.org/10.1787/83fd48ad-en. [106]

Tobias, L. (2008), *Toward Sustainable Financing and Strong Markets for Green Building: US Green Building Finance Review*, Commission for Environmental Cooperation, Montréal, Quebec, http://www.usgbc.org/News/PressReleaseDetails.aspx?ID=3124. [98]

UNECE (2011), *Canberra Handbook on Household Income Statistics*, United Nations Economic Comission for Europe, Geneva, https://unece.org/fileadmin/DAM/stats/groups/cgh/Canbera_Handbook_2011_WEB.pdf. [131]

Waldhart, P. and A. Reschovsky (2012), "Property tax delinquency and the number of payment installments", *Public Finance and Management*, Lincoln Institute of Land Policy, https://www.researchgate.net/publication/313050824_Property_tax_delinquency_and_the_number_of_payment_installments (accessed on 2 November 2021). [29]

Notes

[1] Secondary real estate does not refer exclusively to housing and encompasses real estate assets held at the household level that are not the primary residence of the owner. This includes second and holiday homes, investment real estate, and farmland.

[2] The sample only includes households that report holding mortgage debt on their primary residence. Limiting the analysis to these households removes the population of low-income retirees that have finished paying off their mortgage, and who therefore significantly reduce average housing liabilities in the bottom quintile.

[3] The household head corresponds to the reference person of the household as defined in the Canberra Group Handbook on Household Income Statistics. Specifically, it refers to "a person aged 15 years or over selected to represent the household based on a set of selection criteria related to home ownership, couple or parental status, income and/or age" (UNECE (2011[131])).

[4] Note by Türkiye: The information in this document with reference to "Cyprus" relates to the southern part of the Island. There is no single authority representing both Turkish and Greek Cypriot people on the Islands. Türkiye recognizes the Turkish Republic of Northern Cyprus (TRNC). Until a lasting and equitable solution is found within the context of the United Nations, Türkiye shall preserve its position concerning the "Cyprus issue".

[5] Note by all the European Union Member States of the OECD and the European Commission: The Republic of Cyprus is recognized by all members of the United Nations with the exception of Türkiye. The information in this document relates to the area under the effective control of the Government of the Republic of Cyprus.

[6] According to the HFCS survey, a substantial gift refers to a gift that has made a significant impact on the financial situation of the household (see:)

[7] This analysis is limited to homeowners that are currently living in housing they received as a gift or inheritance, as housing values are the most up-to-date for this group. Future work could draw on detailed multi-country house price indexes to incorporate inherited non owner-occupied housing. The wealth quintiles correspond to levels of household wealth at the time of the survey, which includes the values of the gifted or inherited housing assets under consideration.

3 Housing tax policies in the OECD and options for reform

This chapter provides an overview and an assessment of housing taxes in OECD countries. It covers the wide range of taxes that are commonly levied on housing in the OECD and examines their design from an efficiency, an equity and a revenue perspective. It also looks at the role of specific tax policies in addressing current housing market challenges. The chapter outlines a number of options for reform that governments could consider to enhance the design and functioning of their taxes on housing.

3.1. Key findings

This chapter provides a comparative assessment of housing tax policies in OECD countries and identifies reform options to enhance the design of housing tax systems. The chapter starts by providing an overview of the different types of taxes that are levied on housing in OECD countries and discusses trends in housing-related tax revenues. The chapter then assesses housing tax policies in OECD countries. It examines the efficiency, equity and revenue effects of housing taxes, and evaluates the role of specific tax policy instruments to address current housing challenges. Based on the assessment, the chapter outlines a number of reform options that governments could consider to enhance the design of their housing tax policies.

The design of housing taxes is of growing importance given pressures on governments to raise revenues, improve the functioning of housing markets, and combat inequality. As they continue to navigate the COVID-19 pandemic, many countries are looking to raise tax revenues without threatening the economic recovery. Many governments are also under increasing pressure to address rising inequality and declining housing affordability, which is especially affecting low-income and young households. In addition, the growing international mobility of both capital and people may encourage governments to raise more revenues from less mobile tax bases, in particular real estate (Dolls et al., 2021[1]). This increased attention on housing taxes reinforces the need to design them effectively and fairly.

Overall, this chapter finds that there is significant room to enhance the efficiency, equity and revenue potential of housing taxes in OECD countries. Many countries still levy recurrent property taxes on outdated property values, which significantly reduces their revenue potential (as revenues have not risen in line with property values), their equity (as households whose properties have increased in value may not be paying more tax), as well as their economic efficiency (as property taxes levied on outdated values provide incentives for people to remain in undervalued housing even if it no longer suits their needs). Reliance on transaction taxes is high, despite the potential for these taxes to reduce residential, and to some extent, labour mobility. The majority of countries fully exempt capital gains on main residences, and while there may be justification for such an approach, an uncapped exemption provides vastly greater benefits to the wealthiest households and further distorts the allocation of savings in favour of owner-occupied housing. Other forms of tax relief for owner-occupied housing, in particular mortgage interest relief, have been found to be regressive and ineffective at raising homeownership levels. In some countries, features of rental income taxation and inheritance tax rules applying to housing also reduce progressivity and revenue potential. The assessment also shows that, while housing taxes are often viewed as harder to avoid and evade than other taxes, tax systems leave room for such behaviours, reducing the efficiency, fairness and revenues of housing taxes.

This chapter also finds that some housing tax policies may help address current housing market challenges, although they may not always be the most effective tools. Tax policies may be used to address specific housing market challenges, such as significantly reducing the carbon footprint of housing, encouraging a more efficient use of land and housing, and boosting the supply of affordable housing. However, taxation may be a blunt tool and may even be counterproductive under certain circumstances. In particular, where tax relief is intended to encourage homeownership, it can sometimes contribute to raising house prices and therefore to redistributing wealth to current homeowners if housing supply is fixed. Even where tax policies can play a positive role (e.g. vacant home taxes, tax incentives for energy-efficient housing renovations), they may not be as effective in achieving their desired outcome as alternative policy instruments (e.g. regulations) and will generally need to be complemented by a range of other policy measures.

This chapter identifies a number of reform options that countries could consider to simultaneously enhance the efficiency, equity and revenue potential of housing taxes. Strengthening the role of recurrent taxes on immovable property, in particular by ensuring that they are levied on regularly updated property values, while lowering housing transaction taxes would increase efficiency in the housing market and improve vertical and horizontal equity. Capping the capital gains tax exemption on the sale of main residences at a high capital gain threshold and gradually removing or capping mortgage interest relief for owner-occupied housing would strengthen progressivity. At the same time, these reforms would reduce upward pressure on house prices. Tax incentives for energy efficient housing renovations could be better targeted to ensure that they reach low-income households. This could contribute to greater emissions reductions and enhance the equity of tax incentive schemes. Caution should be exercised when considering tax incentives to encourage homeownership; in most cases, increasing the supply of housing and a more efficient use of the housing stock through both tax and non-tax measures is likely to have a greater impact on housing affordability. Strengthened reporting requirements, including third-party reporting to the tax authority and international exchanges of information for tax purposes, are also key to ensuring that housing taxes are enforced properly. The chapter discusses many other reform options that could help enhance the design, functioning and impact of housing taxes.

Any assessment of housing tax policies should take a holistic view of their interactions with other tax and non-tax policies and with housing market conditions. Interactions between different housing tax policies should be carefully assessed. For instance, residential mobility will be affected directly by both transaction taxes and capital gains taxes, and indirectly by the design of the recurrent tax on immovable property. Reforms aimed at enhancing mobility should therefore consider all three taxes. Carefully assessing interactions between taxes may also help identify cases where, before introducing new tax instruments, countries could consider reforming the design of existing housing taxes. For instance, there may be less need for special taxes to reduce speculation where short-term capital gains are adequately taxed. Similarly, a recurrent tax on immovable property based on regularly updated market values may reduce the need for tax instruments (e.g. infrastructure levies) aimed at capturing property value increases resulting from local public investments. Interactions between tax and non-tax policies are also key. As mentioned, there may be cases where non-tax policies may provide a more effective and equitable alternative to tax measures, especially when the goal is to promote housing affordability. There may also be cases where the success of tax measures depends on other policy settings or housing market conditions.

Housing tax reforms require careful timing and consideration for their impact across different households. Housing tax reforms can have a sizeable impact on house prices, with potentially significant distributional effects as well as wider financial and economic repercussions. A gradual implementation of reforms can help prevent negative macroeconomic shocks while also alleviating the adverse effects of reforms on specific groups of individuals, at least in the short run. Accompanying housing tax reforms with other tax or transfer measures may also help mitigate the impacts of some reforms on more vulnerable people and enhance the public acceptability and political feasibility of policy changes.

3.2. Overview of housing taxes in OECD countries

This section provides an overview of the range of taxes levied on housing in OECD countries and the revenues collected from the main taxes on housing. The section starts by describing the different types of taxes that are commonly levied on the acquisition, holding and disposal of housing. Next, the section examines the revenues that OECD countries collect from property taxes, which include a subset of taxes on housing. The section also looks at the evolution of property tax revenues over time, and compares trends in revenues to house price developments. This overview lays the groundwork for the detailed policy assessment in Section 3.3.

3.2.1. Housing taxes along the housing investment cycle

Across OECD countries, a range of taxes commonly apply at different stages of a housing investment (Figure 3.1). As discussed below, housing tax systems share common features across countries, and the tax treatment differs markedly between owner-occupied and rented property. In the acquisition phase, transaction taxes are commonly applied across countries. In the holding phase, recurrent taxes on immovable property are levied in all OECD countries. The income generated by rental property is also commonly taxed, while imputed rents from owner-occupied housing (i.e. the in-kind income earned by owner-occupiers living in their homes) are typically exempt. Mortgage interest relief is also widespread across countries, particularly for rented property. On the disposal of housing, many countries exempt capital gains on the sale of main residences, while capital gains on secondary properties (e.g rental housing, holiday homes, *pied à terre* in urban centres) are usually taxed, and tax liabilities can often be reduced for longer holding periods. Inheritance and gift taxes may also be levied when immovable property is transferred to heirs. Annex A outlines the tax treatment of housing in all OECD countries.

Figure 3.1. Taxation of housing assets over the asset lifecycle

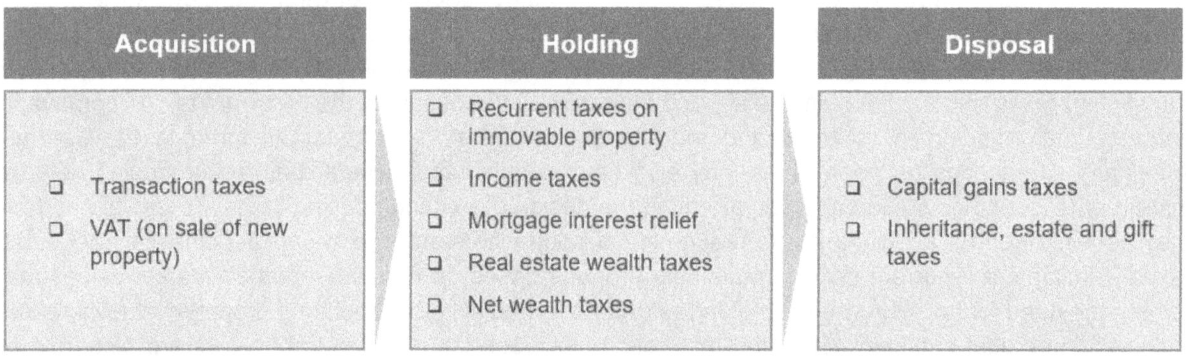

Source: (OECD, 2018[2])

On the acquisition of housing assets, transaction taxes are widely applied across OECD countries. 30 out of 38 OECD countries apply transaction taxes on housing. Transaction taxes are typically levied on the purchase of a housing asset at a flat rate, although in some cases tax rates depend on the value of the housing asset (Australia, Canada, Israel, Korea, Mexico, Portugal, and the United Kingdom). New residential housing is often exempt from transaction taxes, but Value Added Tax (VAT) usually applies on newly built residential property, though sometimes at a reduced rate. A number of countries also apply transaction tax exemptions or concessions for first-time buyers (e.g. Australia, Canada, Italy, and the United Kingdom), which is typically conditional on the value of the property.

During the holding period, all OECD countries levy recurrent taxes on immovable property. Recurrent taxes on immovable property are levied in all 38 OECD countries (though not in all sub-central governments). Recurrent taxes on immovable property are typically paid by property owners (although there are exceptions where the tax is levied on the occupant of a property) and are in most cases levied on both buildings and land, although a few subnational governments and countries levy taxes only on land (New South Wales[1] in Australia and Denmark) or apply different tax rates on land and buildings (Finland and some municipalities in Hawaii and Pennsylvania, United States). In most countries, tax obligations depend on the estimated market value of the property, which in practice can differ significantly from its true market value (see Section 3.3.1), but four countries (the Czech Republic, Israel, Poland, and the Slovak Republic) use area-based systems, where the tax liability is primarily based on the size of the property. A minority of countries levy recurrent taxes on immovable property at progressive rates (e.g. Chile, Denmark, Greece, Korea, Latvia, Mexico), although these taxes also have an element of progressivity in countries that apply a tax-free threshold (e.g. Lithuania).

The approach to the taxation of housing income differs significantly between owner-occupied and rental property. Income from rental property is taxed in the vast majority of OECD countries, with 34 countries levying personal income taxes (PIT) on rental income. Rental income is typically taxed at flat rates in countries with dual income tax systems (e.g. Denmark, Finland) and at progressive PIT rates in countries with comprehensive tax systems (e.g. Canada, Germany, New Zealand). On the other hand, the taxation of imputed rents from owner-occupied property is rare. Only four OECD countries (Denmark, Greece, the Netherlands and Switzerland) tax imputed rents (though generally at lower levels than rental income).

Mortgage interest relief, spread over the asset-holding period, is common across OECD countries. 17 OECD members provide a form of mortgage interest relief (via tax deductions or credits) for owner-occupied housing. In a few countries, mortgage interest relief is capped (Estonia, Finland and Luxembourg) or only applies below an income (Chile) or asset value threshold (Korea). Mortgage interest relief is more commonly available for rented property than for owner-occupied housing, with 26 countries offering a (typically uncapped) tax deduction or credit.

A few OECD countries levy wealth taxes on overall net wealth including the ownership of housing, although preferential tax treatment is typically granted to owner-occupied property. Three OECD countries (Norway, Spain and Switzerland) levy annual taxes on total net wealth above a certain threshold. Owner-occupied properties typically benefit from preferential tax treatment under net wealth taxes. For instance, Spain applies an exemption threshold for the main residence of up to EUR 300 000, in addition to the standard EUR 700 000 net wealth tax exemption threshold. In Norway, only 25% of the owner-occupied property value is subject to the tax,[2] which rises to 95% in the case of secondary housing. A few countries also levy taxes at the national level on overall real estate wealth above a certain threshold (e.g. France, Korea).

On the disposal of housing assets, significant differences exist between the tax treatment of capital gains on main residences and other housing. Twenty countries provide full and unconditional capital gains tax exemptions on sales of main residences, while full exemptions (9 countries) and other favourable tax treatment (5 countries) are available conditional upon a minimum holding period, the value of the gain or the reinvestment of gains in another property. Capital gains on other housing assets are taxed in 33 countries, though again often at concessionary rates subject to a minimum holding period. Where capital gains taxes are levied, countries apply a mix of progressive and flat tax rates.

Inheritance, estate and gift taxes are also levied in many countries when housing assets are passed on to heirs, although the main residence can benefit from preferential tax treatment under specific conditions. A number of countries fully or partially exempt the main residence, while others apply below-market values or lower tax rates. Most countries make tax relief conditional upon certain requirements (e.g. the beneficiary living with the donor prior to, at the time of, or following the donor's death). Other residential property is typically fully included in the inheritance or estate tax base (OECD, 2021[3]).

3.2.2. Property tax revenues in OECD countries

Property tax revenues, which include a subset of taxes on housing, account for a small share of overall tax revenues

Existing data from the OECD Revenue Statistics Database do not allow for all housing tax revenues to be identified, but those property tax revenues that can be identified, provide useful insights into a subset of housing taxes. As discussed above, OECD countries levy a wide range of taxes on housing. For some taxes, in particular income taxes, revenues cannot be disaggregated between housing-related taxes (e.g. taxes on housing capital gains, rental income and imputed rents, if taxed) and non-housing related income taxes. Given these data limitations, this section focuses on property tax revenues, which include revenues from a subset of taxes on housing, in particular recurrent taxes on immovable property and transaction taxes. Importantly, however, property taxes also include a number of non-housing related taxes, including taxes on non-housing assets and taxes on assets held by businesses.

Property taxes typically represent a small source of revenue for OECD countries. On average across OECD countries, property taxes represent around 6% of total tax revenues, a far smaller share than other taxes, including taxes on goods and services (33% of total tax revenues), social security contributions (26%), personal income taxes (23%), and corporate income taxes (10%) (OECD, 2020[4]). However, there is some variation across countries, with a minority of countries raising 10% or more of their total tax revenues from property taxes. Property tax revenues account for around 14% of total tax revenues in Korea, 12% in the United Kingdom, the United States, and Canada and 10% in Luxembourg, while accounting for less than 1% of total tax revenues in the Czech Republic, Estonia and Lithuania (Figure 3.2).

Recurrent taxes on immovable property are the largest component of property tax revenues. Recurrent taxes on immovable property represent the most significant source of property tax revenues in the majority of OECD countries and, on average, account for 62% of countries' total property tax revenues. Taxes on financial and capital transactions, which include transaction taxes on housing, account for 27% of total property tax revenues on average. Both net wealth taxes and inheritance, estate and gift taxes, which are levied on a broad range of assets including housing, generally account for small shares of total property tax revenues in OECD countries (Figure 3.2).

Figure 3.2. Property tax revenue as a share of total tax revenues, 2020

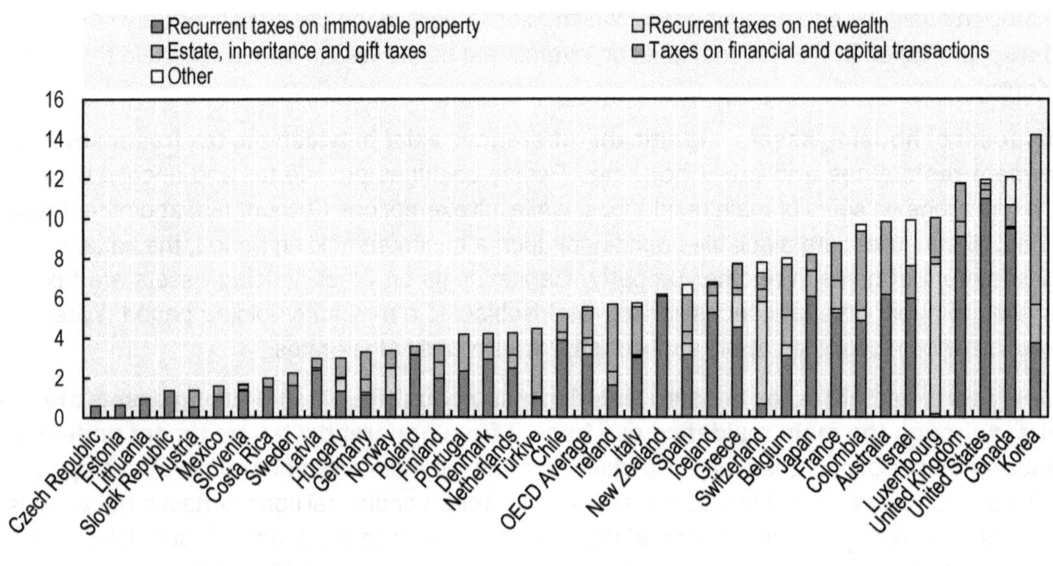

Note: 2019 data for Australia, Greece, Japan, New Zealand and the OECD average. Data include taxes paid by households and non-households and include household and non-household real estate.
Source: OECD Revenue Statistics

StatLink https://stat.link/v0fsxd

Recurrent taxes on immovable property represent a major source of revenue and an important policy lever for sub-central governments. In most countries, revenues from recurrent taxes on immovable property are fully or largely assigned to local governments. As a result, even if revenues from recurrent property taxes are a small part of total tax revenues, they account for a significant share of sub-central government tax revenues. Indeed, recurrent property tax revenues account for 19% of local government revenues and 16% of total sub-national government revenues (local governments and state/regional governments in federal countries) on average across OECD countries (Figure 3.3). Recurrent taxes on immovable property are also the taxes over which local governments have most control, with powers to make decisions on the introduction and removal of the tax, the definition of tax rates and bases, as well as tax reliefs, although the level of autonomy varies across countries (OECD, 2021[5]). This greater autonomy enables subnational governments to adjust their fiscal policy to local demands and contributes to increasing their political accountability (OECD, 2021[5]).

Figure 3.3. Recurrent taxes on immovable property as a percentage of local and state government's revenues, 2019

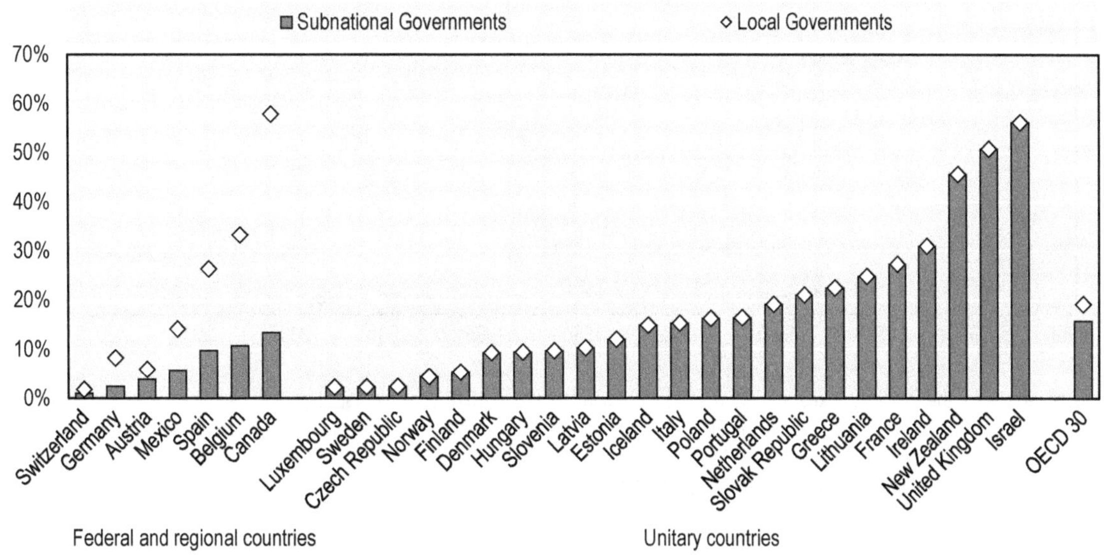

Note: Local and state revenues are consolidated to reflect own-source revenue (defined as total revenue minus the inter-governmental transfer revenue of that government level). The allocation of revenues between different levels of government is specified in the Fiscal Decentralisation Database. Values as of 2019 or closest year with available data.

Source: OECD Revenue Statistics (for recurrent tax on immovable property); OECD Fiscal Decentralisation Database (for SNGs' revenue); Making Property Tax Reform Happen in China: A Review of Property Tax Design and Reform Experiences in OECD Countries (OECD, 2021[5])

StatLink https://stat.link/1jlh7o

Increases in housing values have not been reflected in property tax revenues

Looking at their evolution over time, overall property tax revenues have remained remarkably stable as a share of GDP since the mid-1960s. Total property tax revenues as a share of GDP have remained fairly constant, oscillating between 1.5% and 1.9% over the past six decades (Figure 3.4). Recurrent taxes on immovable property have inched upwards from 0.94% in 1965 to 1.03% of GDP in 2019. On the other hand, between 1965 and 2019, revenues from inheritance, estate and gift taxes declined from 0.25% of GDP to 0.13%, and revenues from net wealth taxes dropped from 0.23% of GDP to 0.16%. This reflects the fact that some countries have abandoned these taxes while others have narrowed their tax bases (OECD, 2018[6]; OECD, 2021[3]). Revenues from financial and transaction taxes have historically exhibited greater volatility than revenues from other property taxes, and have still not recovered from their marked decline after the global financial crisis.

Figure 3.4. Property tax revenue as a share of GDP over time across OECD countries (unweighted average), 1965-2019

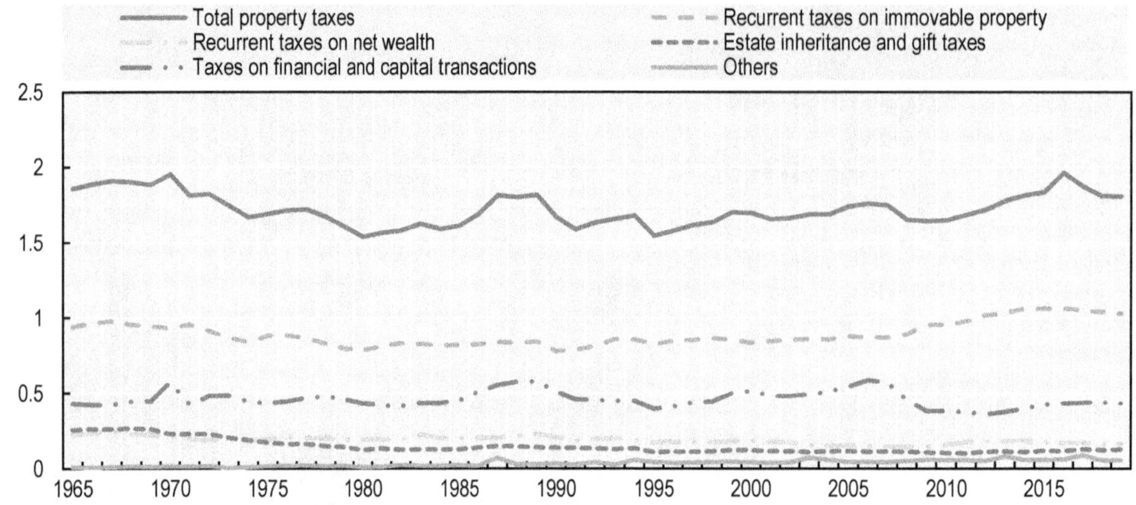

Note: Tax revenues for the Property taxes and Others categories in Iceland in 2016 are calculated as the mean of values for 2015 and 2017. Iceland experienced unusually high tax revenues in 2016 from one-off stability contributions from entities that previously operated as commercial or savings banks and were concluding operations. The tax revenues, equivalent to 15.7% of Iceland's GDP in 2016, led to a spike in the OECD average Property taxes and Others categories (Revenue Statistics, 2018).
Source: OECD Revenue Statistics Database

StatLink https://stat.link/coq7u4

Evidence suggests that revenues from taxes on housing have not kept up with increases in house prices. The sustained growth in property values over recent decades (see Chapter 1) should have been accompanied by a comparable rise in property tax revenues, but the design of these taxes has weakened this relationship in practice. Figure 3.5 displays the average growth in real house prices together with the average growth in recurrent property tax revenues as a percentage of GDP for 15 OECD countries over the period 1995-2020. The two have diverged considerably in recent decades, with the growth of real housing prices far outpacing that of property tax revenues. As discussed in Section 3.3.1, property taxes are often levied on significantly outdated and underestimated property values that do not reflect price developments. Some OECD countries also cap the amount by which property value assessments and tax liabilities can increase in a given year, which further disconnects recurrent property tax revenues from property values (OECD, 2021[5]). These patterns are consistent with existing research finding particularly low levels of buoyancy for recurrent taxes on immovable property (Belinga et al., 2014[7]; Dougherty and de Biase, 2021[8]), as well as a low elasticity of property tax revenues with respect to housing prices (Lutz, 2008[9]). Similar gaps have likely occurred between housing price growth and revenues from other taxes on housing. In particular, capital gains taxes on the sale of main residences are commonly exempt, resulting in substantial forgone revenues (e.g. (Corlett and Leslie, 2021[10]; Grudnoff, 2016[11]; Hungerford, 2010[12])). In a number of countries, other tax incentives typically aimed at promoting homeownership, such as transaction tax exemptions for first-time buyers, have further narrowed tax bases and reduced the revenue raising capacity of housing taxes.

Figure 3.5. Mean growth in real housing prices and mean growth in recurrent property tax revenues (% of GDP) over time, 15 OECD countries, 1995-2020

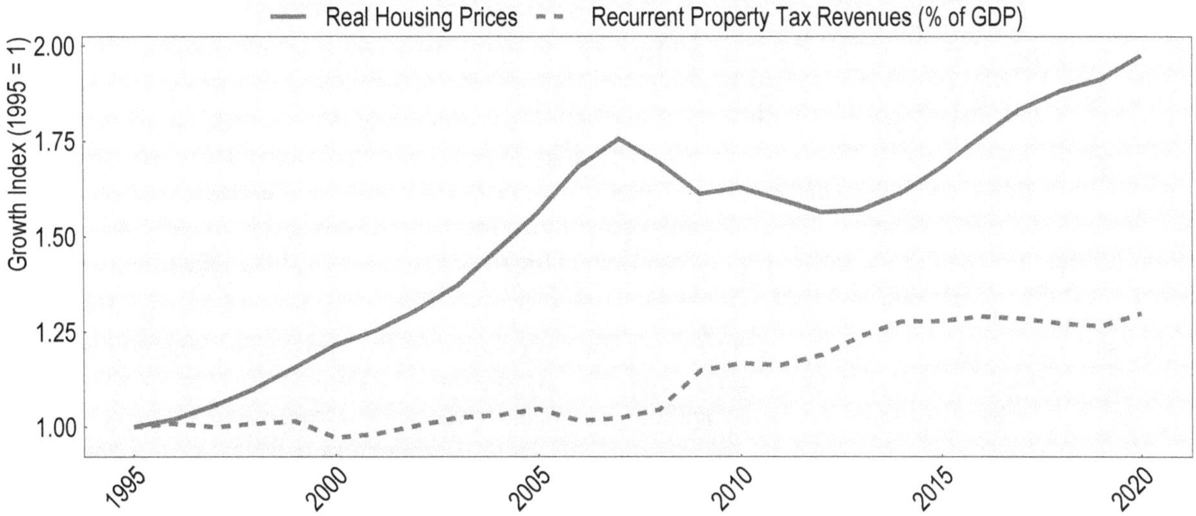

Note: The property tax indicator refers to all recurrent property taxes collected and not just those levied on household assets. Average of Canada, Colombia, Denmark, Finland, France, Germany, Ireland, Israel, Japan, Netherlands, Norway, Spain, Switzerland, United Kingdom, United States. Some countries (e.g. Belgium, Italy, Korea, Portugal, Sweden) that undertook significant reforms of their property tax systems during the period under consideration were removed from this calculation.
Source: The data on real housing prices is taken from the OECD National and Regional House Price Indices dataset. The data on recurrent property tax revenues is taken from OECD Revenue Statistics.

StatLink https://stat.link/0p4ezf

3.3. Policy assessment and options for reform

This section assesses housing tax policies in OECD countries and discusses a range of options for reform. The first part of this assessment (section 3.3.1) examines existing housing tax policies and identifies reform options that could help enhance their efficiency, equity and revenue potential. The second part of this assessment (section 3.3.2) focuses on the role of specific housing tax policy instruments in addressing current housing challenges, in particular housing affordability and environmental sustainability. This section shows that designing housing tax policies requires carefully balancing different objectives and assessing interactions between different types of policies and housing markets. Overall, there is significant room to improve the design and functioning of housing taxes and there are a number of concrete reform options that governments could consider. This section also highlights that housing tax policy instruments have a role to play in addressing current housing market challenges, although in some cases non-tax instruments may be more effective and equitable policy tools.

3.3.1. Assessment of housing tax policies and options to enhance their efficiency, equity and revenue potential

There is significant scope to improve the design and functioning of recurrent taxes on immovable property

Recurrent taxes on immovable property are levied in all OECD countries. All OECD countries, though not all sub-central governments, levy recurrent taxes on immovable property. Recurrent taxes on immovable property are typically paid by property owners, but there are some exceptions (e.g. the Council Tax in the United Kingdom and the *Taxe d'habitation* in France) where the tax is levied on the occupant (regardless of whether they own or rent the property).[3] Most OECD countries apply recurrent taxes on immovable property on the value of both land and buildings. Pure land taxes are found in only three OECD countries (New South Wales[1] in Australia, Denmark and Estonia), while Finland and some municipalities in Hawaii and Pennsylvania, United States, apply higher tax rates on land than on buildings (i.e. split-rate taxation). Most OECD countries apply value-based property tax systems, but four countries (the Czech Republic, Israel, Poland, and the Slovak Republic) use area-based systems, where the property tax is based on the size of the property (although adjustments can be made depending on location or other dwelling characteristics). Recurrent taxes on immovable property are most commonly levied at flat rates, but a minority of countries levy them at progressive rates (Australia, Chile, Colombia, Denmark, Greece, Ireland, Korea, Latvia, Mexico, Slovenia).

Recurrent taxes on immovable property are considered one of the most economically efficient forms of taxation. While the nature of the property tax has long been debated in the theoretical literature (see Box 3.1), extensive research has highlighted its efficiency properties (Grover et al. (2017[13]); Brys et al. (2016[14]), Slack and Bird (2014[15]), Norregaard (2013[16]); Johansson et al. (2008[17]), Diamond and Mirrlees (1971[18]), (Ramsey, 1927[19])). Recurrent taxes on the immovable property of households are a comparatively efficient source of tax revenue because the tax base – typically land and improvements – is highly immobile, which limits the scope for behavioural responses to the tax. This is particularly the case for land, which is in fixed supply. Indeed, in theory a pure land tax would be more efficient as it would not discourage investment in capital improvements, but most countries tax both land and improvements because of the practical difficulties of measuring the value of each separately. Additionally, a recurrent tax on residential property may act to some extent as a "benefits tax", in that it may be seen as a (partial) payment for local public goods (see Box 3.1), and therefore be less distortive than a pure tax. Recurrent taxes on immovable property are also typically capitalised into house prices over time, which suggests that these taxes can help slow house price increases and stabilise fluctuations in the housing market (Oliviero et al., (2019[20]), Blöchliger et al., (2015[21])) and are less distortive than other taxes that are not capitalised into prices (Slack and Bird, 2015[22]). Finally, recurrent taxes are difficult to evade due to the highly visible nature of immovable property, and can also contribute to more efficient land usage. Empirically, recurrent taxes on immovable property have been found to be among the least damaging taxes to long-run economic growth (Johansson, 2016[23]; Cournède, Fournier and Hoeller, 2018[24]; Johansson et al., 2008[17]).

Recurrent taxes on immovable property have also long been identified as a good source of revenue for local governments. Recurrent taxes on immovable property lend themselves to local government taxation for several reasons. First, the tax is borne mainly by local residents with limited spillovers (Norregaard, 2013[16]). Second, as mentioned above, there is a significant link between the tax and the services received, and local public services and investments are to some extent reflected in the property tax base. Third, the property tax tends to be a relatively stable and predictable source of revenue (Blöchliger et al., 2015[21]; Norregaard, 2013[16]). Lastly, recurrent taxes on immovable property may also increase local government accountability. Sub-central and local governments typically have a greater degree of autonomy over the design and implementation of recurrent taxes on immovable property than for other taxes (see Section 3.2), which, coupled with the high salience of the property tax, makes taxpayers more likely and able to hold their local governments accountable.

From a distributional perspective, several studies find that recurrent taxes on immovable property are regressive with respect to income, but these studies have limitations. Several studies find that recurrent immovable property taxes are regressive with respect to income because tax liabilities are a larger share of income for low-income households (Andriopoulou et al. (2020[25]), Kim and Lambert (2008[26]), Palameta and Macredie (2005[27]), Chawla and Wannell (2003[28])). However, there are limitations to these studies that suggest that recurrent property taxes may not be as regressive as generally thought, and may even have some progressive features. Studies typically note that the tax-to-income ratio declines across the income distribution; however, the regressive effect is highest for the lowest-income households and is much less pronounced (although still present) when comparing lower-middle-income households to top income households (Andriopoulou et al. (2020[25]), Palameta and Macredie (2005[27])). This suggests that careful tax design and the provision of tax relief for the lowest income households can alleviate this regressive effect, a finding supported by a few studies (Joumard, Pisu and Bloch (2012[29]), O'Connor et al. (2015[30])). In addition, some studies find that absolute liabilities rise with income because higher-income households own more valuable property (Andriopoulou et al. (2020[25])). More generally, the distributional impacts of recurrent property taxes will differ across countries depending on the distribution of housing assets. Where immovable property is highly concentrated at the top, a shift in the tax mix towards immovable property taxation is expected to have more progressive effects than where housing assets are more equally distributed along the income distribution. Most studies also only look at owner-occupied housing and ignore the impact of taxing secondary real estate, which is likely to be progressive as the highest income households hold significantly more secondary real estate than lower-income households (see Chapter 2).

Property taxes are likely to be progressive with respect to wealth, but empirical research is sparse due to data constraints. While there are a number of studies measuring tax-to-income ratios across the income distribution, there are fewer studies measuring property tax liabilities along the wealth distribution or as a share of wealth. One study finds that in Canada, the ratio of recurrent property tax liabilities to home values is mostly flat across the income distribution (Chawla and Wannell, 2003[28]). While quality data on housing wealth and corresponding tax liabilities are sparse, patterns in homeownership across the wealth distribution suggest that recurrent taxes on immovable property should be progressive with respect to wealth, with tax-to-wealth ratios rising for higher wealth households. As households at the top of the wealth distribution own higher value properties and hold the majority of housing wealth, tax liabilities are likely to be higher as a share of wealth for wealthier households. Low-wealth households tend not to own property, so property taxes are likely to be low at the bottom of the wealth distribution. However, the tax-to-wealth ratio may be higher for households in the upper middle of the wealth distribution, who hold the majority of their wealth in their main residence, than for top wealth households that also hold other assets (e.g. financial and business assets) that are not subject to recurrent taxes on immovable property. As owner-occupied housing wealth is less concentrated than secondary real estate and financial wealth across the wealth distribution, taxing owner-occupied housing may be less progressive than taxing other asset classes.

The distributional effects of recurrent property taxes will also depend on dynamic factors including tax capitalisation and the final economic incidence of the tax. The degree of tax capitalisation, i.e. the extent to which future tax liabilities reduce the price of housing assets, will affect the distributional consequences of recurrent property taxes by determining who bears the tax's final economic incidence. For instance, where full capitalisation occurs (i.e. when after controlling for all housing characteristics, differences in housing prices are exactly equal to the present value of variations in expected tax liabilities), current owners bear the final economic incidence of a tax change, while partial capitalisation suggests that current owners are able to partly shift the incidence onto new buyers. Empirical studies find strong evidence for the capitalisation of recurrent immovable property taxes into house prices, with some studies finding full capitalisation (Borge and Rattsø, 2013[31]; Gallagher, Kurban and Persky, 2013[32]; Palmon and Smith, 1998[33]; Oates, 1969[34])). The distributional effect will therefore depend on the profile of incumbent and prospective owners; if the latter are younger and less wealthy households, a strong degree of tax capitalisation may suggest more progressive effects. In the case of rental housing, the distributional effects of recurrent taxes on immovable property will also depend on whether the owner or the renter bears the final economic incidence of the tax. For instance, a property tax may be more progressive where property owners are unable to shift the full tax burden onto renters in the form of higher rents. In contrast, where property owners can fully shift the property tax onto renters, it will have the same distributional impacts as a tax levied on the occupants of a property (e.g. the Council Tax in the United Kingdom or the *Taxe d'habitation* in France). The degree of tax capitalisation and the final economic incidence of the tax will ultimately depend on demand and supply elasticities as well as other factors including regulations (e.g. rent controls) (Hilber (2017[35])).

Recurrent property taxes also raise liquidity concerns for income-poor but asset-rich households. Evidence shows that low-income households hold housing wealth (Chapter 2), which is an illiquid asset that, in the case of owner-occupied housing, does not generate income. Higher recurrent taxes on immovable property may therefore lead to liquidity issues if taxpayers do not have the necessary income to pay the tax. This issue will be particularly challenging in periods during which house prices increase significantly, as homeowners could see the value of their property increase without necessarily seeing a corresponding increase in their income (European Commission, 2012[36]).This issue has also been raised with regard to retirees who have high owner-occupied housing wealth compared to their incomes (Chapter 2). However, some evidence from Canada shows that low-income retired homeowners do not face higher property tax liabilities than other low-income homeowners (Palameta and Macredie, 2005[27]), which may partly reflect tax design leading to low effective property taxes, resulting for instance from property tax relief for seniors or the fact that they are often levied on outdated property values. Given these features of tax design and tax relief are common across OECD countries, these results could apply in other countries, though further research would be needed.

The efficiency, equity and revenue raising potential of recurrent taxes on immovable property also critically depend on the way they are designed. As discussed in detail below, the efficiency, equity and revenue raising potential of recurrent property taxes ultimately depends on their design including the breadth of the tax base, the applicable tax rates, the availability of tax relief for low-income households, and perhaps more fundamentally on whether the tax is levied on regularly updated property values. The assessment below suggests that there is significant room to improve the design of recurrent taxes on immovable property in the OECD and that countries could consider a number of reforms to boost their efficiency, equity and revenues. There are also various strategies that governments could adopt to enhance the public acceptability of property tax reforms.

Box 3.1. The theoretical conceptualisation of recurrent taxes on immovable property

The theoretical literature can be broadly grouped into three alternative views on the nature of recurrent taxes on immovable property. The different conceptualisations bear important implications for the assessment of the efficiency, equity and final economic incidence of recurrent property taxes.

The traditional view

The "traditional view" conceptualises local property taxes largely as taxes on housing services (Edgeworth, 1897[37]). It is based on a partial equilibrium approach in which the property tax levy is conceptually divided into a tax that falls on immobile land and a tax on mobile capital (i.e. buildings and improvements). While the former is capitalised into land values, the latter is shifted onto the final housing consumer. Empirical work based on this view finds that recurrent property taxes are regressive with respect to income, as the share of taxes paid falls along the income distribution. Property taxes, where they are levied on structures, are also found to be inefficient as they distort the allocation of housing capital.

The capital view

The "capital view" considers the recurrent property tax to be a tax on capital (Mieszkowski, 1972[38]). The approach is based on a general equilibrium model, in which capital is in fixed supply at the national level but mobile across sub-national jurisdictions. While property tax changes on a jurisdictional level may temporarily affect house prices locally (following the mechanisms outlined in the traditional view), capital allocation adjusts over time, equalising after-tax returns of capital. From a national perspective, the tax burden falls on capital owners, which given a higher concentration of capital among high-income and wealth holders implies that property taxes have progressive distributional effects. Regarding their impact on economic efficiency, property taxes are expected to distort the allocation of capital and therefore to generate inefficiency costs.

The benefit view

The "benefit view" conceptualises recurrent taxes on immovable property as a fee for local public services (Hamilton, 1975[39]). Following this view, mobile taxpayers "vote with their feet" and locate in jurisdictions that offer their preferred level of local public services and housing values. Inter-jurisdictional competition coupled with consumer mobility therefore implies that local public services can be provided efficiently as the distortive impact would be small if taxpayers believe the tax aligns with the cost of public services. Moreover, the distributional impact is considered neutral as tax liabilities are offset by gains from consuming public services.

Source: (Edgeworth, 1897[37]; Hamilton, 1975[39]; Mieszkowski, 1972[38]; Norregaard, 2013[16]; Oates and Fischel, 2016[40]; Zodrow, 2001[41])

Value-based property tax systems, particularly those relying on market values rather than annual rental values, are more efficient and equitable than area-based ones. Value-based systems that rely on market values are preferable to area-based systems that rely on the size of the property, which is likely to be a poor proxy for taxpayers' housing wealth and ability to pay as it disregards other physical characteristics of the property and its location,[4] which are key determinants of its value. In practice, area-based property taxes are rare in the OECD (the Czech Republic, Israel, Poland, and the Slovak Republic) and they are typically not purely area-based as they often include adjustments taking into account other characteristics of the property, including its location. Value-based property taxes, on the other hand, include both taxes relying on capital values (i.e. market prices of the property) and taxes relying on annual rental values (i.e. prices at which the property can be rented). While the two values may be mathematically equivalent under certain conditions, most countries rely on capital values as this method allows capturing the highest and best use of a property (rather than current use as is the case with rents) (Slack and Bird, 2014[15]) and can avoid valuation challenges where rent controls are in place (Kelly, White and Anand, 2020[42]).

Regularly updating property values is also key to the efficiency, equity and revenue potential of recurrent taxes on immovable property. Levying the tax on outdated property values creates distortions between older housing that has not been revalued for some time and newer housing that has been recently valued, as well as between properties that were valued at the same time but have experienced varying degrees of price growth. The low tax burdens arising from outdated values also reduce incentives to use the current housing stock efficiently, giving homeowners an incentive to remain in undervalued homes. For instance, in large cities where house prices have increased significantly but property tax burdens (based on outdated property values) have not, older households are not incentivised to downsize to smaller and less valuable homes and free up housing space for younger families. In addition, levying taxes on outdated property values reduces horizontal equity (as households with properties of similar value may not face similar tax liabilities) and vertical equity (as households with more valuable housing may not pay more taxes) (Mirrlees et al., 2011[43]). Empirical evidence finds that outdated property assessments tend to make recurrent property taxes regressive (Hodge et al., 2017[44]; McMillen and Singh, 2020[45]). Levying recurrent property taxes on properties whose values are not regularly updated also means that increases in property values may in some cases go fully untaxed, for instance if capital gains on housing are exempt. Finally, outdated property values undermine the revenue potential of property taxes (see Section 3.2.2) and their ability to limit house price volatility and growth, and infrequent revaluations increase the risks of sudden spikes in tax liabilities when properties are eventually revalued (Slack and Bird (2014[15])). In some cases, these potential spikes can add to the pressures faced by governments to temporarily defer or permanently abandon further revaluations. Thus, ensuring that recurrent property taxes are levied on regularly updated values is a prerequisite to guarantee their efficiency, equity and revenue raising potential.

While experiences across the OECD vary, many countries do not have provisions for regular revaluations or have postponed revaluations. Several countries regularly revalue land and properties, including New South Wales[1] in Australia (yearly; taxable values are the average of the preceding three years), Lithuania (yearly; taxable values are valid for five years[5]), New Zealand (every three years), and Norway (yearly for municipalities using values estimated for net wealth tax purposes; every ten years otherwise). On the other hand, a number of countries rely on significantly outdated property values. For instance, property values used for tax purposes date from 1973 in Austria, 1975 in Belgium, 1970 in France, 1964 in former West Germany and 1935 in former East Germany,[6] 1941 in Luxembourg, and 1991 in the United Kingdom. Several countries index the values with inflation or use a corrective factor (Slack and Bird (2014[15])). While indexing is simple and may help ensure revenue buoyancy, it leads to inequities in the long run as it does not capture varying price growth across different areas or properties. Thus, regular revaluations are the only method guaranteeing that property taxes continue to raise revenue in an efficient and equitable way.

There are different approaches to revaluing properties, but digitalisation is reducing the costs of regular appraisals. The most common valuation approach is the sales (or rent) comparison method, which uses recent sales and property-specific data in order to compare the property being appraised with similar properties (OECD, 2021[5]). Regularly appraising property values according to this method is administratively costly. Digitalisation and the use of computer-assisted mass appraisals (CAMA), which estimate values for a group of properties using mathematical modelling, may reduce the costs associated with frequent property revaluations, although they require high-quality data and significant technical capacity, and may be better undertaken by higher levels of government (OECD, 2021[5]).[7] Data from digital platforms advertising properties for sale (e.g. Zillow, Seloger) may also enhance the ability of governments to accurately undertake regular property valuations. In addition to being technically challenging, property revaluations can be highly unpopular. To address this issue, countries relying on outdated values and wishing to set up a system of regular valuations could consider embedding such a reform in a more comprehensive property tax overhaul, with measures to mitigate potential increases in tax liabilities, as was done in Denmark and Ireland (Box 3.2).

Box 3.2. Recent reforms updating cadastral values for recurrent property taxation

Denmark

Denmark froze property values in 2002, which contributed to booming housing prices in the first decade of the 21st century and a fall in effective tax rates. These tax savings were shown to be unequally distributed across regions, with the largest average benefits accruing to homeowners in the Greater Copenhagen area (Dam et al., 2011[46]).

In 2017, a major property tax reform was passed which entailed a reassessment of properties' fair market values. Under this new system, property values are to be updated every second year (starting in 2020) and updated tax liability assessments began to be issued in 2021. Given the nearly two decade-long tax freeze, reassessments had been expected to significantly raise tax obligations, particularly in areas having witnessed significant house price increases.

To cushion the increase in tax liabilities and increase political support, the government embedded the update of property values in a comprehensive property tax reform. The statutory property tax rate was lowered from 1% to 0.6% and a surtax aimed at high-value properties was applied above a value threshold. To address liquidity concerns and protect owner-occupiers, homeowners whose overall property taxes increase with the new system were compensated through a tax rebate in 2021 and will have the option to defer the future increase in recurrent property tax liabilities until the sale of the property.

The comprehensive approach to Denmark's property tax base reform is likely to have contributed significantly to its political success. While measures compensating adversely affected taxpayers will impact tax revenues in the short run, the reform increases the equity and future revenue-raising potential of the tax, and is expected to reduce house price volatility in the long run.

Ireland

Following the introduction of the Local Property Tax (LPT) in 2013, property values for tax purposes were due to be revalued in 2016. As this revaluation was subsequently delayed, property values were outdated and properties that had been built since 2013 were not subject to the tax.

The LPT reform introduced in 2021 cut tax rates, broadened the base, required taxpayers to update their self-assessed property valuation and brought previously exempt housing (built since 2013) into scope.

The reform is expected to decrease or leave property tax liabilities unchanged for the majority of taxpayers. Around one third of the taxpayers are expected to face an increase in their recurrent property tax burden of up to EUR 100 (USD 118) per year while only 3% should face an increase of more than EUR 100. To support lower-income households, the reform also increased the income threshold below which taxpayers are eligible for property tax deferral and lowered the interest charged on deferred tax payments from 4% to 3%.

Source: (Dam et al., 2011[46]; European Commission, 2012[36]; OECD, 2019[47]; Smidova, 2016[48]; Department of Finance - Ireland, 2021[49])

Allowing for tax payments in instalments may reduce liquidity constraints and salience, while third-party remittance may also enhance tax compliance. Property tax payments often involve one or two large payments, which may raise liquidity issues given insufficient financial planning and tight household budgets (Slack and Bird, 2014[15]). Households may need to save in advance to pay the tax and then bear the responsibility of remitting the tax, which also increases its salience. Tax payments in instalments may therefore help individuals manage their expenses and reduce their liquidity constraints, as well as reduce the salience of the property tax. Studies have found that well-designed instalment schemes can increase tax compliance (OECD, 2021[5]), Reschovsky and Waldhart (2012[50])). The option for third-party remittance (e.g. in Ireland where taxpayers can opt for the property tax to be remitted by their employer or pension provider) may also help reduce compliance costs.

There is a strong case for providing tax deferral in certain cases to alleviate liquidity issues, though deferral programmes may raise some administrative complexities or cause temporary revenue shortfalls. There is a strong case for addressing liquidity issues through tax deferrals to reduce the potential for hardship and the need for less efficient and equitable forms of relief (such as broad exemptions or delaying property revaluations). Several countries offer tax deferrals (typically subject to interest payments) allowing taxpayers to delay some or all of their tax payments to some future period when taxpayers have a greater ability to pay (e.g. until the house is sold or transferred). This effectively gives rise to a tax debt secured against the housing asset. These deferral provisions are typically restricted to certain categories of taxpayers, such as low-income and senior taxpayers (see Box 3.3). Tax deferrals raise some challenges, however. If deferral provisions are targeted, there may be administrative and equity challenges associated with defining and identifying qualifying taxpayers. On the other hand, an automatic right to deferral (i.e. not dependent on income or wealth) may be simpler but poorly targeted and could lead to significant revenue shortfalls in the short-and medium-run (Slack and Bird, 2014[15]; Munnell, Hou and Walters, 2022[51]). Charging interest on unpaid tax liabilities could also discourage people from using tax deferral where interest rates could rise and property values could fall, and raise complexity, although digitalisation has made it much easier to track tax liabilities over time. Countries should charge interest at a rate that ensures that households are neither penalised nor advantaged by their decision to defer. An alternative option for tax deferral could be to register the tax authority's right to an equity share in the property, equal to the tax liability as a share of the housing's market value at that time, which would accrue on sale to the tax authority (Muellbauer, 2018[52]).[8] Such a system would protect individuals from falls in property values, but allow tax authorities to benefit from rising values. At the same time, an equity-based deferral system would expose tax authorities to housing market fluctuations. Administrative considerations aside, some studies of existing deferral programmes show surprisingly low take-up, because elderly households typically wish to leave property to their heirs without substantial tax obligations attached to them (Slack and Bird, 2014[15]) and because liquidity issues may be less of a concern than commonly expected (Bowman, 2006[53]).

Property tax relief can lead to unintended effects if it is not carefully designed, but is an alternative to enhance the equity of recurrent taxes on immovable property. Property tax relief on owner-occupied housing may enhance the equity of property taxes, but there are risks that, in addition to narrowing the tax base, the relief could be capitalised into house prices and weaken the link between taxes paid and local public services received. Relief should be designed in a way that minimises these potential negative effects while strengthening progressivity. One option is to provide a limited exemption to all taxpayers (e.g. homestead exemptions in the United States). Relief should be provided in the form of a flat-amount, rather than as a percentage of the housing value; a flat-amount exemption has a progressive impact on the distribution of property taxes because lower-income households tend to have less valuable properties, so the relief accounts for a larger share of their home values (Langley, 2015[54]). A limited basic exemption would also remove from the tax base very low-value properties on which limited tax revenue is typically collected. Alternatively, a more targeted property tax credit or exemption can be provided. Many countries target relief at low-income homeowners as they are more likely to lack the liquidity to pay the property tax, but additional criteria could be considered. For instance, in the United States, about one-third of states cap property tax liabilities as a share of income, an approach referred to as a circuit breaker, and generally target the tax relief to lower-income households and seniors. This type of income testing could be complemented by wealth testing (e.g. by taking into account the value of the taxpayer's main residence or total housing wealth) to target support to taxpayers who are both low-income and low-wealth and avoid providing relief to households with limited income but sizeable housing wealth. Property tax relief could also take into account the number of occupants or dependent children (e.g. Belgium). Importantly, the need for property tax relief will also depend on other features of property tax systems. Where property tax liabilities tend to be low and where a well-functioning tax deferral system is in place, tax relief may be less necessary (see above).

Box 3.3. Property tax deferrals in different countries

Several OECD countries provide property tax deferral schemes, which are commonly restricted to certain types of taxpayers, including seniors and low-income households. Deferrals can also be used as transitional measures during reforms to protect taxpayers from significant increases in property tax obligations.

- In **Canada**, provincial and local governments administer tax deferral schemes, which are commonly restricted to seniors, widowed and disabled taxpayers. Tax deferrals are commonly capped and interest (at or below market rate) is charged on the unpaid amount. The province of Alberta offers a "Seniors Property Tax Deferral Program" providing taxpayers with a low-interest equity loan on their primary residence, which covers property tax payments until the sale of the house (or any earlier date), at which point the loan is repaid plus interest (the programme charges simple instead of compound interest). Only taxpayers over 65 are eligible under the condition that they hold at least 25% equity in their primary residence and the property is covered by insurance.
- In **Denmark,** a property tax deferral scheme was introduced as part of a comprehensive property tax reform (see Box 3.2), in which property value reassessments risked increasing recurrent property tax liabilities significantly. To alleviate liquidity concerns, the reform allowed deferring increases in tax liabilities until the sale of the property.
- **Ireland** provides full and partial property tax payment deferral to taxpayers who meet certain conditions related to their financial situation and property characteristics (residential vs. rental property). Interest is charged on the unpaid amount while the available deferral duration depends on the specific case and the taxpayer's income (adjusted for mortgage interest payments on the main residence), personal insolvency or hardship (i.e. a significant and unexpected financial loss or expense).
- In the **United States**, many states provide partial or full property tax deferral to eligible seniors, low-income, disabled or widowed taxpayers, or active military personnel. The deferred amount may be capped and may be combined with other tax relief (such as homestead exemptions), and interest charges apply. Payment of the outstanding amount is due on death or sale of the property. Eligibility for the programmes is often tied to both age and income limits (in addition to minimum equity requirements and certain property characteristics).

Source: (Department of Finance - Ireland, 2021[49]; OECD, 2021[5])

Progressive tax rates may be used to enhance the equity of recurrent taxes on immovable property, although progressive taxation might be more effectively achieved at higher levels of government. Progressive property tax rates apply in a minority of OECD countries and may enhance vertical equity, as taxpayers with higher-value properties face proportionately higher tax liabilities. Progressivity can also be achieved through tax relief for poorer and low-wealth households (see above). The effectiveness of progressive tax rates in increasing the overall progressivity of the tax system will depend on the distribution of housing along the income and wealth distributions; it will be enhanced in countries where housing wealth is concentrated at the top (OECD, 2021[5]). However, progressive tax rates may be more distortive than flat rates, as taxpayers may, for instance, bunch below value thresholds or move to lower-tax locations (Best and Kleven, 2018[55]). These behavioural effects will depend on tax design, however. More generally, there is a question as to whether the property tax, which is levied at the local level and intended to finance local public services, should be progressive. Redistribution is typically better achieved at higher levels of government to ensure that residents in poor and rich localities are considered equally. An alternative to progressive property tax rates on individual properties consists in levying progressive taxes on taxpayers' total net housing wealth (e.g. Korea and France both levy national-level progressive taxes on overall real estate wealth above a certain threshold).

Higher recurrent taxes on secondary residences may enhance progressivity, but this depends on tax incidence and could create equity issues regarding renters. In many countries, secondary residences are in practice subject to higher taxation due to exemptions or higher tax-free thresholds for owner-occupied housing. As secondary real estate is highly concentrated at the top of the income and wealth distributions (see Chapter 2), imposing higher recurrent property tax rates on secondary residences could enhance progressivity. However, this could increase the already highly preferential taxation of owner-occupied housing and may lead to equity concerns in the case of rented housing. It is also important to distinguish between secondary property used for long-term rentals and properties used for short-term rentals, as well as secondary residences that do not generate income (e.g. holiday homes, *pied à terre* in urban centres). Higher taxes on long-term rental properties could reduce equity if renters, who tend to have low wealth and lower incomes (Chapter 2), ultimately bear the economic incidence of the tax. In contrast, if the incidence of higher taxes on short-term holiday rentals were to fall on short-term renters, this may be less concerning from an equity perspective. Higher recurrent property taxes on housing not used to generate income would be expected to enhance equity, as the incidence would fall upon the owner.

The use of banding, caps and assessment limits reduces the progressivity and revenue potential of recurrent taxes on immovable property. While property tax caps, assessment limits, and banding have commonly been used to keep property tax liabilities low, alleviate liquidity issues, and smooth property value increases, these policy measures generate a number of issues. In particular, caps limiting the increase in tax liabilities and assessment limits restricting the increase in cadastral values ultimately reduce progressivity, as people with the most valuable property or experiencing the most significant increases in housing values stand to benefit the most (Slack and Bird, 2014[15]). Caps and assessment limits also reduce the extent to which tax liabilities reflect rising house prices, which reduces tax revenues. The use of banding systems (i.e. where properties are assigned to value bands and the same tax is owed for properties within the same band) also raises equity issues. The tax burden is the same for all the properties within each band, which implies that the effective tax burden (measured as the tax liability as a share of the property value) is highest for the lowest-value properties and lowest for the highest-value properties in each value band.

Countries can adopt various strategies to address the unpopularity of property tax reforms and enhance their public acceptability and political feasibility. Recurrent property tax reforms have traditionally been met with strong public resistance due to the taxes' high salience (as it is often the most visible tax that people pay, particularly when it is paid in a lump-sum), the non-direct link to income and potential liquidity issues, its perceived regressivity, and issues around property valuation (Slack and Bird, 2014[15]). There are different options that governments may consider to enhance the public acceptability and political feasibility of property tax reform. One option is to bundle reforms with other tax changes (e.g. reductions in transaction or labour taxes) or improvements in local public service delivery (Slack and Bird, 2014[15]). Indeed, empirical analyses show that taxpayers who directly benefit from their tax contributions, through improvements in local public services for instance, are more willing to pay higher property taxes

(Giaccobasso et al., 2022[56]). Proactive efforts to disseminate information as to how property tax revenues are spent are also critical as taxpayers may not always be aware of how tax revenues are used by local governments (Giaccobasso et al., 2022[56]). More generally, public support and compliance is also promoted by designing a simple, easily understandable and well-enforced property tax, which includes a well functioning and well-communicated property valuation system and appeals process (OECD, 2021[5]). Additional measures to simplify tax compliance, such as the option for property tax withholding by the employer or the pension provider (e.g. Ireland) or the mortgage provider (e.g. escrow accounts in the United States), may also be considered. Measures to mitigate potential regressive effects and liquidity issues, such as property tax deferral and relief to low-income or low-wealth households (see above), are also likely to make property tax reforms more palatable.

Reforms involving shifts from distortive taxes towards recurrent taxes on immovable property may also raise political and governance challenges between different levels of government. There have been frequent calls to shift the tax mix away from taxes deemed distortive (e.g. income taxes or property transaction taxes) towards recurrent taxes on immovable property (Arnold et al., 2011[57]) (Andrews, Caldera Sánchez and Johansson, 2011[58]; Norregaard, 2013[16]; IMF, 2013[59]). However, such shifts often imply reducing taxes mostly raised at central government levels, and increasing revenues from taxes commonly levied by local governments. A shift towards recurrent taxes on immovable property will therefore affect intergovernmental fiscal relations, as it would increase tax revenue and autonomy at sub-central levels. A tax mix shift towards recurrent property taxes may also require some central government co-ordination between municipalities for reform to happen. Indeed, sub-central governments may be reluctant to raise property taxes given the potential for lower intergovernmental transfers, political sensitivity due to their proximity to the taxpayer, and tax competition between municipalities. There may also be regional inequalities between municipalities with different revenue raising capacities (Blochinger, 2018). For instance, municipalities where property values are higher may be able to levy lower property tax rates while maintaining revenues. These adverse effects could be alleviated through coordination whereby common tax base rules are applied across municipalities and the central government sets minimum and maximum tax rates.

Shifts from transaction taxes to recurrent taxes on immovable property can also include transitional measures to reduce potential impacts on house prices and concerns about households paying both high (pre-reform) transaction taxes and high (post-reform) recurrent taxes. Several OECD countries have introduced reforms in recent years aimed at reducing property transaction taxes and raising recurrent taxes on immovable property (OECD, 2021[5]). Such tax shifts may raise concerns about those property owners who paid the higher transaction taxes (before the introduction of the reform) and are liable to increased recurrent taxes on immovable property upon the introduction of the reform. In addition, the capitalisation of lower transaction taxes may not be matched by the capitalisation of higher recurrent immovable property taxes, potentially causing house prices to increase, if taxpayers are myopic about future tax liabilities or value lower taxes today more than future higher taxes. To help taxpayers adjust to tax changes, smooth tax capitalisation and enhance public acceptability, tax shifts can be gradually phased in. For instance, a gradual shift is being implemented in the Australian Capital Territory (ACT) where the property transfer tax (residential conveyance duty) is being phased out over a 20-year period (earlier for some types of properties), while broadening the base and increasing the rates of the recurrent tax on unimproved immovable property (Tax and Transfer Policy Institute et al., 2020[60]), making the tax overall more progressive. Another option may be to let taxpayers choose between tax regimes to limit increases in tax liabilities and enhance support for the reform. For example, in 2021, the New South Wales[1] government in Australia invited taxpayers to comment on a proposed property tax reform that would allow property owners to choose between the existing tax regime, including higher transaction taxes and lower recurrent taxes on immovable property, or the new regime, which abolishes transaction taxes (or refunds transaction taxes recently paid) and increases recurrent property taxes (NSW Treasury, 2021[61]). While allowing taxpayers to choose between systems might raise administrative complexity and create tax minimisation opportunities, the benefits of successfully implementing the reform may outweigh these drawbacks.

The design of property transaction taxes should minimise welfare costs and ensure that residential mobility is not impeded

Transaction taxes on immovable property are common across OECD countries. Transaction taxes on immovable property, which are levied in 30 out of 38 OECD countries, apply nearly always to the market value of the property at the time of sale (that is, the purchase price). Transaction tax rates are generally flat, although seven countries apply progressive tax rates with respect to the property value (Australia, Canada, Israel, Korea, Mexico, Portugal, and the United Kingdom). The tax is due by the buyer of the property[9] at the time of the property purchase. Four countries provide tax exemptions below a certain housing value threshold (Australia, Austria, Canada, and Portugal) while six countries apply exemptions or preferential taxation for first-time buyers (Australia, Canada, Hungary, Italy, and the United Kingdom). New residential housing is commonly exempt from transaction taxes (or subject to lower tax rates, e.g. France), and Value Added Tax (VAT) usually applies, though sometimes at a reduced rate.

Property transaction taxes are attractive from an administrative and political economy perspective. Transaction taxes have a number of administrative advantages. As the tax base is generally the purchase price (or closely related to the purchase price), it is highly visible and precisely measured. Transaction taxes are levied at a time when taxpayers usually have greater liquidity, especially if they are selling a property to purchase a new one, and thus avoid some of the difficulties associated with taxing illiquid housing assets. Additionally, buyers have an incentive to report the housing transaction to acquire the legal documents and guarantee their property rights (Norregaard, 2013[16]) (although there is evidence that some taxpayers declare lower purchase prices to evade transaction taxes; see below). Overall, transaction taxes are commonly associated with high compliance rates and relatively low administrative costs compared to other taxes on housing. Transaction taxes also seem to raise fewer political economy hurdles than other housing taxes. Even though they are highly salient taxes, as taxpayers are responsible for remitting the tax and evidence on tax capitalisation suggests that taxpayers take them into consideration when agreeing on a purchase price, public opposition to transaction taxes seems less pronounced than for some other property taxes. This may be in part because they are levied when taxpayers expect to incur a range of expenses (e.g. taxes, legal fees, moving costs) and have greater liquidity.

However, the literature has repeatedly emphasised the distortive nature of transaction taxes. The conclusion that property transaction taxes are highly distortionary and therefore detrimental to economic growth follows from the well-known Diamond and Mirrlees (1971[18]) finding that taxing intermediate transactions is inefficient. As such, it is always preferable to tax the income and services provided by assets than their purchase or sale. In both cases, taxation discourages asset ownership, but a transaction tax also discourages transactions that would allocate the asset more efficiently. To decrease distortions and enhance efficiency, a reduction in property transaction taxes, financed through increases in less distortive taxes, has therefore been strongly advocated (Brys et al., 2016[14]; Andrews, Caldera Sánchez and Johansson, 2011[58]).

Transaction taxes can have adverse efficiency effects by discouraging housing transactions, which can in turn affect residential and labour mobility. Transaction taxes can deter transactions on housing markets by affecting the payoff of the housing transaction for the buyer and the seller. On the one hand, they can increase the purchase cost for the buyer if the tax-inclusive price of the housing asset increases. On the other hand, they can reduce the price received by the seller if the tax is capitalised, leading to a lower pre-tax house price. The final economic incidence depends on demand and supply elasticities. If buyers are less responsive to higher prices, they will bear a larger share of the tax burden. In contrast, if buyers are more price-elastic than sellers, transaction taxes will be capitalised into house prices and predominantly fall on sellers (and after-tax house prices will not change much in response to the tax change). In either case, however, the tax may discourage an otherwise mutually beneficial transaction, and prevent a more efficient allocation of housing. Transaction taxes may also have wider repercussions on labour markets as higher transaction taxes may prevent relocations allowing people to access employment opportunities.

Empirical evidence generally finds that transaction taxes reduce prices and transaction volumes, but evidence regarding the magnitude of economic distortions is mixed. Across OECD countries, higher transaction taxes are correlated with a reduction in residential mobility (Causa and Pichelmann, 2020[62]). The vast majority of studies exploiting transaction tax reforms or discontinuities in tax rate schedules find a significant negative effect of transaction taxes on transaction volumes, based on evidence from Australia (Davidoff and Leigh, 2013[63]), Canada (Dachis, Duranton and Turner, 2012[64]), Finland (Eerola et al., 2019[65]), Germany (Dolls et al., 2021[1]; Fritzsche and Vandrei, 2019[66]), the United Kingdom[10] ((Best and Kleven, 2018[55]; Besley, Meads and Surico, 2014[67]), and the United States (Kopczuk and Munroe, 2015[68]). Several empirical analyses show that the tax burden is mostly capitalised into house prices (i.e. the tax incidence falls on the seller) (Besley, Meads and Surico, 2014[67]; Dachis, Duranton and Turner, 2012[64]; Davidoff and Leigh, 2013[63]; Dolls et al., 2021[1]; Kopczuk and Munroe, 2015[68]), with some studies even showing a disproportionately higher price decrease relative to the property tax increase (also referred to as over shifting) (Davidoff and Leigh, 2013[63]; Kopczuk and Munroe, 2015[68]) for properties that are expected to be traded frequently in the future (Dolls et al., 2021[1]). However, some empirical analyses question the magnitude of the distortions caused by transaction taxes. Results by Slemrod, Weber and Shan (2017[69]) show that transaction taxes only have small effects on buying and selling behaviours, which is why the authors conclude that transaction taxes generate comparably small welfare costs. Other studies suggest that the negative correlation between transaction taxes and transaction volumes could be driven partly by shifts in the timing of housing transactions (Besley, Meads and Surico, 2014[67]; Fritzsche and Vandrei, 2019[66]) or responses to non-tax factors that accompany transaction tax reforms such as the Great Recession and tighter mortgage market regulations (Haider, Anwar and Holmes, 2016[70]).

The relationship between transaction taxes, residential mobility, and labour mobility is complex as it may depend on relocation motives, homeownership patterns among workers and tax design. Different relocation motives might influence the impact of transaction taxes on residential mobility. For instance, relocation due to significant life events (e.g. changing jobs, retirement) might be less affected by transaction taxes than short-distance moves to better align housing with individual needs. In both the United Kingdom (Hilber and Lyytikäinen, 2017[71]) and Finland (Eerola et al., 2019[72]), evidence shows that short-distance, housing-related relocations are more strongly affected by transaction tax changes than long-distance, job-related moves. While Hilber and Lyytikainen (2017[71]) find no effect of transaction taxes on long-distance moves, results by Eerola et al. (2019[72]) show significant negative effects, suggesting that transaction taxes may also affect labour markets. Eerola et al. (2019[65]) also find evidence that transaction taxes have a stronger effect on property upsizing than on downsizing and on moves involving small adjustments in housing unit size. The effect of transaction taxes on labour mobility might also be influenced by the prevalence of homeownership among workers. In Germany, Petkova and Weichenrieder (2017[73]) find that particularly mobile workers self-select into the rental market, and while transaction taxes lower labour mobility for owner-occupiers, they have a limited effect on typically more mobile renters. The design of transaction taxes may also influence their impact on mobility; for example, Caldera Sanchez and Andrews (2011[74]) find that higher transaction tax rates have a larger effect on mobility than lower rates. Overall, the evidence suggests that the impact of transaction taxes on mobility is complex, depends on country-specific circumstances, and may affect short-distance residential moves more than long-distance labour mobility.

Transaction taxes may help curb speculative activities in overheated housing markets, although empirical findings are mixed. By construction, transaction taxes lower the incentives for short-term trading since the tax liability is effectively spread over the lifetime of the housing investment. The decrease in speculation and short-term trading should moderate price growth and reduce house price volatility (although the effect on price volatility may be more ambiguous, for instance, if lower transaction volumes lead to higher volatility) (Norregaard, 2013[16]). Some governments have designed transaction taxes specifically to disincentivise speculation and short-term trading. For this purpose, transaction taxes may be levied on the seller, which effectively reduces the after-tax return of property resales. For example, Hong Kong levies a Special Stamp Duty (SDD) on real estate sellers, where the tax rate varies inversely with the holding period (up to two years) and is higher for foreign investors and owners of more than one property (Hui, Zhong and Yu, 2017[75]). Empirical evidence shows that the SSD reduces short-term property resales (Agarwal et al., 2022[76]; Hui, Zhong and Yu, 2017[75]), but is less effective at reducing house prices, with some analyses showing no effects on property prices (Ahuja and Nabar, 2011[77]) while others show a reduction of property prices limited to high-value properties. Analyses by Agarwal et al. (2022[76]) even suggest that the SSD ultimately results in house price increases as market liquidity is reduced and property investors strategically defer their property sale, causing bunching of property sales shortly after the two-year holding period. Fu et al. (2013[78]) study the withdrawal of a transaction tax deferral in presale markets in Singapore[11] and find that higher transaction taxes reduce speculative activities in these markets, but that they also increase price volatility.

There is little empirical evidence on the distributional effects of property transaction taxes. Transaction taxes may be somewhat progressive as homeownership is lower for lower income people and property transaction tax burdens increase with the value of the property, which is higher for higher income and wealth households (see Chapter 2). Transaction taxes are also disproportionately borne by frequent property traders, which could suggest progressive effects as speculative trading is more likely to occur among higher income and wealth households. However, some empirical evidence shows that transaction taxes bear more heavily on younger households (Causa and Pichelmann, 2020[62]) who tend to have lower incomes and wealth. In addition, transaction taxes will be disproportionately borne by homeowners who have to relocate more frequently. If more mobile homeowners tend to be poorer households (for instance, low-income workers with less job security who regularly move for work), transaction taxes may have more regressive effects. However, this will not be the case where poorer households are typically renters. Overall, the distributional effects of transaction taxes are uncertain, depending on a range of factors including homeownership and mobility patterns in the country, tax design (for instance, whether tax rates are progressive) as well as tax capitalisation effects, and require further empirical analysis.

From a revenue perspective, transaction tax revenues tend to be pro-cyclical, with risks of funding shortfalls during downturns and excessive spending in times of economic expansion. While transaction taxes allow countries to raise revenue at relatively low administrative cost (see above), revenues tend to be more volatile than those of other taxes on housing, as they depend on property market values and transaction volumes. Developments in house prices and transaction volumes in turn follow closely business cycles (see Chapter 1), which is why transaction tax revenues tend to increase during economic expansions and decrease during downturns. Therefore, governments that rely heavily on transaction tax revenue risk facing funding shortfalls during economic downturns, while increased tax revenue and spending capacity in times of economic expansion might create incentives for unstainable expenditure and unproductive public investments.

There is a strong case for reducing or removing transaction taxes, but it is essential that this be done gradually and accompanied by other tax reforms (e.g. shifts towards recurrent property taxes) to avoid rises in house prices and windfall gains for homeowners. Transaction taxes could be reduced, particularly when they are high, or removed, to improve efficiency in housing and labour markets. However, the isolated reduction or removal of transaction taxes should be avoided as it would create windfall gains for current property owners, as tax reductions would most likely be capitalised into property values. In the current context of high and rising house prices, this would further reduce housing affordability. A gradual reform whereby transaction tax reductions would be financed through an increase in economically more efficient taxes bearing on current homeowners (e.g. recurrent property taxes) could help enhance efficiency and equity simultaneously (Mirrlees et al., 2011[43]), but it would likely require changes to fiscal relations across different levels of government (see above). Several OECD countries provide successful examples of transaction tax reforms, including gradual shifts from transaction taxes to less distortive and more predictable revenue sources.

There may be a case for differentiated transaction taxes for owner-occupied and secondary properties, although this would likely raise a number of issues. One option to address the negative effects of transaction taxes would be to reduce or remove the transaction tax on owner-occupied housing, but maintain it on secondary housing (e.g. Netherlands[12]). This would eliminate the distortions to residential and labour mobility, but still act as a dampener on speculative transactions of second properties. This would also reduce the potentially negative distributional effects of transaction taxes on younger and more mobile households who might be more affected by transaction taxes on owner-occupied housing, but would not be affected by higher taxes on second homes. However, such tax relief would amplify the preferential tax treatment of owner-occupied housing and, like any reduction or removal of transaction taxes, would likely be capitalised into higher house prices in the absence of other reforms (see above). In addition, it could increase the risks of taxpayers mischaracterising second homes as their first home or using "straw buyers" (such as family members that did not own residential property) to evade the higher tax (Thomas, 2021[79]).

An alternative may be to levy progressive transaction tax rates that increase with the value of the property. Recent evidence suggests that progressive property transaction taxes may help enhance equity and reduce distortions by lowering the tax burden on taxpayers who are more constrained by down-payments, while maintaining revenue raising capacity by imposing higher tax rates on higher value properties. Examining the Scottish stamp duty, Borbely (2021[80]) finds that lower tax rates encourage transaction activity in the lower end of the market, where households are more sensitive to transaction taxes that need to be paid upfront, often because they are more highly leveraged and constrained by mortgage down-payments. On the other hand, higher tax rates are not found to have an overall significant negative effect on the transactions in the higher price ranges where tax rates increased, with the exception of very expensive properties, where a negative effect is identified. Importantly, progressive transaction tax rates should avoid introducing sharp discontinuities in the tax schedule. A "slice" system, where the higher marginal tax rate only applies to the portion of the transaction value above a certain threshold, is significantly less distortive than a "slab" system, where the higher marginal tax rate applies to the entire value of the property once above a threshold (see the reform in the United Kingdom (Scanlon, Whitehead and Blanc, 2018[81]).

To address significant and volatile price growth on housing markets, the use of transaction taxes should be carefully assessed against policy alternatives. Transaction taxes have been used to cool down housing markets, but as discussed above, their impact on house price growth and volatility has been mixed. In addition, there may be more effective policies to contain house price growth. These include policies to encourage the supply of housing (see Chapter 1). These also include demand-side tax policies (such as scaling back preferential tax provisions for housing, conditioning preferential capital gains tax treatment upon a minimum holding period, and recurrent property taxes levied on up-to-date market values) and non-tax policy tools (in particular macro-prudential regulations, such as higher capital requirements and limits on loan-to-value and debt-to-income ratios) (Crowe et al., 2011[82]). The impacts of different policy options should be carefully evaluated within the context of the local housing market, the broader macro-prudential policy framework and compatibility with monetary policy (Crowe et al., 2011[82]). If transaction taxes are used to reduce house price growth, speculation and volatility on housing markets, evidence suggests that they could be less distortionary when targeted at a specific market (e.g. pre-sale markets with a substantial presence of speculators) and market segment (e.g. high-value properties) (Hui, Zhong and Yu, 2017[75]; Fu, Qian and Yeung, 2013[78]).

Countries could consider taxing capital gains on main residences above a high threshold and all gains on secondary homes to enhance efficiency and equity

The vast majority of OECD countries exempt owner-occupied housing from capital gains taxation. Twenty OECD countries provide full and unconditional capital gains tax exemptions on owner-occupied housing. Even where capital gains on main residences are taxed, full exemptions can apply in nine countries and other favourable tax treatment can apply in five countries if certain conditions are met. These conditions include minimum holding periods, acquiring another primary residence within a given time (rollover relief), or an exemption for housing or capital gains below a threshold. A far greater number of countries (33 out of 38) levy capital gains taxes on sales of secondary property,[13] although full exemptions apply in nine countries after a minimum holding period and concessionary tax treatment may apply in others. In addition, a small minority of countries exempt capital gains on secondary residences that are not used to generate income (e.g. holiday homes in Norway[14]). As discussed below, while capital gains tax exemptions on the main residence are often justified on the grounds of encouraging homeownership and preventing potential lock-in effects, they raise efficiency and equity concerns. For secondary residential property, the rationale for exempting capital gains is much weaker.

Exempting capital gains on the main residence is often justified on the basis that it supports homeownership and protects people's savings for retirement, but these arguments have significant limitations. Capital gains tax exemptions contribute to the preferential tax treatment of owner-occupied housing (Millar-Powell et al., 2022[83]) and may be justified as a way of promoting homeownership. However, the extent to which capital gains tax exemptions incentivise homeownership is uncertain since it does not address the main barriers to homeownership (e.g. down-payment and income constraints) and the benefits of the exemption only materialise when the home is sold. In addition, there is a risk that exemptions feed into house price inflation if housing supply is not responsive, which would make housing less affordable. Capital gains tax exemptions on owner-occupied housing may also intend to protect people's savings for retirement. Indeed, for many middle-class households, housing and gains accruing on the housing asset represent a major source of wealth (see Chapter 2) as well as an important savings vehicle for retirement (Poterba, Venti and Wise, 2011[84]). However, households also have access to other savings instruments that are specifically aimed at encouraging private pension savings and very favourably taxed in OECD countries (OECD/KIPF, 2014[85]).

From an efficiency perspective, a stronger justification for exempting capital gains on main residences is to reduce potential lock-in effects. Taxing capital gains on a realisation basis may create lock-in effects, discouraging taxpayers from selling property that has appreciated in value. This is true for all assets, but in the case of owner-occupied housing, tax-induced incentives to delay housing sales may have wider implications for residential and labour mobility. In a way that is similar to transaction taxes, there is some empirical evidence that capital gains taxation on residential housing creates lock-in effects in the form of reduced property sales and residential mobility (Cunningham and Engelhardt, 2008[86]; Shan, 2011[87]), although the number of studies is limited. The lock-in effect may be more pronounced among liquidity constrained and less wealthy households, which suggests that there may be a role for maintaining capital gains tax exemptions for some households. Another option to address the lock-in effect is rollover relief, which a few countries provide, whereby capital gains on owner-occupied residences are 'rolled over' if the taxpayer purchases another main residence within a given time.

The extent of the lock-in effect will depend on the level of the tax and other features of the tax system. For instance, lock-in effects are likely to be higher if capital gains tax rates are high and if capital gains taxes are combined with high transaction taxes and a recurrent property tax based on outdated values. As discussed, high transaction taxes can discourage households from selling a house to buy a new one and recurrent property taxes relying on outdated cadastral values create incentives to remain in undervalued homes. If transaction taxes are low and property taxes are based on regularly updated market values, overall lock-in effects will be lower. Lock-in effects will also be stronger, especially for older generations, if capital gains are taxed when the main residence is sold but forgiven when the property is transferred upon death through step-up in basis (i.e. the housing asset is stepped-up to its market value at the time of the bequest). In this case, individuals will have an incentive to hold on to their property until they die and pass it on to heirs to avoid capital gains taxation.

There are also administrative justifications for exempting capital gains on main residences, related to the difficulty of removing inflationary gains and capital improvements from the tax base. Most countries tax nominal capital gains when assets are sold, including real gains and inflation, but this can be more problematic for housing assets that are typically held for long periods. While some countries only tax real gains on housing by indexing capital gains for inflation (Chile and Israel), others avoid the difficulty of inflation adjustment by fully exempting capital gains on main residences (OECD, 2018[2]). Taxing capital gains on main residences also raises the issue of the tax treatment of home improvement costs. Capital improvements are typically deductible for capital gains tax purposes, but this raises recordkeeping issues, as taxpayers need to measure and keep records of the costs related to property improvements. This may pose challenges when homeowners do improvements themselves (e.g. DIY renovations) or have to differentiate between expenditures that affect the basis of the property and maintenance or repair costs (Gravelle, 2022[88])

However, capital gains tax exemptions for main residences, particularly where they are uncapped, raise a number of efficiency, equity and revenue issues. As discussed below, exemptions for capital gains on main residences create distortions across savings instruments, raise vertical, intergenerational and geographical equity issues, and represent significant revenue foregone for governments. In addition, exempting capital gains on main residences may exempt windfall gains, where these exist, further reducing efficiency and equity. The efficiency, equity and revenue concerns associated with the exemption of capital gains on main residences are even more pronounced where countries do not have well-designed recurrent taxes on immovable property based on regularly updated property values. The following paragraphs discuss these various points in greater detail.

Exempting capital gains on main residences creates large distortions across savings instruments. The capital gains tax exemption for owner-occupied property contrasts with the more typical taxation of capital gains on other asset types, such as shares, investment funds, and rented housing (OECD, 2018[2]). The exemption for capital gains on owner-occupied housing creates significant distortions and contributes to lower marginal effective tax rates on owner-occupied housing compared to rented housing and some financial assets (Millar-Powell et al. (2022[83]), OECD (2018[2])). The preferential tax treatment applied to owner-occupied housing, of which the capital gains tax exemption is one element, makes investment in owner-occupied housing more attractive. While very low effective taxation may be justified on the grounds of encouraging homeownership, it also incentivises individuals to divert capital away from other investments and overconsume housing (Gruber, Jensen and Kleven, (2021[89]), Fatica and Prammer (2017[90]), Arnold et al. (2011[57]), (Hungerford, 2010[12])).

Capital gains tax exemptions on owner-occupied housing disproportionately benefit higher income and wealthier households. Compared to lower-wealth and lower-income households, high income and wealth households own more valuable main residences that have experienced larger increases in value in recent decades (see Chapter 2, Corlett and Leslie (2021[10]), Grudnoff (2016[11])). Therefore, a disproportionate share of capital gains on main residences and of the capital gains tax exemption is expected to accrue to top households, a finding that is supported by a limited number of studies. For example, in the United Kingdom, the average nominal capital gain on the main residence between 2000 and 2016-18 was less than GBP 1 000 on average per adult for the first three net wealth deciles, compared to GBP 174 000 for the wealthiest 10% (Corlett and Leslie, 2021[10]). This partly reflects the fact that only homeowners receive a capital gain, and that homeownership rates are 2.7% on average for the bottom three deciles, but reach 98% for the richest decile. In the United States, close to 50% of capital gains on the main residence accrue to households in the top income quintile, while only 5% accrues to the bottom quintile (Hungerford, 2010[12]). In Australia, the bottom half of the income distribution receives around 13%

of the total tax relief for capital gains on the main residence, while the top decile receives 37% (Grudnoff, 2016[11]). Renters, who tend to have lower incomes and wealth (see Chapter 2) do not receive any direct benefit from this exemption.

Capital gains tax exemptions for the main residence reinforce intergenerational and geographical inequality, given that gains have been concentrated among older generations and specific geographical areas. Older households are characterised by high homeownership rates and housing wealth (Chapter 2) and have enjoyed significant growth in property prices. Property value increases in the past three decades have been unprecedented, exceeding inflation and wage growth in a context of historically low interest rates (see Chapter 1), and such gains will most likely not be repeated (Corlett and Leslie, 2021[10]). By contrast, homeownership rates are falling among younger generations, in part due to property value increases that have made it increasingly difficult to access the housing market. Even if younger households are able to access the housing market, they may not experience the large gains of previous generations. Many countries have also witnessed stark differences in the regional distribution of capital gains, with households in large metropolitan areas benefitting from the most significant property price growth on already highly valued property. In the United Kingdom, for example, adults owning property in London benefitted from an average capital increase (GBP 76 000) nearly four times as large as the increase experienced by adults owning property in the North East (GBP 21 000) between 2000 and 2021 (Corlett and Leslie, 2021[10]).

Where windfall gains exist, capital gains tax exemptions for owner-occupied housing leave such gains untaxed, raising further efficiency and equity concerns. While capital gains may arise due to property improvements and partly reflect general price inflation, housing capital gains are primarily the consequence of increases in property values, which are driven by factors over which homeowners have no control. Indeed, rising house prices have been linked to low interest rates, unresponsive supply, and changing demographics, among other factors (see Chapter 1). Positive externalities, particularly from public investments (e.g. improvements in transportation infrastructure, quality of schools), can also contribute to house price increases. Uncapped capital gains tax exemptions on main residences mean that these windfall gains for property owners escape taxation, negatively affecting both efficiency and equity. There may be other tools to capture some windfall gains on property, in particular land value capture taxes, which tax private homeowners (or developers) on the rise in property values that are due to public actions (e.g. infrastructure investments, rezoning), but these fail to capture windfall gains that are due to other factors (see section 3.3.2). The capital gains tax exemption may also amplify incentives for homeowners to oppose new housing construction, where increased housing supply could ease upward pressure on house prices.

Finally, the capital gains tax exemption for main residences represents significant revenue foregone for governments. Some studies have found that the amount of revenue forgone by governments is substantial. In the United States, the revenue cost of the (capped) capital gains tax exemption was estimated at USD 40.3 billion for 2022 (Gravelle, 2022[88]). In Australia, the estimated cost of the capital gains tax exemption for main residences was AUD 64 billion in 2021 (Treasury, 2022[91]). In the United Kingdom, the revenue cost of the Private Residence Relief was estimated to amount to GBP 28.4 billion in 2020-21 (HMRC, (2021[92])), while (Corlett and Leslie, 2021[10]) find that taxing capital gains on all main residences at a flat rate of 28% would raise an estimated GBP 11 billion. In both Australia (Treasury, 2022[91]) and the United Kingdom (HMRC, 2021[92]), the capital gains tax exemption for the main residence is the country's largest tax concession in terms of revenue forgone. However, it should be noted that removing the capital gains tax exemption would not necessarily raise the equivalent of the foregone tax revenue, as additional tax revenues would depend on dynamic effects such as lock-in effects and changing house prices.

The efficiency, equity, and revenue concerns raised by exempting capital gains on main residences are more pronounced where property value increases are not captured under recurrent property taxes. To some extent, recurrent taxes on immovable property can act as an imperfect substitute for an accrual-based capital gains tax so long as property values are regularly updated; the difference being that the recurrent property tax is levied on the overall value of the property, not just the increase in value. By taxing the higher property values on a recurrent basis, recurrent taxes on immovable property avoid the lock-in effects that may arise with realisation-based capital gains taxes. However, in the case where there are no capital gains taxes and where recurrent property taxes are not based on regularly updated property values, increases in housing values gained by homeowners fully escape taxation (assuming no recurrent net wealth tax).

Capping the capital gains tax exemption for main residences to ensure that gains above a very high value are taxed has the potential to simultaneously reduce distortions, enhance equity and raise revenues. The discussion above highlights that capping the capital gains tax exemption on main residences at a high capital gain threshold would yield positive effects for equity and efficiency. In addition, it would allow governments to collect significant amounts of revenue from households with large capital gains, given house price increases. At the same time, exempting a portion of capital gains appears to be a sensible approach to reduce potential lock-in effects and administrative costs. The threshold could be set at a sufficiently high level to continue exempting the vast majority of homeowners but capture those at the top of the distribution, and regularly revalued to take into account house price increases. The tax exemption threshold could be conditional on using the housing as a main residence for a minimum number of years. An alternative would be to exempt gains on main residences earned within a given time regardless of the number of sales. This would prevent tax avoidance that could arise if the capital gains tax exemption applied per transaction, as households could avoid capital gains taxation by regularly selling and buying property and realising gains below the exemption threshold. It would also strengthen horizontal equity between movers and stayers. A capped capital gains tax exemption for the main residence applies in a minority of OECD countries (Table A.1). Israel applies a capital gains tax exemption on the first ILS 4.5 million (approximately USD 1.4 million) of capital gain from residential property, if it is the only property owned by the taxpayer and has been held for more than 18 months. In the United States, capital gains up to USD 250 000 (or USD 500 000 for married couples filing jointly) (not indexed for inflation) on the sale of the main residence can be excluded from taxation, if the home has been owned and used as the main residence for at least two of the previous five years. Mexico exempts capital gains on owner-occupied housing if the gain is below 700 000 investment units (roughly USD 250 000) and if the taxpayer has not disposed of housing within the previous five years. Korea exempts capital gains for houses valued below KRW 900 million (approximately USD 790 000) if they do not qualify for a full exemption based on the holding period.

If countries decide to tax some of the gains on main residences, reforms will likely need to balance these policy objectives with political economy considerations, especially when deciding which gains will be subject to the tax, and take into account interactions with other taxes. If countries decide to broaden the capital gains tax base, governments will need to decide whether the reform only applies to gains that will accrue in the future (e.g. from the date the reform was introduced) or also takes into account past gains. Considering the unprecedented house price growth in recent decades and its implications for intergenerational inequality, it seems warranted for both equity and revenue reasons to include in the tax base capital gains that accrued before the introduction of the tax. However, for practical reasons, gains may be calculated in relation to a specific base date (instead of the full ownership period) (see for example the proposal of Corlett and Leslie (2021[10])). This would reduce the practical difficulties associated with tracking deductible capital improvements over the years as homeowners may not have kept records of these costs, though taxpayers could be allowed to deduct a fixed presumed amount of expenses. At the same time, taxing capital gains in relation to a specific base date would make it more difficult to determine the cost basis of the property than if the original purchase price is used. Taxing capital gains earned after a specific date as opposed to over to the full ownership period would also avoid punishing long-term homeowners, although this would be less of an issue if the capital gains tax exemption is set at a high level. A reform of capital gains taxes also needs to take into account existing rules on unrealised capital gains at death, since taxing capital gains (above a certain threshold) while forgiving capital gains at death through step-up in basis may significantly increase lock-in effects, with individuals holding on to their property until they die to avoid capital gains taxation.

Capital gains on secondary residential property should be taxed to promote neutrality among different asset classes and increase the progressivity of the tax system. Secondary property should be taxed like other capital assets in order to maintain neutrality among different asset types, regardless of whether the housing generates an income (e.g. rented property) or not (e.g. holiday homes). The rationale underlying capital gains tax exemptions or roll-over relief (i.e. prevent lock-in effects that lower residential and potentially labour mobility) is weaker in the case of secondary housing, as the mobility of any occupants (e.g. renters) should be unaffected by capital gains taxes levied on the owners. From an equity perspective, the taxation of capital gains on secondary housing would contribute to enhancing progressivity as secondary real estate wealth is significantly more concentrated at the top of the distribution (see Chapter 2). In the United States, for instance, 70% of accrued capital gains on secondary property go to the top income quintile while just 7% accrues to the first two quintiles combined (Hungerford, 2010[12]). In addition, as capital gains tax is paid upon disposal, the likelihood that the tax burden is largely passed onto renters through higher rents is lower.

Where capital gains are taxed, countries should consider taxing real rather than nominal capital gains. In countries that tax nominal capital gains, the marginal effective tax rate increases with inflation (Millar-Powell et al., 2022[83]). To ensure that only the real gain is taxed, countries should allow the indexation of capital gains using, for example, the Consumer Price Index (CPI). While capital gains indexation might have been less relevant in the low-inflation environment of the past decade, recent trends pointing towards higher inflation may increase the need for inflation indexing. Digitalisation has also significantly reduced the administrative costs associated with indexing capital gains for inflation.

Countries should consider limiting or phasing out mortgage interest relief on owner-occupied housing

Mortgage interest relief for housing is common across OECD countries. Mortgage interest relief is one of the most common tax policy tools to support homeownership across OECD countries (OECD, 2021[93]), which may be explained by the fact that mortgages represent the largest liability in households' debt portfolios and help households access the housing market and accumulate wealth (Causa, Woloszko and Leite, 2019[94]). Out of 38 OECD countries, 17 provide tax relief for mortgage interest on owner-occupied housing via either a tax deduction or a tax credit. In some countries, the total value of the deduction or the credit is capped (e.g. Belgium (mortgage principal repayments), Estonia, Finland, Italy, Luxembourg, and Spain), while two countries restrict eligibility for mortgage interest relief to taxpayers below an income threshold (Chile) or whose housing asset falls below a value threshold (Korea). Mortgage interest relief is more widely available for rented property, as many countries allow taxpayers to deduct the costs they incur to earn taxable rental income. Twenty-six out of 38 countries offer mortgage interest relief for rented properties, and caps or thresholds are less common (OECD, 2018[2]).

Mortgage interest relief can allow taxpayers to deduct the costs that they incur generating taxable income, but there appears to be little justification for this relief in the absence of taxable income. The taxation of net income – gross income minus the costs incurred to generate it – is common practice across OECD countries. In the case of rental property, owners are typically taxed on their net rental income; that is, their rental income after deducting costs such as mortgage interest and local taxes. In the case of owner-occupied property, there is a compelling case for providing mortgage interest relief where imputed rents are taxed. However, imputed rents on owner-occupied housing are rarely taxed for various conceptual and administrative reasons (Box 3.4). In countries where imputed rents on owner-occupied housing are not taxed, the justification for allowing costs, including mortgage interest payments, to be deducted or credited appears limited as there is no corresponding taxable income.[15]

Box 3.4. Imputed rents

Part of the return to an owner-occupier housing investment accrues to the taxpayer in the form of living in the property rent-free. This in-kind return is known as imputed rent. The concept of imputed rent on owner-occupied property is motivated by the idea that the owner-occupier could rent out the property on the market to earn a rental income. However, refraining from doing so indicates that the value of the housing service to the owner-occupier must at least be equal to the forgone rent. While the property owner (making the investment) and the dweller (paying the rental income and consuming the housing service) are two separate individuals in the case of rented housing, they are one and the same person when considering owner-occupied property.

Imputed rent is commonly exempt for tax purposes. This has been found to be one of the most significant drivers of the preferential tax treatment of owner-occupied housing (Millar-Powell et al., 2022[83]). While mortgage interest relief for rental property allows owners to deduct costs that are associated with generating taxable rental income, mortgage interest for owner-occupiers is deducted without a corresponding taxation of imputed rental income. This generous tax treatment of owner-occupied housing results in negative marginal effective tax rates in some countries, effectively providing a tax subsidy for owner-occupied housing (Figure 3.6). To remove distortions in housing investment decisions and eliminate the homeownership bias, the taxation of imputed rents combined with mortgage interest relief has often been suggested as a 'first-best' policy approach.

In practice, a range of conceptual, administrative and political considerations have made the taxation of imputed rental income difficult to implement in practice. Only four OECD countries (Denmark, Greece, the Netherlands and Switzerland) tax imputed rents, although at comparatively low rates and only under certain conditions.

Source: (Goode, 1960[95]; Millar-Powell et al., 2022[83])

Mortgage interest relief on owner-occupied housing provides a large subsidy to homeowners and represents a significant fiscal cost. Mortgage interest relief reduces the financing costs of a debt-financed housing investment (commonly at the taxpayer's marginal tax rate) and therefore reduces the marginal effective tax rate (METR) of debt- relative to equity-financed property (Figure 3.6). On average, the value of the tax relief rises with income, but drops slightly for the highest earners due to capping in some countries. Mortgage interest relief also represents a significant fiscal cost for governments. Forgone tax revenue due to mortgage interest relief amounted to 1.3% of GDP in the Netherlands, 0.3% in Belgium and Luxembourg, and around 0.1% in the United States, Finland and Mexico (OECD, 2021[93]). In the United States, this was equivalent to around 7% of total personal income tax revenue in 2018 (Sommer and Sullivan, 2018[96]). This large fiscal cost has been justified by the expected positive impacts of the tax relief on homeownership, but, as discussed below, evidence suggests that mortgage interest relief is not effective at raising homeownership levels and raises serious efficiency and equity concerns.

Figure 3.6. Marginal effective tax rates and component taxes, owner-occupied debt-financed housing, average for countries with and without mortgage interest relief, 2016

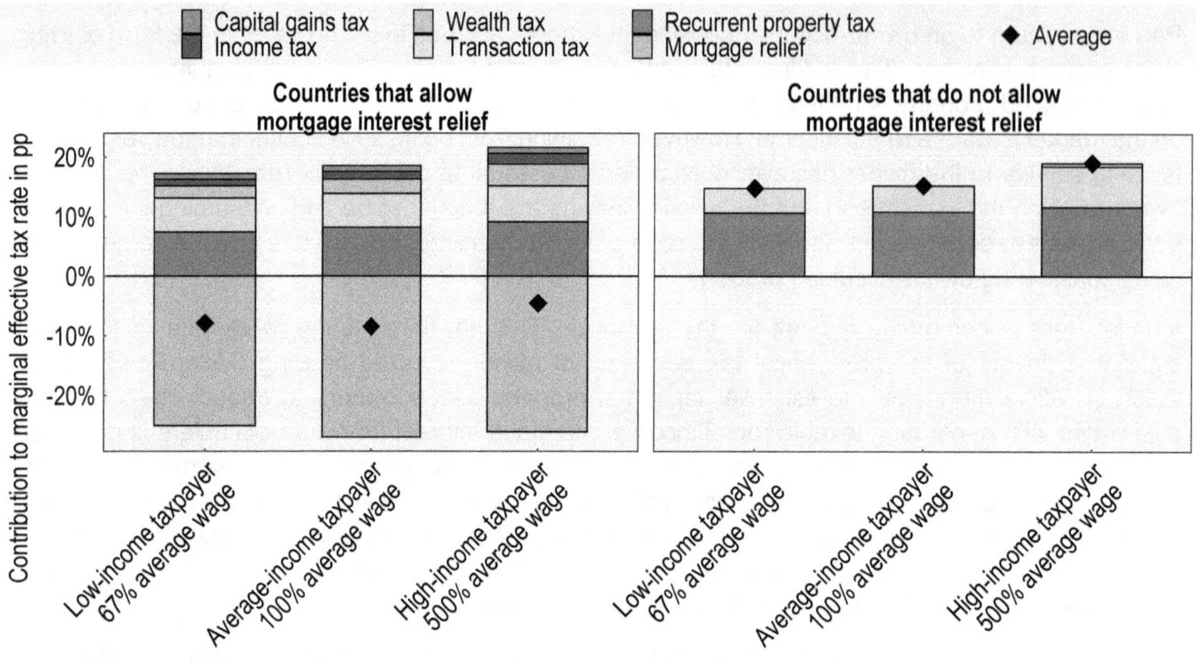

Note: Results are presented for owner-occupied debt financed housing. Results are presented for inflation at the OECD average level; with a 20-year holding period; and the returns stemming 50% from capital gains and 50% from rent or imputed rent. Countries that allow mortgage interest relief on owner-occupied housing are: Argentina, Belgium, Bulgaria, Chile, Colombia, Czech Republic, Denmark, Estonia, Finland, Greece, Italy, Japan, Korea, Luxembourg, Mexico, the Netherlands, Norway, Spain, Sweden, Switzerland, and the United States. Countries that do not allow mortgage interest relief on owner-occupied housing are: Australia, Austria, Canada, France, Germany, Hungary, Iceland, Ireland, Israel, Latvia, Lithuania, New Zealand, Poland, Portugal, Slovak Republic, Slovenia, South Africa, Türkiye, and the United Kingdom.
Source: (Millar-Powell et al., 2022[83])

StatLink https://stat.link/9q5i2p

However, empirical evidence suggests that mortgage interest relief does not raise homeownership rates and results in higher house prices where housing supply is constrained. Descriptive statistics show that homeownership rates among high-income households (e.g. households that benefit the most from deductions) in countries that do not allow mortgage interest relief are high and similar to homeownership rates in comparable countries providing tax relief (Caldera Sánchez and Andrews, 2011[74]). In a study examining the impact of a reform to mortgage interest deductibility in Denmark, Gruber et al. (2021[89]) find causal evidence that changes to mortgage interest relief have no effect on homeownership rates. In the United States, Glaeser and Shapiro (2003[97]) find that mortgage interest relief has not affected homeownership rates, which have remained stable across decades despite significant variations affecting the subsidy, while Hilber and Turner (2014[98]) find that homeownership only increases for higher income groups where the housing supply is elastic. The capitalisation of mortgage interest deductions into higher house prices is evidenced across a range of empirical studies (Berger et al., 2000[99]; Gruber, Jensen and Kleven, 2021[89]) and general equilibrium models (Harris, 2010[100]; Sommer and Sullivan, 2018[96]), particularly where the housing supply is inelastic (see e.g. (Bourassa et al., 2013[101]; Davis, 2019[102]; Hilber and Turner, 2014[98]). As mortgage interest relief is capitalised into higher house prices, it is unlikely to raise homeownership, but it also raises distributional questions, with studies showing that property owners and property developers benefit the most from higher prices (Caldera Sánchez and

Andrews, 2011[74]; Davis, 2019[102]). The impact of mortgage interest relief on homeownership rates is also limited by the fact that such relief fails to address the most important barriers to homeownership, such as households' credit ratings (Barakova et al., 2003[103]) and the availability of down-payments (Gabriel and Rosenthal, 1991[104]).

Empirical evidence also shows that mortgage interest relief encourages purchases of larger and more valuable homes, rather than supporting new entrants into the housing market. Gruber et al. (2021[89]) find that mortgage interest relief affects housing investments at the intensive margin, as households use the tax subsidy to acquire bigger and more expensive properties, rather than at the extensive margin (i.e. acquiring a home). While in theory there may be positive externalities associated with increased home value and property size (e.g. positive effects of nicer homes on the neighbourhood), this is typically not the stated goal of mortgage interest relief. Empirical evidence also shows that intensive margin effects are driven by households moving homes as opposed to improving their home (Gruber, Jensen and Kleven, 2021[89]). Purchases of larger properties may also have negative environmental consequences (e.g. urban sprawl as well as increased energy and water consumption).

Mortgage interest relief has also been found to encourage household indebtedness with potential adverse effects on macroeconomic stability. The demand for housing debt is found to be highly elastic with respect to its tax treatment determining its financing costs (Dunsky and Follain, 2000[105]). General equilibrium models using data from the United States suggest a significant increase in household indebtedness in response to mortgage interest relief (Sommer and Sullivan, 2018[96]). High levels of debt have in turn been found to reduce households' ability to smooth consumption and increase the likelihood of downturns, with recessions tending to be more severe (Sutherland and Hoeller, 2012[106]). Higher leverage ratios also raise after-tax returns and potentially incentivise property speculation (Andrews, Caldera Sánchez and Johansson, 2011[58]). Analysis by Andrews et al. (2011[58]) show that mortgage interest deductibility is correlated with volatility in the housing market, which suggests increased speculative activity.

Mortgage interest relief on owner-occupied housing provides greater benefits to high-income households. As high-income households are more likely to be homeowners, have more valuable homes and hold the largest share of owner-occupied housing debt, they are able to make greater use of mortgage interest relief, while lower-income households who are less likely to own homes, own less valuable properties and hold less housing debt will receive less tax relief (Chapter 2). The design of mortgage interest relief also contributes to the concentration of the tax benefit, as countries commonly provide mortgage interest deductions at the taxpayer's marginal PIT tax rate and do not cap the tax relief on owner-occupied housing (Millar-Powell et al., 2022[83]). A range of studies drawing on different indicators and examining the United States (Carasso, Steuerle and Bell, 2005[107]; Gale, Gruber and Stephens-Davidowitz, 2007[108]; Harris and Parker, 2014[109]; Sommer and Sullivan, 2018[96]) and some European countries (Fatica, 2015[110]; Fatica and Prammer, 2017[90]; Matsaganis and Flevotomou, 2007[111]) find evidence that mortgage interest relief is regressive. Studies find evidence that the share of total tax relief received rises with income. For example, Sommer and Sullivan (2018[96]) estimate that in the United States, 42% of the mortgage interest deduction is captured by taxpayers in the top income quintile, while Matsaganis and Flevotomou (2007[111])estimate that the share of the relief going to the top income quintile ranges from 33% (Sweden) to 59% (Greece) in several European countries. Matsaganis and Flevotomou (2007[111]) also find that tax relief as a share of income is highest for households in the fourth or fifth income quintiles. In the United States, Carasso, Steuerle and Bell (2005[107]) find that tax relief as a share of tax liability rises with income, from 0.3% for the first income quintile to 4.9% for the top income quintile.

However, lower-income and lower-wealth households can derive significant benefit from mortgage interest relief, given household debt levels. It is important to note that while high-income households receive greater relief both as a share of total relief and relative to their incomes (particularly when relief is not capped), lower-income and lower-wealth households may still benefit from tax relief for mortgage interest, as a greater share of low-income households have high debt-to-income ratios and given that housing debt is more substantial relative to gross wealth for low-wealth households (Chapter 2). Fatica and Prammer (2017[90]) find that the tax reduction in some European countries is highest for households with low net wealth and net housing wealth. Capping mortgage interest relief at a low level to target the relief may therefore avoid some of the regressive effects of broad-based relief.

Mortgage interest relief for rented properties allows taxpayers to deduct the costs they incur to earn taxable income, but this relief provides a larger tax reduction to high-income and high-wealth households. Mortgage interest deductions for rented properties ensure tax is levied on taxpayers' net income, that is, after deducting costs incurred to earn the income. However, a tax deduction for mortgage interest results in a greater reduction in tax liability for high-income taxpayers subject to higher marginal PIT rates (in countries that levy progressive tax rates on rental income). In addition, ownership of secondary housing, which includes rented housing, is concentrated among the wealthiest households (see Chapter 2). Due to this concentration of ownership and the design of mortgage interest relief, which is typically uncapped, mortgage interest relief for rented properties primarily flows to top households.

Removing mortgage interest relief for owner-occupied property would simultaneously enhance efficiency, equity, and revenues. Phasing out mortgage interest relief could address many of the negative effects outlined above: reducing tax incentives to overinvest in owner-occupied housing, lowering or mitigating increases in house prices, improving macroeconomic stability, and removing a regressive and costly tax relief. Improved affordability could lower rents and make housing more accessible to households that currently do not make full use of the relief (such as low-income households with low PIT liabilities). Empirical studies suggest that the elimination of mortgage interest relief on main residential properties raises welfare in the long-run (Alpanda and Zubairy, 2016[112]; Floetotto, Kirker and Stroebel, 2016[113]; Gale, Gruber and Stephens-Davidowitz, 2007[108]; Harris, 2010[100]; Karlman, Kinnerud and Kragh-Sørensen, 2021[114]). While removing mortgage interest relief would strengthen progressivity by reducing tax relief that delivers greater benefits to high-income households, capping relief would also help improve progressivity.

Removing mortgage interest relief on owner-occupied housing can nevertheless be complex as it creates winners and losers and risks destabilising the housing market, so a phase-out would need to be gradual. Countries that have removed mortgage interest relief have done so gradually (Box 3.5). Gradually removing mortgage interest relief helps alleviate potential financial difficulties for households repaying their loans. In addition, as mortgage interest relief will likely be capitalised into house prices, its removal could prompt a decline in house prices. This is expected to create winners and losers, particularly in the short run; for example, renters and lower-income households with less borrowing capacity would gain from lower house prices (and not lose much from the repeal of the tax relief for mortgage interest), while highly leveraged homeowners and outright owners may lose (Floetotto, Kirker and Stroebel, 2016[113]; Karlman, Kinnerud and Kragh-Sørensen, 2021[114]). If mortgage interest relief is removed abruptly rather than gradually phased out, benefits accruing to non-homeowners (e.g. renters and prospective owners) will be largest while homeowners, especially those who are highly leveraged, stand to lose the most. On the contrary, gradually phasing out mortgage interest relief will reduce potential house price declines, mitigating the costs of the reform for current homeowners, but also decreasing potential gains in housing affordability for non-homeowners. Besides these welfare effects across different groups, consideration should be given to the wider macroeconomic impact of a sudden repeal of mortgage interest relief as a significant drop in house prices could possibly have wider effects on the economy. The decision on how quickly to remove mortgage interest relief should therefore carefully consider both welfare effects between current homeowners and potential entrants on the housing market, as well as wider macroeconomic risks. In addition to a gradual removal, careful consideration should be given to the timing of reforms. In particular, in the current context of tightening monetary policy, countries need to be attentive to the increased financial vulnerability of some households (see Chapter 1).

Where a full repeal is not possible, countries could scale back mortgage interest relief in a way that reduces its regressive and distortive effects. Countries could limit the amount of mortgage interest that taxpayers are allowed to deduct (e.g. by capping the value of the deduction, limiting the value of the loan on which interest is deductible or limiting the share of interest that is deductible) or restrict eligibility through either a threshold applied to the taxpayer's personal income or a threshold applied to the property value. Alternatively, countries could replace mortgage interest deductions (which reduce taxable income) with capped tax credits (which directly reduce tax liability up to a fixed amount) to make the relief less regressive (e.g. Italy, Spain).

While there is a strong case to maintain mortgage interest relief for rented properties, countries could consider introducing some limitations on this relief to reduce regressivity. There is a strong case for allowing taxpayers to deduct the costs they incur to earn taxable income. However, given the concentration of secondary real estate wealth, countries may consider designing mortgage interest relief so that higher income and wealthy taxpayers do not benefit disproportionately. This could include limiting the amount of the relief (e.g. capping the amount deducted) or shifting to a tax credit. For example, the United Kingdom replaced the mortgage interest deduction with an uncapped tax credit equal to 20% of costs. This ensures that taxpayers with the same costs receive the same tax benefit regardless of the rate at which they pay tax.

Box 3.5. Reforms to mortgage interest relief for owner-occupied housing in Ireland, the Netherlands and the United Kingdom

Ireland

Mortgage interest relief (MIR) for owner-occupied housing was gradually phased out in Ireland starting in 2009 in response to house price inflation and volatile property markets. Within the MIR scheme, the rates and upper thresholds of a qualifying mortgage loan depended on the taxpayers' individual circumstances including if the taxpayer was a first-time buyer, the time at which the property was bought and their civil status. The tax relief was administered through mortgage lenders.

As MIR was phased out, new mortgages taken out after January 2013 did not qualify for MIR and the relief expired for mortgages taken out prior to 2004. The relief continued to apply up to the end of 2020 for households who bought a home on a mortgage between 2004 and 2012, given high property prices and mortgage repayment obligations. The highest rate of relief (capped at a maximum interest amount) was applicable to households that bought a property between 2004 and 2008 at the peak of the housing boom. For property purchases in other years, the rate of relief was between 15% and 25%. Originally, MIR was due to expire in 2017, but it was later decided that it should be phased out more gradually to avoid a spike in mortgage payments for MIR recipients in 2018. Subsequently, the amount of mortgage interest qualifying for relief was gradually reduced from 75% of the existing relief in 2018, to 50% in 2019 and 25% in 2020. Since January 2021, MIR has no longer been available.

Netherlands

In 2013, the Netherlands reformed its approach to mortgage interest relief for owner-occupied housing in an attempt to address deteriorating housing affordability and strengthen macroeconomic stability. The tax reform entailed two major policy shifts. Firstly, the rate at which mortgage interest can be deducted was reduced for both new and existing mortgages. The rate reduction was initially phased in very gradually, targeting a reduction in the marginal income tax rate at which mortgage interest can be deducted from 52% to 38% between 2014 and 2042. Given a continued and accelerating increase in house price growth, particularly in cities, the government agreed on an acceleration of the on-going reduction and a lowering of the rate by one percentage point in 2018. The new target rate was set at 37% to be reached in 2023. The reform was bundled with a reduction in imputed rent taxation, in an attempt to partially compensate homeowners. In 2022, the reduction is continuing and currently mortgage interest can be deducted at a 40% rate. Secondly, the eligibility for new mortgage interest deductions was restricted to mortgages with a regular repayment of the principal (i.e. amortisation) over 30 years. Supporting the amortisation of new mortgages aimed to reduce private debt as well as increase the stability of the financial sector. However, house prices have continued to rise since the reform of mortgage interest deductions in 2013, while residential mortgages fell sharply in 2014 and mortgage growth has remained subdued ever since.

United Kingdom

Mortgage Interest Relief at Source (MIRAS) was introduced in the United Kingdom in 1983, providing a tax deduction of mortgage interest payments for the first GBP 25 000 of a mortgage loan. The relief for owner-occupied housing was abolished in 2000 after a nearly decade-long phase-out. In 1990, the programme had provided tax relief to 10 million households worth on average around GBP 770 per year or around 3% of the property value. Between 1990 and 1999, the gradual phase-out of the programme reduced its value from GBP 7.7 billion to GBP 1.4 billion and included a gradual reduction of the deduction rate from 25% in 1994 to 10% in 1998. Despite the reform, house prices and house price volatility increased, though it is possible that prices and volatility would have increased even more in the absence of the tax reform.

Source: (Brown and Phillips, 2010[115]; OECD, 2014[116]; OECD, 2016[117]; OECD, 2021[118]; OECD, 2009[119])

Taxing net rental income at marginal personal or capital income tax rates and strengthening reporting requirements support efficiency and equity

Rental income generally receives the same tax treatment as other types of capital income. Rental income is taxed with total income at marginal PIT rates in countries with comprehensive tax systems (e.g. Canada, Germany, New Zealand) and at flat rates with other capital income in countries with dual income tax systems (e.g. Denmark, Finland). A few countries offer taxpayers the choice between taxing net rental income at marginal PIT rates and taxing gross rental income at lower flat tax rates (e.g. Israel, Italy, Latvia). A small minority of countries apply a unique set of tax rates and thresholds to rental income (e.g. Greece). Rental income is entirely exempt in some countries for taxpayers who own housing below a size threshold (e.g. Chile[16]) or who earn rental income beneath a threshold (e.g. Israel, Norway[17]), with no requirement to report this income in some places (e.g. Israel).

The tax base is typically realised net rental income, but a minority of countries tax imputed rental income. The majority of countries tax net rental income; that is, income actually received by the taxpayer minus costs. Countries either provide relief for costs incurred (including mortgage interest, maintenance costs, local taxes) or allow taxpayers to deduct a fixed percentage of rental income (e.g. Estonia, Iceland). A few countries allow taxpayers to choose between a fixed deduction and itemising their deductions with actual expenses incurred (e.g. the Czech Republic, Denmark, France, Mexico, Slovenia, Sweden, Türkiye), although this choice may be restricted to taxpayers with rental income below a threshold (e.g. France). The availability of deductions has a significant impact on the taxation of rental income, as taxpayers are far more likely to incur costs such as maintenance and interest (given it is common to borrow to invest in rental housing) compared to other asset classes. While most countries tax rental income actually received (after applicable deductions), a minority of countries instead tax imputed rental income. For instance, rental income is calculated as a multiple of the cadastral value in Belgium and as a deemed return based on a portfolio mix of higher-return investments and lower-return savings in the Netherlands (the share of each category is set by the tax authority and depends on the taxpayer's wealth).

Taxing net rental income at the taxpayer's personal income or capital income tax rate makes sense from an efficiency and horizontal equity perspective. Requiring taxpayers to declare all rental income and related expenses (including mortgage interest payments) and adding rental income to total income (in countries with a comprehensive system) or capital income (in countries with a dual system) ensures actual rental income is taxed in the most efficient and equitable manner. Taxing realised net rental income ensures that tax liabilities align with the taxpayer's actual income. In contrast, there is a significant risk that imputed or deemed rental income would not align with actual income, which could lead to unduly high or low tax liabilities. Tax relief for mortgage interest, depreciation, and other costs allows taxpayers to deduct the expenses they incur to earn taxable income. This ensures taxpayers with the same net return face similar tax liabilities and avoids penalising taxpayers who have higher expenses. Taxing rental income at the same rates as other capital income reduces tax-induced distortions to the allocation of investment across asset classes (OECD/KIPF, 2014[85]). This approach is simpler and more equitable than offering taxpayers the choice between different methods for taxing rental income (i.e. taxing net rental income at marginal PIT rates and gross rental income at low flat rates).

Allowing taxpayers to deduct expenses may increase compliance costs and raise vertical equity concerns, however, these concerns may be addressed through careful tax design. Allowing taxpayers to deduct expenses raises vertical equity concerns, given that wealthier and higher income households are more likely to earn rental income and have more valuable properties and greater deductible expenses. In some countries, higher income taxpayers can also deduct costs at their (higher) marginal PIT rates. Countries concerned with vertical equity could consider capping some deductions or turning some deductions (e.g. mortgage interest relief) into (capped) tax credits. Allowing taxpayers to deduct real expenses also implies a tax administration cost for governments and a tax compliance cost for taxpayers, which will be disproportionately high for taxpayers earning low income. Some countries have addressed this through simplified deduction systems, but these should be designed carefully to avoid significantly eroding the tax base and creating tax minimisation opportunities, particularly where taxpayers have the choice between the regular and simplified regimes.

The rise of short-term rentals has prompted questions over whether and how the resulting income is taxed. Digital platforms such as Airbnb and HomeAway have led to a rise in short-term rentals (Koster, van Ommeren and Volkhausen, 2018[120]), prompting questions over the tax treatment of short-term rental income. While many countries apply the same tax treatment to short-term and long-term rentals, some apply different tax deductions or apply special regimes, such as those relating to holiday rentals or to small businesses. For example, the United Kingdom caps mortgage interest deductibility for long-term rental housing but not for qualifying short-term rentals; in contrast, Spain applies a 60% deduction to taxable rental income earned from long term-rentals but not for short-term rentals. The tax treatment may also depend on the taxpayer's circumstances; for example, whether the rental income exceeds a threshold (e.g. France), whether the owner provides services to guests (e.g. United States), and whether the owner rents out a separate property or part of their home (e.g. Australia). These differences may be necessary to distinguish between the economic reality of different rental arrangements, but they create distortions by incentivising taxpayers to invest in one form of rental housing over another. Deductions for expenses related to short-term rentals are typically available for the full year or are applied on a pro-rata basis with reference to the time that the rental is available to be let (that is, not with reference to the time the housing is actually rented), which creates avoidance opportunities, as taxpayers can claim deductions for the full year even when the property was actually rented for only part of the year. Digital platforms also create risks of tax evasion if taxpayers do not properly declare their incomes.

Countries should ensure that short-term rental income is properly declared and is not taxed more favourably than long-term rental income. While there may be a rationale to apply different tax treatment to short-term and long-term rentals, countries should avoid applying preferential tax treatment to short-term rentals, as this creates distortions and risks affecting the supply of affordable long-term residential housing. To ensure deductions align with taxable income, countries may also consider applying deductions on a pro-rata basis with reference to the period that the rental is actually let, rather than the full year or the period that it is available to be let.

Strengthened reporting requirements may be needed to prevent taxpayers from evading taxes on rental income by inflating their deductible expenses or underreporting their rental income. Income from both long-term and short-term rentals may involve relatively small amounts, spread over many taxpayers who are not typically subject to third party remittance or reporting (Eerola et al., 2019[65]). This leads to risks of taxpayers artificially inflating deductible expenses or underreporting their rental income, which the tax authority may not be able to easily detect. Detection can be even more problematic where taxpayers are not required to declare rental income below a threshold, as taxpayers above the threshold may fail to declare their income and claim ignorance when they are caught (Thomas, 2021[79]). In addition, the absence of reporting can create a data blind spot, as the tax authority cannot measure the prevalence and distributional impact of this tax exemption. Countries could address these issues through expanded reporting obligations from taxpayers, for instance to declare all rental income (even when below the exemption thresholds), and increased third-party reporting requirements (e.g. from rental agencies and digital platforms). The information gathered through expanded reporting would strengthen tax authorities' abilities to identify potential tax evasion as it can be matched with information that taxpayers report. A few countries have recently introduced third-party reporting requirements for digital platforms (e.g. Denmark, France). Third party reporting may also act as a deterrent to taxpayers who may otherwise underreport their income.

The inheritance or estate tax treatment of housing could allow for deferral and payment by instalments, but should avoid exemptions that concentrate the benefits among top wealth households

Half of OECD countries with inheritance and estate taxes apply preferential tax treatment to housing, which is a commonly inherited asset (OECD (2021[3])**).** Many households that receive a gift or inheritance receive housing and the majority of households in some countries use the gifted or inherited asset as their main residence (see Chapter 2). Of the 24 OECD countries that levy inheritance or estate taxes, 12 countries apply preferential tax treatment to the donor's main residence and two of these countries also apply preferential treatment to other real estate (OECD (2021[3])).[18] The most common preferential tax treatment is a full or partial exemption, while a minority of countries apply an additional tax-free allowance, lower tax rates, or below-market valuation. Preferential tax treatment is typically conditional; most countries require the beneficiary to be close family and to live in the housing, while around a third of countries require the beneficiaries not to own other housing. A minority of countries cap the tax benefit by value (Korea, Spain) or size of the housing (Poland).[19]

While including housing in the inheritance or estate tax base improves efficiency and equity, this could lead to hardship for co-habitants. Preferential tax treatment for the main residence is distortive and increases the incentives for households to invest in their residence. This type of relief can be complex to administer; for example, if countries also wish to provide relief on housing that was sold shortly before the donor's death. The condition to remain in the inherited housing also creates lock-in effects, discouraging heirs from relocating if more adapted housing is found elsewhere. From an equity perspective, the preferential tax treatment of inherited housing is likely to reduce wealth equality as the wealthiest households own most inherited main residence wealth (see Chapter 2) and relief is typically uncapped. However, taxing inherited housing wealth upon the donor's death may lead to hardship for beneficiaries who live in the residence, owing to the illiquid nature of housing wealth and the potential for forced sale. The political economy of taxing inherited housing wealth may also be challenging, as people have an emotional bond to housing and wish to pass it to their heirs unencumbered by taxes.

Countries may consider tax deferral and tax payment in instalments to reduce hardship risks. Given the illiquid nature of housing wealth and the importance of the shelter it provides, countries may consider providing a standard inheritance or estate tax deferral period, followed by payment of taxes by instalments over a number of years. This would allow taxpayers the flexibility of selling and relocating if needed, while minimising distortions and liquidity problems. There may be less need for tax deferral for taxpayers who were not living in the housing prior to the donor's death. Countries wishing to extend this tax treatment to non-co-habitants should apply interest to the deferred tax liability to ensure taxpayers are not advantaged by delaying payment. Countries that wish to maintain the favourable inheritance or estate tax treatment for inherited housing should consider applying a cap to ensure that the benefits are not concentrated among heirs receiving large wealth transfers.

Tax avoidance and evasion can be addressed through increased transparency and detection efforts, and removing incentives to use corporate structures and trusts

There is evidence that taxpayers use a range of strategies to minimise, avoid and evade taxes on housing. Taxpayers can minimise taxes on housing by using incentives provided by tax systems, such as holding housing for long periods of time to defer the realisation of capital gains. In contrast, aggressive tax avoidance exploits loopholes in the tax system, for example, through use of sophisticated structures like trusts. Taxpayers may also illegally evade taxes, whether it is by under-declaring housing values or through complex schemes obfuscating asset ownership. Policy makers should improve detection tools to be better aware of the prevalence and revenue costs of these practices and more effectively target compliance actions. Combatting aggressive forms of tax avoidance and evasion through a multi-pronged approach is also key to improving the efficiency and equity of housing tax systems.

Tax systems may encourage certain tax minimising behaviours, such as holding assets for long periods and using mortgage debt to offset income. Holding housing assets for long periods allows taxpayers to effectively spread the cost of transaction taxes over time and defer the realisation of taxable capital gains. After a given holding period, taxpayers may also become eligible for special tax rates and deductions linked to long-term capital gains. The evidence of bunching around the thresholds where taxpayers become eligible for special tax treatment confirms the attractiveness of this behaviour (Levy (2021[121]), Dowd and McClelland (2017[122])). In countries where capital gains are taxed at progressive PIT rates, taxpayers can lower their tax liability by timing the realisation of the capital gain during a lower income year, which highlights the importance of lifecycle income when assessing tax minimisation. Other features of tax systems can provide opportunities for taxpayers to minimise their tax burden on housing investments. For example, taxpayers can typically use mortgage interest relief to reduce their taxable rental income from debt-financed rental properties. Taxpayers can continue minimising their taxable rental income by investing in additional debt-financed property to keep deductible interest costs high.

Even when tax minimising behaviours are encouraged by current housing tax systems, understanding their prevalence and revenue impact is important. Taxpayers may respond to features of housing tax design by, for example, selling their housing once they become eligible for preferential treatment on long-term capital gains or favouring debt over equity finance. Statistical analysis can help measure the prevalence of such behaviours, for example identifying where there are more sellers after a particular holding period than would be expected without the preferential tax treatment (e.g. through bunching analysis). It is important for countries to understand the broader effects of the design of their housing taxes, as this may have implications for asset allocation, affordability, mobility, and the use of housing. Policy makers may opt to maintain housing tax provisions and incentives to support certain policy outcomes, but may also find that there is scope to increase neutrality in housing taxation with regard to the holding period (long or short), different types of return (rent or capital gains), and different types of finance (debt or equity).

More aggressive tax avoidance strategies can involve sophisticated techniques, such as the use of corporate structures. By holding in or transferring housing assets into a legal structure, taxpayers may avoid taxes that would otherwise apply to natural persons. For instance, individuals may purchase the shares in a corporate structure that owns housing rather than the underlying housing asset, to avoid transaction taxes if transaction taxes only apply to the sale of property rather than shares. This may also allow taxpayers to circumvent special housing taxes due by some categories of taxpayers, such as stamp duty surcharges that may apply to foreign nationals or non-residents. While some countries apply transaction taxes to the purchase of shares in "housing rich" companies, recent leaks indicate that this strategy remains used in certain jurisdictions (e.g. Pandora Papers). In addition, rental income may be taxed at lower CIT rates when the housing is held by a company, compared to higher marginal PIT rates for natural persons (the overall level of taxation would depend on the tax treatment of dividends, though decisions over the extent and timing of dividend payments could still allow for considerable deferral). Taxpayers may also reduce inheritance taxes by owning housing through corporate structures, if preferential tax treatment applies to business assets compared to housing assets.

Trusts and similar legal arrangements may be used to avoid taxes on housing, but this will depend on how countries define and tax trusts and related structures.[20] The tax treatment of trusts differs substantially among countries with common law systems, where trusts are a native concept, while other countries may only recognise foreign trusts or not recognise trusts at all. As a result, tax avoidance strategies involving trusts are highly country-specific. For example, by holding housing in a trust, taxpayers can confer the benefits of property on beneficiaries without transferring legal ownership and incurring transaction or capital gains taxes (e.g. Switzerland, United Kingdom). However, some countries deem that placing housing in a trust is a transfer of ownership and apply transaction and capital gains taxes (e.g. Australia). Trusts generally allow a flexible allocation of income among beneficiaries, so trusts can lower the overall taxation of the returns to housing by channelling income to beneficiaries who are taxed at the lowest marginal rates. This is true whether trust distributions are treated as income (e.g. Australia) or as gifts (e.g. in parts of Switzerland), although in the latter case the beneficiary's relationship to the settlor also affects the tax treatment of the distribution. Depending on the countries, losses and certain allowances (e.g. depreciation allowances, deductions for long-term capital gains) may or may not flow through to trust beneficiaries. Taxpayers can minimise tax by taking this into consideration when selecting the portfolio of housing assets that they place in a trust. The tax treatment of inheritances and capital gains at death will also influence the tax minimising strategies that taxpayers can employ; trusts may be used to delay the realisation of taxable capital gains or to transfer housing assets to the next generation without incurring wealth transfer taxes.

Countries can combat tax avoidance through corporate structures or trusts by reducing the attractiveness of holding housing through these vehicles. Countries may restrict the availability of some housing tax exemptions and deductions to property owned by natural persons. This could include denying preferential treatment for recurrent taxes on immovable property and capital gains taxes (e.g. tax-free thresholds, full or partial exemptions, and lower tax rates) that may apply to natural persons. Countries could also deny valuation discounts (which may apply to account for minority ownership or lack of marketability when acquiring a stake in a closely-held business) for "housing rich" firms, so housing is not valued (and taxed) less when inherited via a business structure than if it were inherited directly. Countries could treat the transfer of assets into a trust as a change of ownership, applying transaction taxes, capital gains taxes, and gift taxes as though the transfer occurred between two individuals. Other measures include periodic asset taxation or deemed realisation of capital gains, and limiting the lifespan of trusts to ensure housing held in trust is not subject to more favourable taxation than housing held by natural persons. Applying anti-avoidance measures to the sale and disposal of shares in "housing rich" firms can prevent taxpayers from avoiding transaction taxes by purchasing the corporate structure instead of the underlying housing asset.

Taxpayers may also engage in illegal tax evasion, which in its simplest form involves under-declaring property values. Evidence suggests tax evasion is widespread in the housing sector, due in part to the attractiveness of housing as an asset class and lower levels of transparency and third party reporting compared to financial assets (OECD, (2007[123]), Remeur (2019[124]), Ernesto U. and Michele (Eds.) (2015[125]), De Simone, Lester and Markle (2020[126]), Maloney, Somerville and Unger (2019[127]), O'Reilly, Parra Ramirez and Stemmer (2019[128])). A simple tax evasion scheme involves the buyer and seller agreeing to declare a purchase price that is lower than the real price, with the buyer paying the difference in cash. The seller evades some of their capital gains tax liability and the buyer evades some transaction taxes. There is evidence that this type of tax evasion is widespread (Montalvo, Piolatto and Raya (2020[129]), Ben-Shahar, Golan and Sulganik (2020[130]), Agarwal et al. (2020[131])). For example, Ben-Shahar, Golan and Sulganik (2020[130]) find that among all reported housing transactions in Israel from 1998-2015, 8% of transactions involved under-reporting, with the average reported price 30% below the estimated true price. Individuals may evade other taxes levied on the basis of the property's value (i.e. wealth taxes, inheritance and estate taxes, and recurrent taxes on immovable property) by under declaring property values. Other simple strategies include not declaring rental income (to evade income taxes) or fraudulently declaring rental housing is a main residence (to take advantage of the preferential tax treatment granted to owner-occupied housing).

Sophisticated tax evasion schemes use businesses or trust structures to conceal beneficial ownership and undertake fraudulent transactions. Taxpayers may set up or acquire multiple structures to make it difficult for the tax authority to identify owners and levy taxes, and some of the structures may be located offshore to further obfuscate ownership. Individuals can undertake transactions (e.g. loan agreements and service agreements) among the different companies and trusts they control, for example, creating fraudulent deductible costs or losses to offset taxable income. Individuals could also loan themselves their own undeclared funds that are held offshore through a corporate structure, using interest expenses to reduce their taxable income while not paying tax on the interest income received by the offshore corporate structure (OECD, (2007[123])). Sophisticated tax avoidance and tax evasion strategies generally require professional expertise, which highlights the role for "professional enablers" such as lawyers and real estate agents, who may use their expertise to facilitate evasion of taxes on housing (OECD (2021[132]), Maloney, Somerville and Unger (2019[127])).

A combination of detection tools are needed to identify and help combat aggressive tax avoidance and tax evasion. To identify potential under-valuations, tax authorities can undertake statistical analysis to compare housing transaction prices to similar properties and to the property's past purchase prices. Tax authorities can match data from sources such as other government bodies (e.g. property records) and private institutions (e.g. bank accounts) to better understand taxpayer profiles and identify potential inconsistencies in reported information. Red flag analysis may help the tax authority target audits by identifying where further investigation is warranted, for example because of the person involved (e.g. the person has a history of tax evasion) or characteristics of the purchase (e.g. lower than expected valuations or no mortgage finance[21]).

Greater transparency through increased reporting requirements is core to identifying and discouraging tax evasion. Information on the natural person(s) who ultimately own the real estate, which is covered by the concept of "beneficial ownership"[22], is a key element of greater transparency. This may include different types of reporting, such as beneficial owner registers of companies or real estate, and may have crossovers with initiatives taken in relation to Anti-Money Laundering and Combating the Financing of Terrorism (AML/CFT). For example, to prevent money laundering through real estate, the United States has opened a consultation on a proposal to require housing purchases that do not involve mortgage finance to be reported (purchases involving mortgage finance are already reported by financial institutions).[23] Land ownership registries, such as the recently established Land Owner Transparency Registry operating in British Columbia, Canada, are also a valuable source of information about beneficial ownership of property. Recent scandals suggest the real estate sector would benefit from better supervision and enforcement of existing requirements (e.g. Suspicious Transaction Reports (STRs) that are underused). A "whole of government approach" involving information sharing and coordination between authorities (such as those responsible for tax, AML/CFT) would increase the effectiveness and impact of these actions. This may require changes to inter-governmental agreements, such as those that restrict the use of information obtained under Exchange of Information (EOI). Countries also have in place strategies to detect professional enablers, including risk assessments, data mining, and whistle-blower programmes, which are complemented by international standards such as the Financial Action Task Force recommendations regarding professionals involved with real estate transactions[24] and mandatory disclosure rules for intermediaries (OECD (2018[133])).

International tax transparency initiatives have greatly improved tax authorities' understanding of the nature and extent of wealth held abroad, but gaps remain in reporting on real estate wealth. EOI includes two main standards: Exchange of Information on Request (EOIR), which allows tax authorities to request a broad range of information on assets that their taxpayers hold abroad when the information is foreseeably relevant, and Automatic Exchange of Information (AEOI), where countries exchange each year a standard set of information on foreign taxpayers with their tax residence jurisdiction. These standards represent a significant step forward in international tax transparency. However, there is no minimum standard for AEOI on real estate, while EOIR requires tax authorities to have reasonable suspicions to request specific information on real estate in other jurisdictions. As real estate is typically taxed where it is physically located, international tax transparency standards have targeted higher-risk financial assets. These standards mean that some proceeds of real estate investments (e.g. rental income paid into a bank account) would be reported, but ownership of real estate assets would not. There are some OECD countries, however, that do exchange such information spontaneously or automatically (and the OECD has produced an electronic format for doing so). Evidence suggests that EOI has led to a reduction in offshore bank deposits (O'Reilly, Parra Ramirez and Stemmer (2019[128])), but it may have increased the popularity of real estate, which is typically not subject to automatic reporting (De Simone, Lester and Markle (2020[126]), Bomare and Le Guern Henry (forthcoming)). Future work on improving countries' ability to detect tax evasion in the real estate sector could involve exploring the expansion of AEOI to real estate.

3.3.2. Assessment of the role of housing tax policies in addressing current housing challenges and reform options

> ***Tax support for homeownership should be carefully evaluated against local housing market characteristics, as some of these tax measures may be counterproductive when supply is inelastic***

Tax and non-tax measures intended to support homebuyers have become increasingly popular in recent decades. In addition to mortgage interest relief, discussed in section 3.3.1, countries provide a range of tax and non-tax measures to encourage homeownership. Tax measures commonly include one-off tax reliefs and tax-favoured savings schemes, which are conditioned on the purchase of residential property. These policies are often targeted at specific groups such as first-time homebuyers or individuals and households below a certain age and are typically capped with reference to the property value. A few countries target lower-income earners by conditioning one-off tax reliefs upon taxable income (e.g. France, Belgium, and Ireland). In several countries, one-off tax measures take the form of exemptions or concessions from transaction taxes for first-time buyers (sometimes subject to further eligibility criteria) (e.g. Australia, Finland, Greece, Netherlands, the United Kingdom). In Australia, Canada, Colombia, Luxembourg, Norway, the United Kingdom and the United States, governments offer first-time buyer savings schemes, which provide preferential tax treatment (interest and/or capital gains tax exemptions) to savings directed towards a first home purchase. Non-tax policies aimed at supporting homeownership are also common, including measures such as equity loan programmes, mortgage guarantees, shared ownership schemes (which allow people to buy a share of their home while paying rent on the remaining share), or the option to make advance pension withdrawals or pledge pension assets to buy a home (e.g. Switzerland) (OECD, 2021[93]).

However, evidence suggests that measures promoting homeownership may be limited in their effectiveness and can contribute to increased house prices where there are housing supply constraints. While studies looking at the impact of the tax reliefs described above are lacking, studies assessing the effects of non-tax policies aimed at encouraging homeownership may provide useful guidance. For instance, studies evaluating the effect of increased credit supply on the housing market, through eased restrictions for first-time buyers, show that increased credit supply raises house prices (Duca, Muellbauer and Murphy, 2011[134]; Di Maggio and Kermani, 2016[135]; Mian and Sufi, 2009[136]). However, in areas where supply is elastic, the housing stock increases and house price growth is more contained (Favara and Imbs, 2015[137]). Analyses of the effectiveness of the equity loan scheme in the United Kingdom lead to similar conclusions (Carozzi, Hilber and Yu, 2020[138]). Results suggest that where housing supply is inelastic due to regulatory or geographical constraints, the equity loan scheme has no significant effect on construction and private lending activity, but is associated with a price increase of 6% for newly constructed buildings (Carozzi, Hilber and Yu, 2020[138]). Conversely, in areas with responsive housing supply, sales of newly built homes increased by 6-7%, with no effect on house price developments. Carozzi et al. (2020[138]) also provide evidence on the distributional effects of the scheme and conclude that in the regions with the highest housing costs, the scheme has primarily benefited landowners and developers while housing affordability has deteriorated.

Measures aimed at increasing housing supply should be prioritised to address housing affordability and encourage homeownership. The empirical evidence emphasises the need to address the inelastic supply of housing, for instance through reforms to land use and housing market regulations and the construction of social housing (see Chapter 1). In environments where such reforms may be difficult or take a long time, phasing-out some of the policies that subsidise housing costs and fuel demand, particularly those are not targeted at specific groups such as low-income households or first-time buyers and predominantly benefit higher-income households (e.g. mortgage interest relief), could help improve housing affordability, but a careful assessment and a gradual approach would be needed (as discussed above). As with restricting or removing mortgage interest relief, removing other housing cost subsidies will affect specific groups differently and might therefore require a transition period and potential compensation measures.

A careful blend of tax and non-tax policies may be needed to increase supply of affordable housing

Some countries provide tax incentives to increase the supply of affordable housing. Governments may need to support the provision of affordable housing, as the potentially lower returns available compared to other forms of housing may lead to under-provision by the private sector. Tax policies to encourage the supply of affordable housing often take one of two forms. One approach consists of providing corporate tax relief to housing developers that undertake the construction of affordable housing projects. The most researched example of this type of policy is the Low-Income Housing Tax Credit (LIHTC) in the United States, which offers participating developers an annual income tax credit of either 30% or 70% of their project's costs spread over a ten-year period.[25] To qualify, owners or developers must ensure that sufficient shares of tenants earn below specified income thresholds and must rent the units at below-market rates over a 15-year period. Tax incentives targeted to housing developers can also be found in other OECD countries including, for instance, Chile[26], Colombia, Germany, Türkiye, Portugal and Spain, and depending on policy makers' goals, may be targeted towards increasing the supply of rental or owner-occupied housing. Another category of tax support measures for affordable housing involves providing tax breaks directly to homeowners who commit to renting out residential properties for a minimum length of time. These policies typically require rents to be set below-market prices and may either be restricted to newly-acquired dwellings (e.g. buy-to-let schemes, as with the *dispositif Pinel*[27] in France), or applicable regardless of whether rental units were purchased for this purpose (e.g. the capital gains tax discount for affordable housing in Australia[28]).

Tax incentives for housing developers can have important effects on the supply of affordable housing. Evidence shows that measures such as the LIHTC can increase the share of affordable housing within the housing stock. Baum-Snow and Marion (2009[139]) find that greater financial support for LIHTC projects increases the number of low-income housing units and O'Regan and Horn (2013[140]) find that households benefiting from the LIHTC face significantly lower rent burdens than comparable tenants in non-LIHTC housing. This suggests that this credit has indeed resulted in more affordable housing. In contrast, studies show that although 57% of rented housing units built under the *dispositif Pinel* were let at below-market rents, the amount of reduced rent was very small; for every EUR 10 spent on the scheme, renters benefited from a EUR 1 reduction to their rent (Deniau et al., 2019[141]). This is due in part to the design of the provisions; the incentive set a maximum rent per square metre at the regional level, but in areas of cheaper rents, units benefitting from the incentive could effectively be rented at close to market rates while remaining below the cap (Deniau et al., 2019[141]).

However, the subsidisation of affordable housing construction has the potential to crowd out non-subsidised housing developments and create concentrations of low-income housing. Incentives to build affordable housing may crowd out non-eligible private housing developments, both within the area targeted by the incentives and in non-eligible locations (Deniau et al., 2019[141]). If increases in affordable housing are offset by comparable declines in the construction of unsubsidised units, tax incentives increase access to cheaper housing but have no impact on the net supply of dwellings. Subsidies may also create high concentrations of low-cost housing, depending on the types of housing that the measures allow (McClure, 2019[142]). Research into the prevalence of crowding out has led to mixed conclusions. From a theoretical perspective, higher crowding-out is expected in regions with a more elastic supply of housing or areas where demand is more inelastic (Eriksen and Rosenthal, 2010[143]). Some empirical investigations find a near one-to-one substitution rate between private housing investments and construction projects benefiting from the LIHTC (Eriksen and Rosenthal, 2010[143]), while others find more modest effects and point to important heterogeneities in crowding-out rates depending on local market specificities. For example, empirical evidence suggests that crowding-out is particularly high in gentrifying communities (where investors benefiting from the LIHTC may offer affordable housing to take advantage of the tax credit while expecting to later benefit from a large capital gain (Baum-Snow and Marion, 2009[139])) and in areas with low excess demand for subsidised housing (Sinai and Waldfogel, 2005[144]).

Tax incentives for housing developers need to be carefully designed and may not be the most effective tools if the overall profitability of investment is very low. First, to ensure that they achieve their stated objectives, tax incentives need to include clear eligibility criteria and monitoring (e.g. minimum shares of a project's units qualifying as social housing, criteria determining the tenants that are eligible for affordable housing, regulated rents, length of time the unit is available for affordable housing), even if this requires additional administrative resources. There may also be some provisions to ensure a greater diversity of household types among newly constructed housing developments (such as, for example, required levels of middle-income units or higher maximum income thresholds for a selection of units), to avoid homogeneous concentrations of low-income housing. Second, tax incentives need to be carefully designed as their effectiveness will depend on investment profitability, which may be low in the case of affordable housing (and may decrease even further if construction costs continue to rise, see Chapter 1). Investment allowances or tax credits are of no immediate benefit to companies that have no profits or tax liability against which they can be offset. They are useful to these taxpayers only if they can be applied to profits derived from other projects not related to affordable housing or can be carried forward to offset future profits or tax liabilities. Where profitability is expected to remain very low or negative in the long run, however, other provisions may be required to ensure that tax incentives effectively encourage affordable housing supply. In this regard, there are a range of options, such as making tax credits refundable, which comes at greater fiscal cost to government, or allowing tax credits to be sold to outside investors (who can use the tax credits to offset their tax liabilities) in exchange for equity financing (e.g. United States), which increases the complexity and enforcement costs of tax incentive schemes. In addition, or as an alternative, to tax incentives, governments may encourage the supply of affordable housing through direct subsidies to developers or regulations mandating minimum shares of affordable housing in buildings or municipalities. As discussed in Chapter 1, additional measures to address housing supply shortages, including the revision of land-use and zoning regulations, will also be key to enhancing housing affordability.

Tax breaks for owners of affordable rental units have raised concerns over their equity and ability to address local housing needs. Tax incentives targeting property owners raise distributional concerns, as they are directed towards individuals who can afford secondary properties and tend to be high-income earners and holders of high-wealth (see Chapter 2). In France, for example, over 50% of investors benefiting from the *dispositif Pinel* belong to the top decile of the income distribution (Deniau et al., 2019[141]). Any type of policy that provides supply-side tax incentives to landlords will raise similar equity concerns, which should be carefully weighed against the potential equity gains that may result from increasing the stock of affordable rental housing. In France, the *dispositif Pinel,* while clearly accelerating the construction of private collective housing developments, was found to lead to the construction of housing that seemed to meet the needs of investors more than those of potential tenants (Deniau et al., 2019[141]). As local authorities had very little control over the location and number of subsidised apartments, new developments were sometimes at odds with local development plans, suggesting that centrally-administered tax incentives would benefit from coordination with local authorities (Deniau et al., 2019[141]).

Well-targeted tax incentives for energy efficient housing could help reduce energy use in the residential sector

The residential sector has a sizeable carbon footprint. In 2019, it accounted for 22% of global final energy consumption and 17% of total CO_2 emissions (see Chapter 1). Transitioning to zero carbon housing[29] (also called zero energy housing) by reducing energy consumption and switching to renewable energy sources will therefore be a key element of achieving climate goals. A combination of tools is needed to achieve zero carbon residential dwellings, including enhanced insulation technologies, optimised ventilation strategies, solar panels, and heat pumps (Economidou et al., 2020[145]).

Policies designed to encourage investments in the energy efficiency of housing units have become increasingly popular over recent years. Given the low level of annual construction relative to the existing building stock in OECD countries (see Chapter 1), undertaking renovations to enhance the energy efficiency of existing housing units (a process known as "retrofitting") is critical. However, evidence shows that households' investments in energy efficiency remain well below optimal levels, in part due to the difficulties of financing the upfront investment and high discounting of future gains in the form of lower energy bills (Wilson, Crane and Chryssochoidis, 2015[146]). To address barriers to investments in energy efficiency, governments have implemented a range of tax policies (e.g. tax rebates for energy efficient installations) and non-tax measures (e.g. grants and low-interest loans).

Tax relief for energy-efficient housing renovations is available in several OECD countries. The tax relief is intended to prompt investments in energy efficient housing infrastructure by providing the incentives and financial support that taxpayers may need. Several OECD countries currently provide tax incentives for energy-efficient retrofitting through the personal income tax, including Denmark, Germany, Greece, Italy, Mexico, Poland, and the United States. In these countries, tax incentives for retrofitting are generally capped as a percentage of the project's costs, up to a fixed limit, and may take the form of a deduction or credit. In addition, a minority of countries apply reduced or zero VAT rates to materials used in retrofitting.

There is evidence that tax incentives for retrofitting increase energy-efficient housing renovations. Studies in France (Risch, 2020[147]; Charlier, Risch and Salmon, 2018[148]; Clerc, Mauroux and Marcus, 2010[149]) Italy (Alberini, Bigano and Boeri, 2014[150]) Mexico (Boomhower and Davis, 2014[151]) and the United States (Hassett and Metcalf, 1995[152]) find that tax incentives encourage households to undertake renovations in energy-efficient housing. Tax incentives also have substantial rates of take-up. For example, Clerc, Mauroux and Marcus (2010[149]) find that between 2005 and 2008, eligible energy efficient renovations were undertaken in one in ten main residences in France, of which one third occurred in buildings built before 1975.

However, tax incentives for retrofitting often subsidise, at least partially, investments that would have occurred anyway. Tax incentives to encourage housing retrofits carry the risk of redundancy, where households receive tax relief for renovations that they would have undertaken in the absence of the tax incentive. Risch (2020[147]) provides an overview of existing studies and finds ample empirical evidence of this phenomenon across a range of countries, with estimates of redundancy rates ranging from 40% to 92%. Some research, however, finds a considerable increase in renovation expenditure despite a high incidence of redundancy, which suggests that beneficiaries of these policies may undertake more significant renovations than they would otherwise (Risch, 2020[147]).

The disproportionate uptake of these tax incentives by high-income households has raised concerns over their equity and effectiveness. Research on the Non-Business Energy Property Credit and the Residential Energy Efficient Property Credit in the United States, as well as the former *Crédit d'impôt pour la transition énergétique* in France, has found that the upper quintile of the income distribution has figured disproportionately among their beneficiaries (Borenstein and Davis, 2016[153]; Charlier, Risch and Salmon, 2018[148]; Clerc, Mauroux and Marcus, 2010[149]). This poses an equity concern as these tax credits have overwhelmingly subsidised housing upgrades for higher-income households, whose gains will compound over time as they spend relatively less of their income on energy than households who have not retrofitted for energy efficiency. The greater take-up of tax incentives by higher-income households could also reduce the effectiveness of the tax relief as higher-income households are more likely to afford the investments without additional support, whereas lower-income households are less likely to undertake these projects without financial assistance (Charlier, Risch and Salmon, 2018[148]). In addition, while the majority of existing housing stock may need some form of energy efficient renovation at some point, lower-income households are more likely to occupy dwellings with a greater scope for reductions in energy usage and should therefore be a higher priority for retrofitting incentives (Giraudet, Bourgeois and Quirion, 2021[154]).

These incentives could better target lower-income households, although this may be less effective where low-income households are predominantly renters. The lower uptake of tax incentives for energy-efficient housing at the bottom of the income distribution suggests that low-income households face barriers to accessing tax incentives for retrofits. This may be due in part to the design of these policies; for instance, where tax credits are non-refundable (i.e. the maximum value of the credit cannot exceed the taxpayer's tax liability), households with negative or limited tax liabilities cannot take full advantage of these incentives. In addition, the financial incentives provided may simply be too small to induce renovations among poorer households (Charlier, Risch and Salmon, 2018[148]). To address some of these issues, countries could consider income-based eligibility criteria as well as the provision of refundable tax credits. Low-income households may also struggle to finance up-front investments and may be sensitive to the time delay between when they make the investment and receive the tax benefit. Measures providing immediate financial assistance may be considered as an alternative. Some of these considerations fed into the recent design of *MaPrimeRénov* in France, which offers higher grants for retrofitting projects performed by lower-income households and an advance payment to undertake the renovations for the lowest-income households. It is important to note, however, that the success of targeting retrofitting measures at lower-income households will depend on homeownership levels at the bottom of the income distribution, which vary widely across countries (Chapter 2). Indeed, targeting retrofitting tax incentives at low-income households will prove less effective in countries where they are predominantly renters.

Carbon pricing encourages low-carbon investment and consumption choices and, if well-designed, is a complementary approach to improve the energy and emissions performance of residential buildings, including rental housing. Pricing emissions from the residential sector could encourage property owners to invest in renovations that reduce the emissions-intensity of their building (though this would need to be accompanied by measures to ensure taxpayers are aware of the value of low-emission housing and can afford to make the investments). Pricing emissions also encourages occupants to reduce energy usage or switch to clean fuels, to the extent they are able to do so given the existing energy and emissions performance of the building (OECD, 2019[155]; OECD, 2021[156]). For instance, in addition to existing energy taxes on fuels used in buildings, Germany introduced in 2021 a national emissions trading system that effectively puts a carbon price on heating in the building and transport sector. In 2022, the German government announced that the carbon tax liability would be split between landlords and tenants as of 2023 depending on the quality of the building's emissions performance. Tenants in low-emission housing will bear most of the price, while landlords will be liable for the majority of the additional price for carbon-intensive rental dwellings. This measure is intended to alleviate the carbon price burden on tenants and to encourage landlords to undertake investments to improve the emissions performance of their home, while still incentivising tenants to reduce their carbon footprint. A key success factor for such a measure is to ensure that landlords are not able to pass their higher tax burden onto their tenants (e.g. through higher rents) without making the associated investments. The design of these types of tax measures should also aim to remain relatively simple.

To encourage the supply of new energy-efficient housing, some governments offer tax incentives to housing developers that build energy-efficient housing, but other instruments may be considered. Tax incentives can encourage developers to implement minimum energy efficiency standards in newly built housing. For example, the 45L Tax Credit in the United States provides developers with USD 2 000 for each new dwelling that meets guidelines for energy performance (Goldstein et al., 2012[157]; Tobias, 2008[158]). Although the credit has not been thoroughly evaluated, analysis suggests that it may have helped expand the stock of environmentally efficient dwellings (Goldstein et al., 2012[157]). In general, however, the introduction of stricter building codes may present the most effective way to ensure that new dwellings are constructed with energy performance objectives in mind, and there is significant scope for improvement in that area given that almost two-thirds of countries globally were lacking such regulations as of 2019 (OECD, 2021[159]). Governments can also introduce other compulsory instruments, such as carbon taxes, as well as voluntary instruments, including eco-labelling and industry-set standards to encourage the construction of new energy-efficient housing (Lee and Yik, 2004[160]).

Recurrent taxes on vacant homes can help increase housing supply, though more research is needed to assess their effectiveness relative to alternative policies

In the context of rising house prices and declining affordability, some cities have introduced recurrent taxes on vacant dwellings to encourage a more efficient use of the housing stock. Long-term residential vacancies reduce the supply of dwellings available for purchase or rent, which can put upward pressure on house prices in supply-constrained areas. Recurrent taxes on vacant homes are one of the policy tools that a handful of municipalities have introduced to increase the supply of housing.[30] The primary goal of these taxes is to incentivise owners of vacant dwellings to return these properties to the rental or housing market, though these measures can also yield tax revenues that may be re-directed towards initiatives aimed at further alleviating housing concerns (Housing Vancouver, 2020[161]). They are typically designed as an annual tax levied on residential properties (either as a lump sum, or as a share of the property's value) that are unoccupied for a minimum length of time over a given period. To prevent landlords from circumventing the tax by converting their housing into short-term rental units, these policies may only take long-term tenancies into consideration when assessing whether a unit has been occupied. Vacant home taxes are also likely to have progressive effects as they are levied on owners of secondary real estate, which is highly concentrated at the top of the income and wealth distributions (Chapter 2), and cannot be passed onto tenants.

Analyses of existing vacant home taxes suggest that some taxes have been successful in increasing housing supply, while others have had a limited impact. The Empty Homes Tax[31] levied by the City of Vancouver aims to discourage speculative investments and provide a much-needed increase in the supply of rental housing (Housing Vancouver, 2020[161]). Following its introduction, the city saw a 25.4% reduction in residential vacancies that was largely driven by an increase in the number of rented properties (Housing Vancouver, 2020[161]). A likely factor behind the policy's success is the fact that false declarations can be fined up to CAD 10 000 per day of non-compliance if caught during the city's routine audit process (City of Vancouver, 2022). Likewise, the *Taxe sur les Logement Vacants*[32] levied in several French municipalities was found to reduce vacancies by 13% on average in the four years following its implementation (Segú, 2020[162]). Other instances of vacant homes taxes have proven to be less effective, however. A recent analysis of the Vacant Residential Property Tax[33] in Melbourne, Australia, found that the policy has had a limited impact on residential vacancy rates (Fitzgerald, 2020[163]). According to the study, this stems from the lack of robust enforcement measures to verify homeowners' declarations, which have not led to any non-compliance penalties since the policy's introduction and resulted in only a fraction of the true number of vacancies being declared.

Evidence shows that successful vacant home taxes require extensive monitoring and compliance checks, which can increase administrative costs. The definition of vacant dwellings typically relies on a time-based occupancy test, which can be challenging for taxpayers to keep track of and for tax administrations to monitor. Ensuring that self-declarations are accurate will require extensive compliance checks. If certain types of properties are excluded (e.g. holiday homes, properties purchased as future main residences upon retiring), which narrows the tax base and reduces the efficiency of the tax, monitoring costs will be even higher for tax administrations. In practice, the tax design, administration, and compliance costs associated with vacant home taxes are likely to be high in comparison to the revenue raised. Nonetheless, vacant home taxes are primarily intended to increase the stock of housing, while raising revenue tends to be a secondary objective (even more so given that a successful vacant home tax will lead to declining revenues over time, as vacancy rates decrease in response).

When considering taxes on vacant homes, it is important to first establish that local housing concerns are driven by excess vacancies and would not be better addressed through alternative policies. When vacant homes are not a major driver of housing supply shortages, this tax will not meaningfully increase housing supply and alternative policy levers are likely to help achieve these aims more effectively. Even where vacant home taxes have been successful in returning dwellings to the housing market, their effectiveness in mitigating large-scale housing affordability concerns relative to policy alternatives is unclear. The relaxation of zoning restrictions and other land use controls, for example, may have a far greater impact on the supply of housing and could present a better option for governments seeking to combat rising housing prices. In addition, a well-designed recurrent tax on immovable property, where property values are based on regularly updated market values, can already encourage a more efficient use of the current housing stock and reduce the need for taxes on vacant homes (see section 3.3.1). Further research would be helpful to assess which policies should be prioritised among the broader set of measures aimed at tackling housing supply and affordability issues.

Where governments decide to introduce taxes on vacant homes, it is crucial that these policies include credible measures to monitor compliance and ensure that targeted dwellings return to the long-term rental and housing markets. Where vacant home taxes rely on self-declarations, particularly where taxpayers are not required to provide supporting evidence such as rental income receipts, the tax administration may receive inaccurate information. Failing to capture a sufficient share of vacancies through these measures will significantly limit their impact on the stock of housing, in addition to reducing the tax base. While ensuring that homeowners adhere to their reporting obligations will increase administrative costs, high rates of compliance from owners of vacant dwellings are essential for these policies to be effective. It will also be critical to design policies that prevent owners of vacant dwellings from converting their units into short-term rentals as a way of avoiding the tax. This may include restricting exemptions to dwellings that have been occupied for a minimum number of consecutive days, or simply considering properties to be vacant if they are registered as short-term rental units.

Where countries provide preferential tax treatment for unoccupied housing, removing these reliefs should be the first priority. Vacant housing may benefit from preferential tax treatment compared to occupied housing in some countries. For instance, some municipalities in the United Kingdom provide a Council Tax discount for empty properties (although households can be charged an extra amount if their property remains empty for two years or more). Preferential tax treatment for unoccupied housing reduces the tax burden on secondary housing owners who consume few local services, but it effectively rewards taxpayers who keep housing vacant and reduces their incentives to return these dwellings to the market. Such measures should therefore be removed.

Split-rate taxes could help enhance housing supply and contain urban sprawl, but their success will partly depend on interactions with other land-use policies

Tax measures offer a potential policy lever to shape the design and environmental impact of urban areas. As discussed in Chapter 1, urban sprawl can lead to significant environmental degradation, including natural land loss, reduced biodiversity, and water pollution, as well as greater transport emissions and congestion from increased car use. Tax policies encouraging higher urban densities could help discourage urban sprawl while also promoting housing affordability in large cities. It is worth mentioning, however, that denser urban areas may be associated with reduced housing quality (e.g. increased congestion in city centres, noise) and should therefore be accompanied by policies to reduce these potential costs in large cities (e.g. investment in public transportation and green spaces).

In this context, split-rate taxes are increasingly being discussed as tools that could encourage denser developments (OECD, 2021[5]). Split-rate taxes are a hybrid of pure land value taxes and regular recurrent taxes on immovable property, where both the land and improvements on the land are taxed, but land is typically taxed at a higher rate. As the supply of land is highly inelastic, taxes on the unimproved value of land are economically efficient and therefore contrast with taxes on improvements (i.e. buildings), which may affect investment. Split-rate taxes have been suggested as a tool that could encourage greater urban densities; if land is taxed at higher rates than improvements, owners will have an incentive to reduce their average property tax rate by, for example, constructing new units on vacant or under-used land, or converting existing single-unit structures into multi-unit properties. Individuals owning low-density properties with high land values may also prefer to sell this land to housing developers. A split-rate property tax could over time lead to an increase in residential densities. Since split-rate taxes will have a larger impact on owners' financial incentives in areas where the relative value of land is high, they may be particularly effective at maximising the density of downtown cores. However, given that split rate taxes levy lower rates on buildings, they may also encourage increases in the average dwelling size depending on community housing preferences and local market conditions. Split-rate taxes will only have a positive effect on housing density and limiting urban sprawl if the growth in the number of housing units per area is higher than growth in dwelling size (Banzhaf and Lavery, 2010[164]).

In spite of their potential benefits, split-rate property taxes are a seldom-used policy tool. In practice, these policies have been concentrated in the U.S. states of Pennsylvania (where almost two dozen municipal governments have introduced split-rate taxes to date) and Hawaii (where regional governments may choose to levy split-rate taxes). Split-rate taxes also apply at the national level in Finland.

A few studies suggest that split-rate taxes may help increase residential densities and have positive distributional effects. An empirical analysis of the effects of split-rate taxes in Pennsylvania confirms the theoretical predictions discussed above, finding a rise in both the total number of housing units and the average number of rooms per dwelling (Banzhaf and Lavery, 2010[164]). Banzhaf and Lavery (2010[164]) further note that the increase in housing units outweighs the increase in average dwelling size and has led to an overall increase in housing density. Moreover, as high tax rates on land are thought to disproportionately affect wealthier households, whose property holdings tend to feature higher land-to-building value ratios on average (Bowman and Bell, 2004[165]), these measures can be expected to be progressive. Among homeowners affected by the Pennsylvanian split-rate taxes, 85% experienced a decrease in property tax liabilities following the introduction of these measures (Hartzok, 1997[166]), while simulations performed in other settings conclude that poorer homeowners stand to benefit the most in this respect (Bowman and Bell, 2004[165]).

However, there are practical difficulties associated with split-rate taxes and their success depends on interactions with other housing market and policy settings. A common concern is the fact that the valuation of land independent of its improvements poses a significant practical challenge for local governments, which may not be equipped to perform these appraisals in an accurate way (Bowman and Bell, 2004[165]; Cohen and Coughlin, 2005[167]; Kwak and Mak, 2011[168]). In contrast to traditional housing markets, there is no sizeable competitive market for land that can be drawn upon to easily determine land values. In addition to the costs incurred from adopting novel methods of land valuation, it may be difficult for governments to know *ex-ante* how much revenue a split-rate tax could raise if they do not already have access to quality data on land values. Moreover, whether urban sprawl will indeed slow down following the introduction of split-rate taxes depends on the maturity of the housing market and the location of the municipality within its broader urban area. Split-rate taxes may have less effect in developed urban areas or neighbourhoods with restrictive zoning regulations than in urban areas where there is still scope for significant construction or redevelopment. Banzhaf and Lavery (2010[164]) note that if split-rate taxes levied in municipalities on the fringes of a metropolitan area increase population density on the outskirts of the city centre, this would give the impression of increased sprawl.[34]

While the evidence on split-rate taxes is limited and context-specific, several policy lessons can be drawn for policy makers interested in exploring their introduction. First, policy makers must be mindful of the interaction of property taxes with existing land-use policies. Split-rate measures are likely to be ineffective when, for example, existing height restrictions limit the possibility for greater housing densities (OECD, 2021[159]). Policy makers should also ensure that these policies do not primarily translate into the construction of larger housing units, which could worsen urban sprawl. In general, involving higher levels of government in the design of split-rate taxes may be helpful to ensure that measures implemented by local administrations align with the interests of the broader region (OECD, 2021[159]). Higher levels of government may also help overcome some of the practical concerns surrounding land valuation by providing technological and financial resources that work to increase the accuracy of this process. In Australia, for example, land value taxes are administered by state authorities, which have developed sophisticated mass appraisal techniques that combine historical sales records with Geographic Information Systems (GIS) software and increased assessment accuracy. Finally, if split-rate property taxes pose too great of a practical challenge, a simpler alternative may be to levy higher taxes on vacant land (e.g. Colombia, South Korea), which forgoes the problem of evaluating land independent of its improvements but would still incentivise new construction.

Infrastructure levies can provide an important source of funding for local government projects, although conventional housing tax policies may offer a better alternative

Infrastructure levies are a type of land value capture instrument that can help fund investments in urban infrastructure, while capturing some of the private gains from such investments. Land value capture refers to the process by which governments recover increases in property values that directly result from public interventions, such as investments in new transit projects or changes to zoning regulations. While land value capture includes a wide range of instruments,[35] including many applying to developers, this section focuses only on infrastructure levies. Infrastructure levies are a type of land value capture instrument that applies through the tax system, wherein property owners pay a one-off or temporary surcharge on properties whose values have increased due to a specific public infrastructure project. As the revenues gained from infrastructure levies can offset the costs of the initial investment or help fund future public investment projects, these measures present a valuable revenue-raising tool for governments looking to meet their infrastructure needs. They can also be justified on equity grounds, since infrastructure levies prevent property owners from receiving untaxed windfall gains while ensuring that these benefits are returned to the public.

The use of infrastructure levies in OECD countries is limited, but there have been a few examples of successful policies. The experiences of some local governments in OECD countries with infrastructure levies has shown that these policies can generate significant revenues and contribute to the financing of public investments. In past years, for instance, infrastructure levies have constituted up to 25% of local government revenue in Bogotá, Colombia (Borrero Ochoa, 2011[169]). In general, studies have highlighted the effectiveness of these measures to fund key public investments in Colombian cities (Amirtahmasebi et al., 2016[170]). The design of infrastructure levies has varied significantly between these municipalities. Some cities, for example, divide the costs of infrastructure projects among all households deemed to be within an area of influence, while others conduct dedicated surveys before and after undertaking a project to determine the resulting increases in individual property values (Haas and Kriticos, 2019[171]). A variation of this levy collected annually over a period is the *Taxe spéciale d'équipement* in Île-de-France, France, which was introduced to help fund the *Grand Paris Express* transit project and is designed to generate EUR 117 million in revenue each year.

The introduction of infrastructure levies may face important practical challenges. Municipal governments may lack the immediate capacity to implement infrastructure levies and will likely need to develop new tools, such as large-scale property value surveys or ways to identify the geographic scope of windfall gains, which will increase the costs of this policy (Blanco et al., 2016[172]; GFDRR, 2018[173]). In addition to the general issues associated with property value appraisals (see section 3.3.1), attributing a change in these values to specific public investment projects is even more challenging (Amirtahmasebi et al., 2016[170]), and the accuracy of these estimates cannot be reasonably confirmed by alternative means of assessment. Approaches that do not assess benefits on an individual basis may also ignore important heterogeneities in the size of windfall gains and overlook the fact that the values of some properties (e.g. those beside a newly constructed highway extension) may be negatively impacted by the developments. In general, governments designing infrastructure levies are likely to face a significant trade-off between accuracy and cost-effectiveness, and may experience political resistance from property owners. Further concerns relate to the fact that landlords may respond to infrastructure levies by passing the tax burden onto tenants through higher rents, which could potentially have negative distributional consequences.

While infrastructure levies may provide an option to fund specific projects, a recurrent tax on immovable property based on regularly updated property values is key to capturing property value increases. Capturing windfall gains from public investment is key from an efficiency, equity and revenue raising perspective. However, there are other housing tax policies that can achieve this objective. Under a recurrent property tax based on accurate and regularly updated property values, property value increases stemming from nearby government spending will automatically be captured. In this case, an additional infrastructure levy tax may not be needed to capture windfall gains, although it may have other benefits for spatial planning and sustainable development. Section 3.3.1 highlights, however, that many OECD countries continue to levy their recurrent property taxes on outdated values, which means that many of these taxes need to be reformed to successfully capture property value increases. In addition, even where a recurrent property tax is based on regularly updated property values, it is important to note that it is not a perfect substitute for an infrastructure levy. Indeed, a recurrent property tax is not used to fund specific projects, it provides a more stable but less rapid source of funding for local governments than infrastructure levies that may be collected prior to the start of a project, and it captures all property values increases (not just those related to public investments). Overlap between infrastructure levies and capital gains taxes should also be carefully considered, as property value increases (including those stemming from local public investment) will be taxed if capital gains taxes apply when properties are sold.

References

Agarwal, S. et al. (2022), "Tobin Tax Policy, Housing Speculation, and Property Market Dynamics", *SSRN*, https://doi.org/10.2139/ssrn.3641624. [76]

Agarwal, S. et al. (2020), "Tax evasion, capital gains taxes, and the housing market", *Journal of Public Economics*, Vol. 188, p. 104222, https://doi.org/10.1016/j.jpubeco.2020.104222. [131]

Ahuja, A. and M. Nabar (2011), "Safeguarding Banks and Containing Property Booms: Cross-Country Evidence on Macroprudential Policies and Lessons From Hong Kong SAR", *IMF Working Papers*, No. WP/11/284, International Monetary Fund, https://ideas.repec.org/p/imf/imfwpa/2011-284.html (accessed on 2 November 2021). [77]

Alberini, A., A. Bigano and M. Boeri (2014), "Looking for free riding: energy efficiency incentives and Italian homeowners", *Energy Efficiency*, Vol. 7/4, pp. 571-590, https://doi.org/10.1007/s12053-013-9241-7. [150]

Alpanda, S. and S. Zubairy (2016), "Housing and Tax Policy", *Journal of Money, Credit and Banking*, Vol. 48/2-3, pp. 485-512, https://doi.org/10.1111/JMCB.12307. [112]

Amirtahmasebi, R. et al. (2016), *Regenerating Urban Land: A Practitioner's Guide to Leveraging Private Investment*, World Bank, Washington, DC, https://doi.org/10.1596/978-1-4648-0473-1. [170]

Andrews, D., A. Caldera Sánchez and Å. Johansson (2011), "Housing Markets and Structural Policies in OECD Countries", *OECD Economics Department Working Papers*, No. 836, OECD Publishing, Paris, https://doi.org/10.1787/5kgk8t2k9vf3-en. [58]

Andriopoulou, E. et al. (2020), "The distributional impact of recurrent immovable property taxation in Greece", pp. 506-526, https://doi.org/10.3326/pse.44.4.4. [25]

Arnold, J. et al. (2011), "Tax Policy for Economic Recovery and Growth", *The Economic Journal*, Vol. 121/550, pp. 59-80, https://doi.org/10.1111/J.1468-0297.2010.02415.X. [57]

Banzhaf, H. and N. Lavery (2010), "Can the land tax help curb urban sprawl? Evidence from growth patterns in Pennsylvania", *Journal of Urban Economics*, Vol. 67/2, pp. 169-179, https://doi.org/10.1016/j.jue.2009.08.005. [164]

Barakova, I. et al. (2003), "Does credit quality matter for homeownership?", *Journal of Housing Economics*, Vol. 12/4, pp. 318-336, https://doi.org/10.1016/J.JHE.2003.09.002. [103]

Baum-Snow, N. and J. Marion (2009), "The effects of low income housing tax credit developments on neighborhoods", *Journal of Public Economics*, Vol. 93/5-6, pp. 654-666, https://doi.org/10.1016/j.jpubeco.2009.01.001. [139]

Belinga, V. et al. (2014), "Tax Buoyancy in OECD Countries", *IMF Working Papers*, Vol. 14/110, p. 1, https://doi.org/10.5089/9781498305075.001. [7]

Ben-Shahar, D., R. Golan and E. Sulganik (2020), "Tax Evasion in the Housing Market: Identification and Exploration", *Journal of Real Estate Research*, Vol. 42/3, pp. 315-340, https://doi.org/10.1080/08965803.2020.1840899. [130]

Berger, T. et al. (2000), "The Capitalization of Interest Subsidies: Evidence from Sweden", *Journal of Money, Credit and Banking*, Vol. 32/2, p. 217, https://doi.org/10.2307/2601239. [99]

Besley, T., N. Meads and P. Surico (2014), "The incidence of transaction taxes: Evidence from a stamp duty holiday", *Journal of Public Economics*, Vol. 119, pp. 61-70, https://doi.org/10.1016/J.JPUBECO.2014.07.005. [67]

Best, M. and H. Kleven (2018), "Housing Market Responses to Transaction Taxes: Evidence From Notches and Stimulus in the U.K.", *The Review of Economic Studies*, Vol. 85/1, pp. 157-193, https://doi.org/10.1093/RESTUD/RDX032. [55]

Blanco, A. et al. (2016), *The Potential of Land Value Capture for Financing Urban Projects: Methodological Considerations and Case Studies*, Inter-American Development Bank, Washington, D.C., https://doi.org/10.18235/0000597. [172]

Blöchliger, H. et al. (2015), "The stabilisation properties of immovable property taxation: Evidence from OECD countries", *OECD Economics Department Working Papers*, No. 1237, OECD Publishing, Paris, https://doi.org/10.1787/5js0cqq93djg-en. [21]

Boomhower, J. and L. Davis (2014), "A credible approach for measuring inframarginal participation in energy efficiency programs", *Journal of Public Economics*, Vol. 113, pp. 67-79, https://doi.org/10.1016/j.jpubeco.2014.03.009. [151]

Borbely, D. (2021), "Limiting the distortionary effects of transaction taxes: Scottish stamp duty after the Mirrlees Review", *Fiscal Studies*, Vol. 42/2, pp. 265-290, https://doi.org/10.1111/1475-5890.12270. [80]

Borenstein, S. and L. Davis (2016), "The Distributional Effects of US Clean Energy Tax Credits", *Tax Policy and the Economy*, Vol. 30/1, pp. 191-234, https://doi.org/10.1086/685597. [153]

Borge, L. and J. Rattsø (2013), "Capitalization of Property Taxes in Norway", *Public Finance Review*, Vol. 42/5, pp. 635-661. [31]

Borrero Ochoa, O. (2011), "Betterment Levy in Colombia Relevance, Procedures, and Social Acceptability", *Land Lines*, Vol. 23, pp. 14-19. [169]

Bourassa, S. et al. (2013), "Mortgage Interest Deductions and Homeownership: An International Survey", *Swiss Finance Institute Research Papers*, No. 12-06, Swiss Finance Institute, https://doi.org/10.2139/SSRN.2002865. [101]

Bowman, J. (2006), "Property Tax Policy Responses to Rapidly Rising Home Values: District of Columbia, Maryland, and Virginia", *National Tax Journal*, Vol. 59/3, pp. 717-733. [53]

Bowman, J. and M. Bell (2004), "Implications of a Split-Rate Real Property Tax: An Initial Look at Three Virginia Local Government Areas", Lincoln Institute of Land Policy. [165]

Brown, J. and D. Phillips (2010), "Tax and Benefit Reforms Under Labour", *2010 Election Briefing Note*, No. 1 (IFS BN88), Institute for Fiscal Studies. [115]

Brys, B. et al. (2016), "Tax Design for Inclusive Economic Growth", *OECD Taxation Working Papers*, No. 26, OECD Publishing, Paris, https://doi.org/10.1787/5jlv74ggk0g7-en. [14]

Caldera Sánchez, A. and D. Andrews (2011), "To Move or not to Move: What Drives Residential Mobility Rates in the OECD?", *OECD Economics Department Working Papers*, No. 846, OECD Publishing, Paris, https://doi.org/10.1787/5kghtc7kzx21-en. [74]

Carasso, A., C. Steuerle and E. Bell (2005), "How to Better Encourage Homeownership", *Tax Policy Issues and Options*, No. 12, Urban Brookings Tax Policy Center, http://www.taxpolicycenter.org/TaxModel/income.cfm. (accessed on 3 November 2021). [107]

Carozzi, F., C. Hilber and X. Yu (2020), "On the economic impacts of mortgage credit expansion policies: evidence from help to buy", *CEP Discussion Papers*, No. 1681, Centre for Economic Performance, LSE, https://ideas.repec.org/p/cep/cepdps/dp1681.html (accessed on 3 November 2021). [138]

Causa, O. and J. Pichelmann (2020), *Should I stay or should I go? Housing and residential mobility across OECD countries*, OECD Publishing, Paris, https://doi.org/10.1787/acf95e90-en. [62]

Causa, O., N. Woloszko and D. Leite (2019), "Housing, wealth accumulation and wealth distribution: Evidence and stylized facts", *OECD Economics Department Working Papers*, No. 1588, OECD Publishing, Paris, https://doi.org/10.1787/86954c10-en. [94]

Charlier, D., A. Risch and C. Salmon (2018), "Energy Burden Alleviation and Greenhouse Gas Emissions Reduction: Can We Reach Two Objectives With One Policy?", *Ecological Economics*, Vol. 143, pp. 294-313, https://doi.org/10.1016/j.ecolecon.2017.07.002. [148]

Chawla, R. and T. Wannell (2003), *Property taxes*, Statistics Canada, https://www150.statcan.gc.ca/n1/en/catalogue/75-001-X200310713094 (accessed on 2 November 2021). [28]

Clerc, M., A. Mauroux and V. Marcus (2010), *Le recours au crédit d'impôt en faveur du développement durable*, Insee Première, Paris, France, https://www.insee.fr/fr/statistiques/1283214. [149]

Cohen, J. and C. Coughlin (2005), "An Introduction to Two-Rate Taxation of Land and Buildings", *Federal Reserve Bank of St. Louis Review*, Vol. 87/3, pp. 359-374, https://doi.org/10.20955/r.87.359-374. [167]

Corlett, A. and J. Leslie (2021), "Home county: Options for taxing main residence capital gains", Resolution Foundation. [10]

Cournède, B., J. Fournier and P. Hoeller (2018), "Public finance structure and inclusive growth", *OECD Economic Policy Papers*, No. 25, OECD, Paris. [24]

Crowe, C. et al. (2011), "How to Deal with Real Estate Booms: Lessons from Country Experiences", *IMF Working Paper*, No. WP/11/91, International Monetary Fund, https://doi.org/10.5089/9781455253302.001.A001. [82]

Cunningham, C. and G. Engelhardt (2008), "Housing capital-gains taxation and homeowner mobility: Evidence from the Taxpayer Relief Act of 1997", *Journal of Urban Economics*, Vol. 63/3, pp. 803-815, https://doi.org/10.1016/J.JUE.2007.05.002. [86]

Dachis, B., G. Duranton and M. Turner (2012), "The effects of land transfer taxes on real estate markets: evidence from a natural experiment in Toronto", *Journal of Economic Geography*, Vol. 12, pp. 327-354, https://doi.org/10.1093/jeg/lbr007. [64]

Dam, N. et al. (2011), "The Housing Bubble that Burst: Can House Prices be Explained? And Can Their Fluctuations be Dampened?", *Monetary Review*, Nationalbank Denmark, Copenhagen. [46]

Davidoff, I. and A. Leigh (2013), "How Do Stamp Duties Affect the Housing Market?", *IZA Discussion Paper*, No. 7463, Institute for the Study of Labor (IZA), https://docs.iza.org/dp7463.pdf. [63]

Davis, M. (2019), "The Distributional Impact of Mortgage Interest Subsidies: Evidence from Variation in State Tax Policies", *Job Market Paper*, The Wharton School, University of Pennsylvania, https://faculty.wharton.upenn.edu/wp-content/uploads/2016/11/MDavis_MID.pdf (accessed on 3 November 2021). [102]

De Simone, L., R. Lester and K. Markle (2020), "Transparency and Tax Evasion: Evidence from the Foreign Account Tax Compliance Act (FATCA)", *Journal of Accounting Research*, Vol. 58/1, pp. 105-153, https://doi.org/10.1111/1475-679X.12293. [126]

Deniau, F. et al. (2019), *Évaluation du dispositif d'aide fiscale à l'investissement locatif Pinel*, Inspection générale des finances, Paris, France. [141]

Department of Finance - Ireland (2021), *Minister Donohoe announces changes to Local Property Tax*. [49]

Di Maggio, M. and A. Kermani (2016), "Credit-Induced Boom and Bust", *The Review of Financial Studies*, https://doi.org/10.2139/SSRN.2463516. [135]

Diamond, P. and J. Mirrlees (1971), "Optimal Taxation and Public Production I: Production Efficiency", *The American Economic Review*, Vol. 61/1, pp. 8-27, https://www.jstor.org/stable/1910538?seq=1#metadata_info_tab_contents (accessed on 2 November 2021). [18]

Dolls, M. et al. (2021), "Who Bears the Burden of Real Estate Transfer Taxes? Evidence from the German Housing Market", *CESifo Working Papers*, No. 8839, CESifo. [1]

Dougherty, S. and P. de Biase (2021), "Who absorbs the shock? An analysis of the fiscal impact of the COVID-19 crisis on different levels of government", *International Economics and Economic Policy*, Vol. 18/3, pp. 517-540, https://doi.org/10.1007/s10368-021-00518-1. [8]

Dowd, T. and R. McClelland (2017), "The Bunching of Capital Gains Realizations", *SSRN Electronic Journal*, https://doi.org/10.2139/ssrn.2899093. [122]

Duca, J., J. Muellbauer and A. Murphy (2011), "House Prices and Credit Constraints: Making Sense of the US Experience", *The Economic Journal*, Vol. 121/552, pp. 533-551, https://doi.org/10.1111/J.1468-0297.2011.02424.X. [134]

Dunsky, R. and J. Follain (2000), "Tax-Induced Portfolio Reshuffling: The Case of the Mortgage Interest Deduction", *Real Estate Economics*, Vol. 28/4, pp. 683-718, https://doi.org/10.1111/1540-6229.00816. [105]

Economidou, M. et al. (2020), "Review of 50 years of EU energy efficiency policies for buildings", *Energy and Buildings*, Vol. 225, https://doi.org/10.1016/j.enbuild.2020.110322. [145]

Edgeworth, F. (1897), "The pure theory of taxation", *The Economic Journal*, Vol. 7, pp. 46-70. [37]

Eerola, E. et al. (2019), "Tax Compliance in the Rental Housing Market: Evidence from a Field Experiment", *SSRN Electronic Journal*, https://doi.org/10.2139/ssrn.3464295. [65]

Eerola, E. et al. (2019), "Effects of Housing Transfer Taxes on Household Mobility", *CESifo Working Paper*, No. 7750, CESifo. [72]

Eriksen, M. and S. Rosenthal (2010), "Crowd out effects of place-based subsidized rental housing: New evidence from the LIHTC program", *Journal of Public Economics*, Vol. 94/11-12, https://doi.org/10.1016/j.jpubeco.2010.07.002. [143]

Ernesto U., S. and R. Michele (eds.) (2015), *From Illegal Markets to Legitimate Businesses: The Portfolio of Organised Crime in Europe. Final Report of Project OCP – Organised Crime Portfolio*, Transcrime – Università degli Studi di Trento, Trento. [125]

European Commission (2012), "Possible reforms of real estate taxation: Criteria for successful policies", *Occasional Papers*, No. 119, European Commission, Brussels, https://doi.org/10.2765/24556. [36]

Fatica, S. (2015), "Housing taxation: from micro design to macro impact", *Quaterly Report on the Euro Area*, No. 14(1), Directorate General Economic and Financial Affairs - European Commission, https://ideas.repec.org/a/euf/qreuro/0141-03.html (accessed on 3 November 2021). [110]

Fatica, S. and D. Prammer (2017), "Housing and the tax system: how large are the distortions in the euro area?", *ECB Working Paper*, No. 2087, European Central Bank, https://doi.org/10.2866/456421. [90]

Favara, G. and J. Imbs (2015), "Credit Supply and the Price of Housing", *American Economic Review*, Vol. 105/3, pp. 958-92, https://doi.org/10.1257/AER.20121416. [137]

Fitzgerald, K. (2020), *Speculative Vacancies 10: A Persistent Puzzle*, Prosper Australia, Melbourne, Victoria. [163]

Floetotto, M., M. Kirker and J. Stroebel (2016), "Government intervention in the housing market: Who wins, who loses?", *Journal of Monetary Economics*, Vol. 80, pp. 106-123, https://doi.org/10.1016/J.JMONECO.2016.04.005. [113]

Fritzsche, C. and L. Vandrei (2019), "The German real estate transfer tax: Evidence for single-family home transactions", *Regional Science and Urban Economics*, Vol. 74, pp. 131-143, https://doi.org/10.1016/j.regsciurbeco.2018.08.005. [66]

Fu, Y., W. Qian and B. Yeung (2013), "Speculative Investors and Tobin's Tax in the Housing Market", *NBER Working Paper*, No. 19400, National Bureau of Economic Research. [78]

Gabriel, S. and S. Rosenthal (1991), "Credit rationing, race, and the mortgage market", *Journal of Urban Economics*, Vol. 29/3, pp. 371-379, https://doi.org/10.1016/0094-1190(91)90007-T. [104]

Gale, W., J. Gruber and S. Stephens-Davidowitz (2007), "Encouraging Homeownership Through the Tax Code", *Tax Notes*, No. Vol.115, No.12, https://papers.ssrn.com/sol3/papers.cfm?abstract_id=1758888 (accessed on 3 November 2021). [108]

Gallagher, R., H. Kurban and J. Persky (2013), "Small Homes, Public Schools, and Property Tax Capitalization", *CES Papers*, No. 13-04, US Census Bureau Center for Economic Studies. [32]

GFDRR (2018), *Land Value Capture*, Global Facility for Disaster Reduction and Recovery, Washington, DC. [173]

Giaccobasso, M. et al. (2022), *Where Do My Tax Dollars Go? Tax Morale Effects of Perceived Government Spending*, National Bureau of Economic Research, Cambridge, MA, https://doi.org/10.3386/w29789. [56]

Giraudet, L., C. Bourgeois and P. Quirion (2021), "Policies for low-carbon and affordable home heating: A French outlook", *Energy Policy*, Vol. 151, https://doi.org/10.1016/j.enpol.2021.112140. [154]

Glaeser, E. and J. Shapiro (2003), "The Benefits of the Home Mortgage Interest Deduction", *Tax Policy and the Economy*, Vol. 17, pp. 37-82, https://doi.org/10.1086/tpe.17.20140504. [97]

Goldstein, D. et al. (2012), *A Retrospective Look at Federal Energy Efficiency Tax Incentives: How Do Cost and Performance-Based Incentives Compare in Their Ability to Transform Markets?*, ACEEE Summer Study on Energy Efficiency in Buildings. [157]

Goode, R. (1960), "Imputed rent of owner-occupied dwellings under income tax", *The Journal of Finance*, Vol. 15/4, pp. 504-530, https://doi.org/10.1111/J.1540-6261.1960.TB02766.X. [95]

Gravelle, J. (2022), *The Exclusion of Capital Gains for Owner-Occupied Housing*, Congressional Research Service. [88]

Grover, R. et al. (2017), "Achieving successful implementation of value-based property tax reforms in emerging European economies", *Journal of European Real Estate Research*, Vol. 10/1, pp. 91-106. [13]

Gruber, J., A. Jensen and H. Kleven (2021), "Do People Respond to the Mortgage Interest Deduction? Quasi-experimental Evidence from Denmark", *American Economic Journal: Economic Policy*, Vol. 13/2, pp. 273-303, https://doi.org/10.1257/POL.20170366. [89]

Grudnoff, M. (2016), "CGT main residence exemption Why removing the tax concession for homes over $2 million is good for the budget, the economy and fairness", The Australia Institute, https://www.tai.org.au (accessed on 2 November 2021). [11]

Haas, A. and S. Kriticos (2019), *Considerations for land value capture reform in the Greater Amman Municipality*, International Growth Centre, London. [171]

Haider, M., A. Anwar and C. Holmes (2016), "Did the Land Transfer Tax Reduce Housing Sales in Toronto?", *IMFG Papers*, No. 28, Institute on Municipal Finance & Governance, http://munkschool.utoronto.ca/imfg/ (accessed on 2 November 2021). [70]

Hamilton, B. (1975), "Zoning and Property Taxation in a System of Local Governments", *Urban Studies*, Vol. 12/2, pp. 205-2011. [39]

Harris, B. (2010), *The Effect of Proposed Tax Reforms on Metropolitan Housing Prices*, Tax Policy Center - Urban Institute and Brookings Institute. [100]

Harris, B. and L. Parker (2014), *The Mortgage Interest Deduction Across Zip Codes*, Brookings, https://www.brookings.edu/research/the-mortgage-interest-deduction-across-zip-codes/ (accessed on 3 November 2021). [109]

Hartzok, A. (1997), "Pennsylvania's Success with Local Property Tax Reform", *American Journal of Economics and Sociology*, Vol. 56/2, https://doi.org/10.1111/j.1536-7150.1997.tb03461.x. [166]

Hassett, K. and G. Metcalf (1995), “Energy tax credits and residential conservation investment: Evidence from panel data”, *Journal of Public Economics*, Vol. 57/2, pp. 201-217, https://doi.org/10.1016/0047-2727(94)01452-T. [152]

Hilber, C. (2017), “The Economic Implications of House Price Capitalization: A Synthesis”, *Real Estate Economics*, Vol. 45/2, pp. 301-339, https://doi.org/10.1111/1540-6229.12129. [35]

Hilber, C. and T. Lyytikäinen (2017), “Transfer taxes and household mobility: Distortion on the housing or labor market?”, *Journal of Urban Economics*, Vol. 101, https://doi.org/10.1016/j.jue.2017.06.002. [71]

Hilber, C. and T. Turner (2014), “The mortgage interest deduction and its impact on homeownership decisions”, *Review of Economics and Statistics*, Vol. 96/4, pp. 618-637, https://doi.org/10.1162/REST_A_00427. [98]

HMRC (2021), *Tax relief statistics (December 2021)*, Official Statistics, accessed 5 April 2022 https://www.gov.uk/government/statistics/main-tax-expenditures-and-structural-reliefs/estimated-cost-of-tax-reliefs-statistics#contents. [92]

Hodge, T. et al. (2017), “Assessment Inequity in a Declining Housing Market: The Case of Detroit”, *Real Estate Economics*, Vol. 45/2, pp. 237-258, https://doi.org/10.1111/1540-6229.12126. [44]

Housing Vancouver (2020), *Empty Homes Tax Annual Report*, City of Vancouver, Vancouver, British Colombia. [161]

Hui, E., J. Zhong and K. Yu (2017), “Property prices, housing policies for collateral and resale constraints”, *International Journal of Strategic Property Management*, Vol. 21/2, pp. 115-128, https://doi.org/10.3846/1648715X.2016.1249984. [75]

Hungerford, T. (2010), *The Economic Effects of Capital Gains Taxation*, Congressional Research Service, Washington, DC. [12]

IMF (2013), *Fiscal Monitor: Taxing Times - World Economic and Financial Surveys.* [59]

Johansson, Å. (2016), “Public Finance, Economic Growth and Inequality: A Survey of the Evidence”, *OECD Economics Department Working Papers*, No. 1346, OECD, Paris. [23]

Johansson, Å. et al. (2008), “Taxation and Economic Growth”, *OECD Economics Department Working Papers*, No. 620, OECD Publishing, Paris, https://doi.org/10.1787/241216205486. [17]

Joumard, I., M. Pisu and D. Bloch (2012), “Tackling income inequality: The role of taxes and transfers”, *OECD Journal: Economic Studies*, https://doi.org/10.1787/eco_studies-2012-5k95xd6l65lt. [29]

Karlman, M., K. Kinnerud and K. Kragh-Sørensen (2021), “Costly reversals of bad policies: The case of the mortgage interest deduction”, *Review of Economic Dynamics*, Vol. 40, pp. 85-107, https://doi.org/10.1016/J.RED.2020.08.003. [114]

Kelly, R., R. White and A. Anand (2020), *Property Tax Diagnostic Manual*, World Bank Group, Washington, D.C. [42]

Kim, K. and P. Lambert (2008), “Redistributive Effect of U.S. Taxes and Public Transfers, 1994-2004:”, *http://dx.doi.org/10.1177/1091142108324423*, Vol. 37/1, pp. 3-26, https://doi.org/10.1177/1091142108324423. [26]

Kopczuk, W. and D. Munroe (2015), “Mansion Tax: The Effect of Transfer Taxes on the Residential Real Estate Market”, *American Economic Journal: Economic Policy*, Vol. 7/2, pp. 214-257, https://doi.org/10.1257/pol.20130361. [68]

Koster, H., J. van Ommeren and N. Volkhausen (2018), “Short-Term Rentals and the Housing Market: Quasi-Experimental Evidence from Airbnb in Los Angeles”, *CEPR Discussion Paper*, No. DP13094, Centre for Economic Policy Research, London. [120]

Kwak, S. and J. Mak (2011), “Political Economy of Property Tax Reform: Hawaii's Experiment with Split-Rate Property Taxation”, *American Journal of Economics and Sociology*, Vol. 70/1, https://doi.org/10.1111/j.1536-7150.2010.00761.x. [168]

Langley, A. (2015), *How Do States Spell Relief?*, pp. 24-31. [54]

Lee, W. and F. Yik (2004), “Regulatory and voluntary approaches for enhancing building energy efficiency”, *Progress in Energy and Combustion Science*, Vol. 30/5, pp. 477-499, https://doi.org/10.1016/j.pecs.2004.03.002. [160]

Levy, A. (2021), “The tax elasticity of capital gains: Evidence from millions of housing sales”, MIT. [121]

Lutz, B. (2008), “The Connection Between House Price Appreciation and Property Tax Revenues”, *Finance and Economics Discussion Series*, Vol. 2008/48, pp. 1-32, https://doi.org/10.17016/FEDS.2008.48. [9]

Maloney, M., T. Somerville and B. Unger (2019), *Combatting Money Laundering in BC Real Estate*, Expert Panel on Money Laundering in BC Real Estate. [127]

Matsaganis, M. and M. Flevotomou (2007), “The impact of mortgage interest tax relief in the Netherlands, Sweden, Finland, Italy and Greece”, *EUROMOD Working Papers*, No. EM2/07, Institute for Social and Economic Research, https://ideas.repec.org/p/ese/emodwp/em2-07.html (accessed on 3 November 2021). [111]

McClure, K. (2019), “What Should Be the Future of the Low-Income Housing Tax Credit Program?”, *Housing Policy Debate*, Vol. 29/1, pp. 65-81, https://doi.org/10.1080/10511482.2018.1469526. [142]

McMillen, D. and R. Singh (2020), “Assessment Regressivity and Property Taxation”, *Journal of Real Estate Finance and Economics*, Vol. 60/1-2, pp. 155-169, https://doi.org/10.1007/S11146-019-09715-X. [45]

Mian, A. and A. Sufi (2009), “The Consequences of Mortgage Credit Expansion: Evidence from the U.S. Mortgage Default Crisis”, *The Quarterly Journal of Economics*, Vol. 124/4, pp. 1449-1496, https://doi.org/10.1162/QJEC.2009.124.4.1449. [136]

Mieszkowski, P. (1972), “The property tax: An excise tax or a profits tax?”, *Journal of Public Economics*, Vol. 1/1, pp. 73-96, https://doi.org/10.1016/0047-2727(72)90020-5. [38]

Millar-Powell, B. et al. (2022), “Measuring effective taxation of housing: Building the foundations for policy reform”, *OECD Taxation Working Papers*, No. 56, OECD, Paris. [83]

Mirrlees, J. et al. (2011), "The Taxation of Land and Property", in *Tax by design*, Oxford University Press, Oxford. [43]

Montalvo, J., A. Piolatto and J. Raya (2020), "Transaction-tax evasion in the housing market", *Regional Science and Urban Economics*, Vol. 81, p. 103526, https://doi.org/10.1016/j.regsciurbeco.2020.103526. [129]

Muellbauer, J. (2018), "Housing, debt and the economy: a tale of two countries", *National Institute Economic Review*, Vol. 245, pp. R20-R33, https://doi.org/10.1177/002795011824500112. [52]

Munnell, A., W. Hou and A. Walters (2022), "Property Tax Deferral: Can a Public/Private Partnership Help Provide Lifetime Income?", in Mitchell, O. (ed.), *New Models for Managing Longevity Risk: Public-Private Partnerships*, Oxford University Press, Oxford, UK. [51]

Norregaard, J. (2013), "Taxing Immovable Property: Revenue Potential and Implementation Challenges", *IMF Working Paper*, No. 13/129, IMF. [16]

NSW Treasury (2021), *NSW Property Tax Proposal -Progress Paper for June 2021 Making Home Ownership More Achievable in NSW*, NSW Treasury, Sydney. [61]

O'Connor, B. et al. (2015), "Searching for the inclusive growth tax grail: The distributional impact of growth enhancing tax reform in Ireland", *Economics Department Working Papers*, No. 1270, OECD Publishing, Paris, https://doi.org/10.1787/5jrqc6vk3n30-en. [30]

O'Reilly, P., K. Parra Ramirez and M. Stemmer (2019), "Exchange of information and bank deposits in international financial centres", *OECD Taxation Working Papers*, No. 46, OECD Publishing, Paris, https://doi.org/10.1787/025bfebe-en. [128]

Oates, W. (1969), "The Effects of Property Taxes and Local Public Spending on Property Values: An Empirical Study of Tax Capitalization and the Tiebout Hypothesis", *Journal of Political Economy*, Vol. 77/6, pp. 957-971. [34]

Oates, W. and A. Fischel (2016), "Are local property taxes regressive, progressive, or what?", *National Tax Journal*, Vol. 69/2. [40]

OECD (2022), *Affordable Housing Database*, https://www.oecd.org/housing/data/affordable-housing-database/ (accessed on 21 February 2022). [175]

OECD (2021), *Brick by Brick: Building Better Housing Policies*, OECD Publishing, Paris, https://doi.org/10.1787/b453b043-en. [159]

OECD (2021), *Effective Carbon Rates 2021: Pricing Carbon Emissions through Taxes and Emissions Trading*, OECD Publishing, Paris, https://doi.org/10.1787/0e8e24f5-en. [156]

OECD (2021), *Ending the Shell Game: Cracking down on the Professionals who enable Tax and White Collar Crimes*, OECD, Paris. [132]

OECD (2021), *Inheritance Taxation in OECD Countries*, OECD Tax Policy Studies, No. 28, OECD Publishing, Paris, https://doi.org/10.1787/e2879a7d-en. [3]

OECD (2021), *Making Property Tax Reform Happen in China: A Review of Property Tax Design and Reform Experiences in OECD Countries*, OECD Fiscal Federalism Studies, OECD Publishing, Paris, https://doi.org/10.1787/bd0fbae3-en. [5]

OECD (2021), *OECD Economic Surveys: Netherlands 2021*, OECD Publishing, Paris, https://doi.org/10.1787/dd476bd3-en. [118]

OECD (2021), "Tax relief for homeownership", *OECD Affordable Housing Database*, No. PH2.2, OECD, Paris, https://www.oecd.org/els/family/PH2-1-Public-spending-support-to-home-buyers.pdf (accessed on 3 November 2021). [93]

OECD (2020), *Revenue Statistics 2020*, OECD Publishing, Paris, https://doi.org/10.1787/8625f8e5-en. [4]

OECD (2019), *OECD Economic Surveys: Denmark 2019*, OECD Publishing, Paris, https://doi.org/10.1787/eco_surveys-dnk-2019-en. [47]

OECD (2019), *Taxing Energy Use 2019: Using Taxes for Climate Action*, OECD Publishing, Paris, https://doi.org/10.1787/058ca239-en. [155]

OECD (2018), *Model Mandatory Disclosure Rules for CRS Avoidance Arrangements and Opaque Offshore Structures*, OECD Publishing, Paris, https://www.oecd.org/tax/exchange-of-tax-information/model-mandatory-disclosure-rules-for-crs-avoidance-arrangements-and-opaque-offshore-structures.htm. [133]

OECD (2018), *Taxation of Household Savings*, OECD Tax Policy Studies, No. 25, OECD Publishing, Paris, https://doi.org/10.1787/9789264289536-en. [2]

OECD (2018), *The Role and Design of Net Wealth Taxes in the OECD*, OECD Tax Policy Studies, No. 26, OECD Publishing, Paris, https://doi.org/10.1787/9789264290303-en. [6]

OECD (2016), *OECD Economic Surveys: Netherlands 2016*, OECD Publishing, Paris, https://doi.org/10.1787/eco_surveys-nld-2016-en. [117]

OECD (2014), *OECD Economic Surveys: Netherlands 2014*, OECD Publishing, Paris, https://doi.org/10.1787/eco_surveys-nld-2014-en. [116]

OECD (2009), *OECD Economic Surveys: Ireland 2009*, OECD Publishing, Paris, https://doi.org/10.1787/eco_surveys-irl-2009-en. [119]

OECD (2007), *Tax Fraud and Money Laundering Vulnerabilities Involving the Real Estate Sector*, OECD Publishing, Paris, https://www.oecd.org/ctp/crime/realestatesectortaxfraudandmoneylaunderingvulnerabilities.htm (accessed on 13 July 2022). [123]

OECD (forthcoming 2022), *Global Compendium on Land Value Capture*, OECD, Paris. [174]

OECD/KIPF (2014), *The Distributional Effects of Consumption Taxes in OECD Countries*, OECD Tax Policy Studies, No. 22, OECD Publishing, Paris, https://doi.org/10.1787/9789264224520-en. [85]

Oliviero, T. et al. (2019), "House prices and immovable property tax: Evidence from OECD countries", *Metroeconomica*, Vol. 70/4, pp. 776-792, https://doi.org/10.1111/meca.12253. [20]

O'Regan, K. and K. Horn (2013), "What Can We Learn About the Low-Income Housing Tax Credit Program by Looking at the Tenants?", *Housing Policy Debate*, Vol. 23/3, pp. 597-613, https://doi.org/10.1080/10511482.2013.772909. [140]

Palameta, B. and I. Macredie (2005), *Property taxes relative to income*, Statistics Canada. [27]

Palmon, O. and B. Smith (1998), "New Evidence on Property Tax Capitalization", *Journal of Political Economy*, Vol. 106/5, pp. 1099-1111, https://doi.org/10.1086/250041. [33]

Petkova, K. and A. Weichenrieder (2017), "Price and Quantity Effects of the German Real Estate Transfer Tax", *WU International Taxation Research Paper Series*, No. 2, https://papers.ssrn.com/sol3/papers.cfm?abstract_id=2988888 (accessed on 2 November 2021). [73]

Poterba, J., S. Venti and D. Wise (2011), "The Composition and Draw-down of Wealth in Retirement", *NBER Working Paper Series*, No. 17536, National Bureau for Economic Research, https://doi.org/10.3386/W17536. [84]

Ramsey, F. (1927), "A Contribution to the Theory of Taxation", *The Economic Journal*, Vol. 37/145, p. 47, https://doi.org/10.2307/2222721. [19]

Remeur, C. (2019), *Understanding money laundering through real estate transactions*, European Parliamentary Research Service. [124]

Risch, A. (2020), "Are environmental fiscal incentives effective in inducing energy-saving renovations? An econometric evaluation of the French energy tax credit", *Energy Economics*, Vol. 90, https://doi.org/10.1016/j.eneco.2020.104831. [147]

Scanlon, K., C. Whitehead and F. Blanc (2018), *A sustainable increase in London's housing supply?*, London School of Economics and Political Science, London. [81]

Segú, M. (2020), "The impact of taxing vacancy on housing markets: Evidence from France", *Journal of Public Economics*, Vol. 185, p. 104079, https://doi.org/10.1016/j.jpubeco.2019.104079. [162]

Shan, H. (2011), "The Effect of Capital Gains Taxation on Home Sales: Evidence from the Taxpayer Relief Act of 1997", *Journal of Public Economics*, Vol. 95, p. 188, https://doi.org/10.1016/J.JPUBECO.2010.10.006. [87]

Sinai, T. and J. Waldfogel (2005), "Do low-income housing subsidies increase the occupied housing stock?", *Journal of Public Economics*, Vol. 89/11-12, pp. 2137-2164, https://doi.org/10.1016/j.jpubeco.2004.06.015. [144]

Slack, E. and R. Bird (2015), "How to Reform the Property Tax: Lessons from around the World", *IMFG Papers*, No. 21, Institute of Municipal Finance and Governance, http://munkschool.utoronto.ca/imfg/ (accessed on 2 November 2021). [22]

Slack, E. and R. Bird (2014), "The Political Economy of Property Tax Reform", *OECD Working Papers on Fiscal Federalism*, No. 18, OECD Publishing, Paris, https://doi.org/10.1787/5jz5pzvzv6r7-en. [15]

Slemrod, J., C. Weber and H. Shan (2017), "The behavioral response to housing transfer taxes: Evidence from a notched change in D.C. policy", *Journal of Urban Economics*, Vol. 100, pp. 137-153, https://doi.org/10.1016/J.JUE.2017.05.005. [69]

Smidova, Z. (2016), "Betting the house in Denmark", *OECD Economics Department Working Papers*, No. 1337, OECD Publishing, Paris, https://doi.org/10.1787/5jln042vd3kk-en. [48]

Sommer, K. and P. Sullivan (2018), "Implications of US Tax Policy for House Prices, Rents, and Homeownership", *American Economic Review*, Vol. 108/2, p. 274, https://doi.org/10.1257/AER.20141751. [96]

Sutherland, D. and P. Hoeller (2012), "Debt and Macroeconomic Stability: An Overview of the Literature and Some Empirics", *OECD Economics Department Working Papers*, No. 1006, OECD Publishing, Paris, https://doi.org/10.1787/5k8xb75txzf5-en. [106]

Tax and Transfer Policy Institute et al. (2020), *Analysis of the Impacts and Outcomes of the ACT Tax Reform*. [60]

Thomas, A. (2021), "Reforming the taxation of housing in Israel", *OECD Taxation Working Papers*, No. 53, OECD Publishing, Paris, https://doi.org/10.1787/83fd48ad-en. [79]

Tobias, L. (2008), *Toward Sustainable Financing and Strong Markets for Green Building: US Green Building Finance Review*, Commission for Environmental Cooperation, Montréal, Quebec, http://www.usgbc.org/News/PressReleaseDetails.aspx?ID=3124. [158]

Treasury (2022), *2021 Tax Benchmarks and Variations Statement*, Australian Government Treasury, Canberra. [91]

Waldhart, P. and A. Reschovsky (2012), "Property tax delinquency and the number of payment installments", *Public Finance and Management*, Lincoln Institute of Land Policy, https://www.researchgate.net/publication/313050824_Property_tax_delinquency_and_the_number_of_payment_installments (accessed on 2 November 2021). [50]

Wilson, C., L. Crane and G. Chryssochoidis (2015), "Why do homeowners renovate energy efficiently? Contrasting perspectives and implications for policy", *Energy Research & Social Science*, Vol. 7, pp. 12-22, https://doi.org/10.1016/j.erss.2015.03.002. [146]

Zodrow, G. (2001), "The Property Tax as a Capital Tax: A Room with Three Views", *National Tax Journal*, Vol. 54/1, pp. 139-156. [41]

Notes

[1] The representative state chosen for Australia is New South Wales, the most populous state. While other states have some similar housing tax policies as New South Wales, states have significant autonomy over the design and administration of certain taxes and there are important differences across states.

[2] As of 2022, for primary residences valued above NOK 10 million, 50% of the value of the property is subject to the wealth tax in Norway.

[3] In Germany, recurrent taxes on immovable property may be paid by the occupant (as part of the additional charges) if agreed upon in the rental contract.

[4] Consider, for example, two apartments of identical area in square metres, but one on the ground floor and the other on the top floor of a large apartment building. The apartment on the top floor will likely be worth significantly more (and generate a higher imputed or actual return) than the ground floor apartment.

However, this greater value (and return) will not be taken into account in an area-based recurrent immovable property tax (Thomas, 2021[79]).

5 Annual property revaluations are used as inputs for a range of purposes, including tax, statistical, and social support purposes. Property revaluations are valid for five years for the purpose of the recurrent tax on immovable property.

6 Note that the calculation of recurrent property tax liabilities (which also takes into account the type of property and a factor determined by the respective municipalities) based on outdated property values was deemed unconstitutional in April 2018. With effect in January 2025, a tax reform was introduced to update property tax values with reference to their market value on 1st January 2022.

7 High levels of government typically bear the responsibility for valuation, even in countries where local governments have substantial autonomy over the design of recurrent immovable property taxes. This ensures consistent valuation methods across municipalities and in the context of CAMA valuations, there is the added advantage of economies of scale and availability of personnel with the necessary technical skills (OECD, 2021[5]).

8 For example, a 1% recurrent immovable property tax is levied on a property worth USD 100 000. Rather than pay USD 1 000, the taxpayer gives the tax authority an equity share equal to 1% of the value of the property. Later, the taxpayer sells the property for USD 120 000 and remits USD 1 200 (1% of the sale value) to satisfy the tax liability.

9 In Türkiye, the seller and buyer may share the tax burden.

10 Note that the empirical studies on the United Kingdom evaluate a temporary transaction tax cut introduced in response to the Global Financial Crisis while other analyses study permanent transaction tax reforms.

11 Private condominium properties may be sold before project completion in Singapore, with investors having been able to defer the transaction tax until the completion or sale of the property before the tax reform

12 The Netherlands introduced a transaction tax reform in 2021, which made the lower transaction tax rate of 2% conditional on the long-term occupation of the property by the buyer. The standard transaction tax rate, on the other hand, was progressively increased from 6% in 2020 to 9% in 2022.

13 Table A.2 describes the tax treatment of rented secondary housing and does not capture specific treatment that may apply to secondary housing that does not generate rental income.

14 Holiday homes are exempt from capital gains taxes if they are used as holiday homes for at least five of the eight years before sale.

15 Note that recurrent taxes on immovable property could be considered as roughly equivalent to an imputed tax on the rental income (although it does not account for different rates of return or for costs).

16 Individuals are exempt from taxes on rental income earned from housing with a surface equal to or lower than 140 m2, up to a maximum of two new or existing dwellings per person.

17 Rental income is exempt from personal income taxes where the taxpayer lets part of their primary residence on a long-term basis (more than 30 days) and the rental income is less than 50% of the home's rental value.

[18] Main residence: Belgium (exempt [spouse] or lower tax rates [co-owners that are lineal heirs or cohabitants]), France (partially exempt), Germany (exempt), Greece (additional tax-free threshold), Ireland (exempt), Japan (partially exempt), Korea (exempt, capped at KRW 600 million), Poland (exempt [immediate family] or exemption capped at 110 m2 [extended family and carers]), Portugal (partially exempt, then lower tax rates), Spain (partially exempt, capped at EUR 122 606), Switzerland (valued slightly below market value), and United Kingdom (partially exempt). Other housing: Poland (exempt [immediate family] or exemption capped at 110 m2 [extended family and carers]) and Switzerland (valued slightly below market value).

[19] Beneficiary lives in the house before/after donor's death: At time of death (Belgium [spouse], France), 3 years before & 6 years after (Ireland), 5 years after (Poland [extended family and carers only]), 10 years before (Korea), 10 years after (Germany, Spain). Not own other housing: Greece, Ireland, Korea, Poland [extended family and carers only]. Eligible beneficiaries: Spouse (Belgium [exemption]); spouse and children (France, Germany, Greece); lineal descendants (Korea, United Kingdom); spouse, ascendants, and descendants (Spain); immediate family (Poland [exemption]); extended family and carers (Poland [exemption capped at 110m2]); co-owners that are lineal heirs or cohabitants (Belgium [lower tax rates]); all beneficiaries (Ireland, Japan, Portugal, Switzerland).

[20] Countries typically recognise multiple types of trusts or similar legal arrangements. The strategies discussed in this section refer to arrangements that function like discretionary trusts, where the trustee determines how income is distributed to beneficiaries, though some strategies will also apply to other types of arrangements such as those that function like unit trusts. Some strategies may depend on whether the trust is revocable or irrevocable.

[21] Buyers who can finance a housing purchase without a mortgage have greater opportunities to evade taxes by under-declaring the purchase price, as they are more likely to have the cash needed to make undeclared payments to the seller. Liquidity-constrained buyers who rely on mortgage finance have an incentive to obtain higher valuations (to unlock mortgage credit) and report an accurate purchase price (to avoid falling above required loan-to-value limits). For this reason, transactions without mortgage finance and with lower valuations relative to sale price may warrant closer attention (Montalvo, Piolatto and Raya, 2020[129]).

[22] The Glossary to the Financial Action Task Force (FATF) Recommendations defines beneficial owners as to the natural person(s) who ultimately owns or controls a customer and/or the natural person on whose behalf a transaction is being conducted. It also includes those persons who exercise ultimate effective control over a legal person or arrangement. For more information see https://www.fatf-gafi.org/media/fatf/documents/reports/Guidance-transparency-beneficial-ownership.pdf

[23] https://www.federalregister.gov/documents/2021/12/08/2021-26549/anti-money-laundering-regulations-for-real-estate-transactions

[24] FATF number 22 recommends that customer due diligence and record-keeping requirements (outlined in recommendations 10, 11, 12, 15, and 17) apply to real estate agents, accountants, lawyers, notaries, and other independent legal professionals involved in real estate transactions

[25] The extent of the reduction is determined by a set of criteria linked to the project's scope. Larger credits are applied to new construction or substantial rehabilitation and smaller credits are applied to properties acquired for rehabilitation and for projects funded using tax-exempt bonds.

[26] The *Crédito Especial a Empresas Constructoras* allows construction companies to deduct from their income 65% of VAT on the sale (net of land value) of new residential properties. The tax relief is capped

at UF 225 per housing unit and the maximum dwelling value is UF 2 000 (for subsidised housing, the maximum dwelling value is UF 2 200 and the VAT deduction is 12.35%). The tax credit will be abolished from January 1, 2025.

27 The *dispositif Pinel* provides an income tax credit following the purchase or construction of new housing worth up to EUR 300 000 in an eligible zone. The housing must be rented to households whose income falls under a threshold at a capped price per m^2 and the total credit varies between 12% and 21% of the purchase price, depending on the duration it is rented (6 to 12 years).

28 Taxpayers are eligible for an additional 10% capital gains discount if they rent their housing at below-market rates for three years and a registered Community Housing Provider managed the property. Taxpayers must also be eligible for the 50% capital gains discount that applies to assets held for more than 12 months.

29 Zero carbon housing refers to housing with very high energy performance, where the very low amount of energy required is entirely or mostly produced from renewable sources on-site or nearby (Economidou et al., 2020[145]).

30 To date, taxes on vacant dwellings can be found in Vancouver, Canada; Oakland, U.S.; Melbourne, Australia; and a number of French urban areas (e.g. Paris, Lyon, Lille, Bordeaux, Toulouse).

31 The Empty Homes Tax, also known as the Vacancy Tax, was introduced in 2017 as an annual 1% tax (later raised to 1.25% in 2020 and to 3% in 2021) that is levied on the assessed taxable value of dwellings deemed to be vacant for more than six months of the year.

32 The *Taxe sur les Logement Vacants* (TLV) is levied on the deemed rental value (calculated by the tax administration) of unfurnished properties that have been occupied for less than 30 days in the previous 2 years. The rate increases with each year of vacancy and applies in large metropolitan areas where demand significantly outstrips supply.

33 The Vacant Residential Property Tax is a flat 1% tax levied on the value of the land and buildings as determined by the state's general valuation process, where the property was unoccupied for more than six months in the preceding year.

34 It is important to note that denser developments at the urban periphery may have some benefits, such as facilitating the development of transport networks that increase connectivity between regions.

35 Governments may apply land value capture through tax and non-tax measures, such as requiring cash payments in exchange for development rights, obliging developers to provide in-kind contributions in exchange for project approval, or strategically purchasing and developing land with the intention of selling or leasing it once the value increases. See OECD (forthcoming 2022[174]) for a comprehensive overview of value capture instruments.

Annex A. Tax treatment of housing in OECD counries

Table A A.1. Tax treatment of owner-occupied residential property, 2022

As at 1 January 2022

Country	Acquisition of asset	Holding of asset				Disposal of asset	
	Transaction tax	PIT		Other taxes		Capital gains	Estate and inheritance tax
		Income from asset	Interest expense deductible	Income from asset	Value of asset		
Australia	Y	N	N	N	Y	N	..
Austria	Y	N	N	N	Y	N	..
Belgium	Y[1]	N	Y	N	Y	N	Y[2]
Canada	Y	N	N	N	Y	N	..
Chile	N	N	Y[3]	N	Y[4]	Y[5]	Y
Czech Republic	Y	N	Y	N	Y	Y[6]	..
Colombia	N	N	Y	N	Y[7]	Y	..
Costa Rica	Y	N	N	N	Y	Y	..
Denmark	Y	N	Y	Y[8]	Y	N	Y
Estonia	N	N	Y[9]	N	Y	N	..
Finland	Y	N	Y[10]	N	Y	N	Y
France	Y	N	N	N	Y[11]	N	Y[12]
Germany	Y	N	N	N	Y	N[13]	Y[14]
Greece	Y	N	N	Y[8]	Y	N	Y[15]
Hungary	Y	N	N	N	Y[16]	Y[17]	Y
Iceland	Y	N	N	N	Y	N	Y
Ireland	Y	N	N	N	Y	N	Y[18]
Israel	Y[19]	N	N	N	Y	Y[20]	..
Italy	Y	N	Y[21]	N	Y[22]	N	Y
Japan	N	N	Y[23]	N	Y	Y	Y[24]
Korea	Y	N	Y[25]	N	Y	Y[26]	Y[27]
Latvia	Y	N	N	N	Y	N[28]	..
Lithuania	N	N	N	N	Y	Y[29]	Y
Luxembourg	N	N	Y[30]	N	Y	N	Y
Mexico	Y	N	Y	N	Y	N[31]	..
Netherlands	Y	Y[8]	Y	N	Y[32]	N	Y
New Zealand	N	N	N	N	Y	N	..
Norway	Y	N	Y	N	Y[33]	N	..
Poland	Y	N	N	N	Y[34]	N[35]	Y[36]
Portugal	Y	N	N	N	Y	N	Y[37]
Slovak Republic	N	N	N	N	Y	N	..
Slovenia	Y	N	N	N	Y	Y	Y
Spain	Y	N	N[38]	N	Y[39]	Y[40]	Y[41]
Sweden	Y	N	Y	N	Y[42]	Y[43]	..

Switzerland	Y[44]	Y[8]	Y	N	Y[7,44]	Y[45]	Y[46]
Türkiye	Y	N	N	N	Y	N	Y
United Kingdom	Y	N	N	N	Y	N	Y[47]
United States	Y	N	Y	N	Y	Y[48]	Y

Note: In addition to the information in this table, special tax provisions may apply to some taxpayers. This could include tax exemptions, credits and caps, and may be conditional on fulfilling certain criteria (e.g. transaction tax exemptions for first time buyers, inheritance tax exemptions for close relatives of deceased donors).

1 The first EUR 175 000 of the value of the housing is exempt from transaction taxes, where housing is acquired by a natural person for their primary residence and is worth EUR 500 000 or less.

2 Owner-occupied housing is exempt if inherited by the spouse who was living in the housing at the time of the donor's death. It is taxed at lower rates if inherited by co-owners that are lineal heirs or cohabitants.

3 Interest not deductible if taxpayer earns above CLP 97 507 800. Limit of interest deductible equal to CLP 5 200 416. Values on December 31st, 2021.

4 Recurrent property tax applies if house value is greater than CLP 47 360 490 (on January 1, 2022).

5 Accumulated capital gains are tax exempt up to a value of CLP 247 933 920 (on January 1, 2022).

6 Gains are taxable if held for five years or less; or two years or less if the taxpayer's main residence (unless the gains are used to finance a new residence in which case not taxable even if held for two years or less).

7 Recurrent property tax plus net wealth tax.

8 Tax on imputed rental income.

9 Mortgage interest is deductible up to EUR 300 per year and limited to 50% of the taxpayer's taxable income in the respective tax year.

10 10% of mortgage interest is deductible against capital income. Of the excess of deductible interest over capital income, 30% (32% for first-time homebuyers) can be credited against earned income tax up to a maximum of EUR 1 400.

11 Recurrent property tax plus net housing wealth tax. The taxable threshold for the net housing wealth tax is set at EUR 1.3 million, but once this threshold has been achieved, the assets are taxed as of EUR 800 000.

12 Partly exempt (20%) if inherited by the donor's spouse or children who lived in the housing at time of the donor's death.

13 No taxation if occupied by the owner since acquisition or construction, or for at least 2 years before the year of sale or if held for more than 10 years.

14 Exempt if inherited by the donor's spouse or children who live in the housing for 10 years after the donor's death.

15 An additional tax-free threshold applies when inherited by the spouse or children, who do not own other housing.

16 Recurrent property tax (building tax on dwellings) due in only some municipalities. In 2017 only 548 municipalities out of 3 178 levied building tax on dwellings.

17 The taxable capital gain is reduced by an increasing percentage each year and is exempt after five years.

18 Exemption for beneficiaries who live in the housing for 3 years before and 6 years after the donor's death and do not own other housing.

19 Buyers who own more than one property are subject to higher transaction taxes.

20 CGT only applies on gains above a sale price of ILS 4.5 million.

21 A tax credit of 19% of mortgage interest is provided up to a max of EUR 4 000 of interest payment.

22 Only luxury homes subject to recurrent property tax.

23 Tax credit equal to 1% of the remaining mortgage balance at the end of each year. Only available when the taxable income of the year is less than or equal to JPY 30 million. The tax credit is capped at JPY 400 000 per year if the taxpayer started living in the house between 2014 and 2019, and acquired the housing after the consumption tax hike in 2014. In other cases, the tax credit is capped at JPY 200 000 per year.

24 Partially exempt (80%)

25 Deductible at taxpayer's marginal rate unless house cost more than KRW 400 million and up to a limit depending on years being paid off.

26 40% tax rate for short-term holdings of less than 1 year. No CGT if held for 2 years or more. CGT is however still applicable if house is worth more than KRW 900 million.

27 Exemption capped at KRW 600 million for children and lineal descendent who lived in the housing for 10 years before the donor's death and do not own other housing.

28 Capital gains from the alienation of the real estate were not taxable, if the following criteria were fulfilled: ownership ≥ 60 months and the declared place of residence for at least 12 months until entering into the alienation contract; ownership ≥ 60 months and the only real estate owned for the last 60 months before the alienation; the only real estate has been replaced with another functionally similar real estate 12 months before or after the alienation of the first real estate; income from the disposal of real estate has occurred in relation to the division of property in the case of dissolution of marriage, provided that it is the declared place of residence of both spouses at least 12 months until the day of entering into the alienation contract; there has been a disposal of the real estate in accordance with the procedures specified in the Law On Alienation of Immovable Property for the Public Needs, provided that ownership ≥ 60 months or the income is invested anew in functionally similar real estate within 12 months after alienation of immovable property for the public needs.

29 Taxable unless place of residence for at least 2 years; or if less than 2 years and income is used within one year to purchase a new place of residence.

30 Mortgage interest is deductible below a threshold (EUR 2 000 years 1-5; EUR 1 5000 years 5-10; then EUR 1 000).

31 Unless gain exceeds 700 thousand investment units, or have sold a house within the previous five years.

32 Recurrent property tax.

[33] Recurrent property tax and net wealth tax. Only 25% of the owner-occupied property value is subject to the tax. As of 2022, for primary residences valued above NOK 10 million, 50% of the value of the property is subject to the wealth tax.
[34] Recurrent property tax is not levied on the value of the real property. The tax base is area in case of land and usable area in case of buildings.
[35] Realised income from disposal of real property is subject to taxation, if disposal takes place less than five years after acquisition or construction of the asset.
[36] Fully exempt for immediate family. Exempt for up to 110 m2 of residential property for extended family and carers who do not own residential property and live in the housing for five years after the donor's death. Carers refer to non-related persons who have taken care of the donor for at least two years, where a written and signed agreement has been attested by a notary.
[37] Owner-occupied housing is partially exempt under a cap and then is subject to lower tax rates than standard inheritance tax rates.
[38] A tax credit (which covered interest and amount of acquisition) was repealed in 2013. However, it can still be applied as a temporary regime by taxpayers who were applying the credit prior to 2013. According to their legal competences, the majority of regional governments (Comunidades Autónomas) apply the tax credit.
[39] Recurrent property tax and net wealth tax. For net wealth tax, an exemption threshold of EUR 300 000 applies for the main residence.
[40] However, full rollover relief applies in respect of capital gains from disposals by any taxpayer of his primary residence. The exemption requires that the entire proceeds be reinvested within a 2-year period in the acquisition of another primary residence. Full exemption applies for taxpayers over 65 years old (see above).
[41] Partially exempt (95%), capped at EUR 122 606, for spouses, ascendants, and descendants who live in the housing for 10 years after the donor's death.
[42] Recurrent property tax has a maximum amount of SEK 8 874 for a house and SEK 1 519 for an apartment.
[43] Only a proportion (22/30) of the capital gain is taxable.
[44] Transaction taxes and recurrent property taxes are applied in many, but not all cantons.
[45] All cantons levy an immovable property gains tax (Grundstückgewinnsteuer). The tax treatment of property gains may depend on factors including the holding period
[46] Valued slightly below market value.
[47] Partial exemption for lineal descendants.
[48] Untaxed if capital gain of less than USD 250 000 (or USD 500 000 for married filing jointly) and held for at least 2 of the last 5 years. Otherwise taxed at marginal PIT rates for short-term gains, and at preferential long-term rates for long-term gains.
Source: Taxation of Household Savings Questionnaire, 2016, updated to January 2022 in consultation with country delegates. Inheritance, Estate, and Gift Taxes Questionnaire, 2020.

Table A A.2. Tax Treatment of rented residential property, 2022

As at 1 January 2022

Country	Acquisition of asset	Holding of asset				Disposal of asset	
	Transaction tax	PIT		Other taxes		Capital gains	Estate and inheritance tax
		Income from asset	Interest expense deductible	Income from asset	Value of asset		
Australia	Y	Y	Y	N	Y	Y	..
Austria	Y	Y	Y	N	Y	Y	..
Belgium	Y	Y[1]	Y[2]	N	Y	Y[3]	Y
Canada	Y	Y	Y	N	Y	Y	..
Chile	N	Y[4]	Y[5]	N	Y[6]	Y[7]	Y
Czech Republic	Y	Y	Y	N	Y	Y[8]	..
Colombia	N	Y	Y	N	Y[9]	Y	..
Costa Rica	Y	Y	Y	Y	Y	Y[10]	..
Denmark	Y	N	Y	Y[11]	Y	Y[12]	Y
Estonia	N	Y[13]	Y[14]	N	Y	Y	..
Finland	Y	Y[15]	Y[16]	N	Y	Y	Y
France	Y	Y	N	N	Y[17]	Y[18]	Y
Germany	Y	Y	Y	N	Y	Y[19]	Y
Greece	Y	Y	N	N	Y	N	Y
Hungary	Y	Y	N	N	Y[20]	Y[21]	Y
Iceland	Y	N	N	Y[22]	Y	Y	Y
Ireland	Y	Y	Y	N	Y	Y	Y
Israel	Y[23]	Y[24]	N	N	Y	Y	..
Italy	Y[25]	Y[26]	N	Y[26]	Y	Y[27]	Y
Japan	N	Y	Y	N	Y	Y	Y
Korea	Y	Y[28]	Y[29]	N	Y	Y[30]	Y
Latvia	Y	Y[31]	N	N	Y	Y	..
Lithuania	N	Y	N	N	Y	Y[32]	Y
Luxembourg	N	Y	Y	N	Y	Y	Y
Mexico	Y	Y	Y	N	Y	Y	..
Netherlands	Y	N	N	Y[33]	Y	N	Y
New Zealand	N	Y	Y	N	Y	N	..
Norway	Y	Y	Y	N	Y[34]	Y	..
Poland	Y	Y	Y[35]	N	Y[36]	Y[37]	Y[38]
Portugal	Y	Y	N	N	Y	Y[39]	Y
Slovak Republic	N	Y[40]	N	N	Y	N	..
Slovenia	Y	N	N	Y	Y	Y[41]	Y
Spain	Y	Y[42]	Y	N	Y[43]	Y	Y
Sweden	Y	Y	Y	N	Y[44]	Y[45]	..
Switzerland	Y[46]	Y	Y	N	Y[9,46]	Y	Y[47]
Türkiye	Y	Y	Y	N	Y	N	Y
United Kingdom	Y	Y	Y	N	Y	Y	Y
United States	Y	Y	Y	N	Y	Y[48]	Y

Note: In addition to the information in this table, special tax provisions may apply to some taxpayers. This could include tax exemptions, credits and caps, and may be conditional on fulfilling certain criteria (e.g. transaction tax exemptions for first time buyers, inheritance tax exemptions for close relatives of deceased donors).

[1] Imputed income is taxed at progressive PIT rates.

[2] Mortgage principal repayments for rented residential property benefit from a tax credit of 30%, limited to the first EUR 78 440 of the loan and for a maximum tax credit of EUR 2 350. Mortgage interest can be deducted in full from taxable rental (and other property) income.

[3] If held less than five years.

[4] A large number of owners are exempt from taxes on rental income earned from housing with a surface equal to or lower than 140 m2. This benefit can be used on a maximum of two new or existing dwellings per person.
[5] Interest not deductible if taxpayer earns above CLP 97 507 800. Limit of interest deductible equal to CLP 5 200 416. Values on December 31st, 2021.
[6] Recurrent property tax applies if house value is greater than CLP 47 360 490 (on January 1, 2022).
[7] Accumulated capital gains are tax exempt up to a value of CLP 247 933 920 (on January 1, 2022).
[8] Taxable if held <5 years; or <2 years if taxpayer's main residence (unless used to finance new residence).
[9] Recurrent property tax plus net wealth tax.
[10] The tax does not apply if income is used for the acquisition of another property for residential purposes.
[11] A splitting system applies.
[12] Taxed at flat rate as "net capital income" under semi-dual system.
[13] Income tax only applies to 80% of rental income.
[14] Mortgage interest is deductible up to EUR 300 per year and limited to 50% of the taxpayer's taxable income in the respective tax year.
[15] Rental income is taxed as investment income, but at a flat 30% rate.
[16] Deductible against capital income.
[17] Recurrent property tax plus net housing wealth tax. The taxable threshold for the net housing wealth tax is set at EUR 1.3 million, but once this threshold has been achieved, the assets are taxed as of EUR 800 000.
[18] Subject to flat withholding tax plus social taxes. A reduction is provided if held more than six years. Untaxed if held for more than 22 years (withholding tax) and 30 years (social taxes).
[19] No CGT if held more than 10 years.
[20] Recurrent property tax (building tax on dwellings) due in only some municipalities. In 2017 only 548 municipalities of 3178 levied building tax on dwellings.
[21] The taxable capital gain is reduced by an increasing percentage each year and is exempt after five years.
[22] 50% of rental income is exempt and 50% is subject to a flat 20% capital income tax rate.
[23] Buyers who own more than one property are subject to higher transaction taxes.
[24] Taxpayer has three options: exemption of rental income up to a ceiling of ILS 5 030; 10% tax on gross rental income, with no deductions; or marginal tax rate (30% to 48%) on rental income net of expenses.
[25] Higher transaction tax rate for second homes than owner-occupied home.
[26] Actual rental income from residential property is taxed under ordinary PIT, with 95% of the annual rent included in the tax base. Alternatively, the taxpayer can choose to pay a 21% "coupon tax" on rental income. (10% in the case of pre-agreed controlled rents).
[27] Exempt from CGT if held at least five years.
[28] Exempt if rental income does not exceed KRW 20 million income until 2016.
[29] 40% of interest and principle is deductible against salary and wage income.
[30] 40% tax rate if held <1 year. For 5 years, taxable but get 15% reduction; if 10 years get 38% reduction
[31] Two possibilities – PIT applied to rental income (general treatment) or special PIT rate applied at flat concessionary rate.
[32] If held less than 10 years.
[33] Deemed return on net asset value (value less debt) is taxed. First EUR 24 437 of total assets excluding pensions and owner-occupied housing is exempt.
[34] Recurrent property tax and net wealth tax. 95% of the value of secondary housing is subject to the tax.
[35] Mortgage interest deductibility for natural persons (not engaged in business activity) only available until 31 December 2022.
[36] Recurrent property tax is not levied on the value of the real property. The tax base is area in case of land and usable area in case of buildings.
[37] Realised income from disposal of real property is subject to taxation, if disposal takes place less than five years after acquisition or construction of the asset.
[38] Fully exempt for immediate family. Exempt for up to 110 m2 of residential property for extended family and carers who do not own residential property and live in the housing for five years after the donor's death. Carers refer to non-related persons who have taken care of the donor for at least two years, where a written and signed agreement has been attested by a notary.
[39] Half of capital gains are indexed.
[40] Rental income less than EUR 500 is untaxed.
[41] The tax rate for capital gains depends on the holding period: 25% for up to 5 years; 15% from 5 to 10 years; 10% from 10 to 15 years; 5% from 15 to 20 years; and non-taxation for greater than 20 years.
[42] 60% reduction in tax on rental income.
[43] Recurrent property tax and net wealth tax. For net wealth tax, an exemption threshold of EUR 700 000 is applied in general for all assets, including rented residential property.
[44] Recurrent property tax has a maximum amount of SEK 8 874 for a house and SEK 1 519 for an apartment.
[45] Only 90% of the capital gain is taxable when used mainly for business.
[46] Transaction taxes and recurrent property taxes are applied in many, but not all cantons. Neither are applied in Zurich, which is used as the representative canton in the ETR modelling.
[47] Valued slightly below market value.
[48] Lower rate schedule applies for long term gains of more than one year. Gain attributable to any accelerated depreciation is taxable at ordinary rates. Gain attributable to straight-line depreciation is taxed at ordinary rates up to 25%.

Source: Taxation of Household Savings Questionnaire, 2016, updated to January 2022 in consultation with country delegates. Inheritance, Estate, and Gift Taxes Questionnaire, 2020.

www.ingramcontent.com/pod-product-compliance
Lightning Source LLC
Chambersburg PA
CBHW061218240926
51846CB00006B/1269